# Chilcotin Diary

*This book is for Mildred—the light at the end of my tunnel.*

# Chilcotin Diary
## Forty Years of Adventure

*Written and Illustrated*
*by*
*Will D. Jenkins, Sr.*

ISBN 0-88839-409-6

**Cataloging in Publication Data**
Jenkins, Will D., 1899-
Chilcotin diary

ISBN 0-88839-409-6

1. Jenkins, Will D., 1899- 2. Frontier and pioneer life—British
Columbia—Chilcotin River Region. 3. Chilcotin River Region
(B.C.)—Biography. I. Title.
FC3845.C445Z49 1997    971.1'75    C97-910520-X
F1089.C445J46 1997

Printed in Canada—Jasper

Edited: Karen Kloeble and Nancy Miller
Production: Nancy Miller
Cover Design: Andrew Jaster

Published simultaneously in Canada and the United States by

**HANCOCK HOUSE PUBLISHERS LTD.**
19313 Zero Avenue, Surrey, B.C. V4P 1M7
(604) 538-1114  Fax (604) 538-2262

**HANCOCK HOUSE PUBLISHERS**
1431 Harrison Avenue, Blaine, WA 98230
(604) 538-1114  Fax (604) 538-2262
Web site: *www.hancockhouse.com* email: *hancockhouse.com*

# Contents

# Acknowledgments

I wish to express grateful appreciation for assistance in the preparation of this manuscript by my niece Dena Fleurichamp, my granddaughter Maria Jenkins, Mrs. Joy Graham of Tatla Lake, Mrs. Irene Bliss of Willow Springs Ranch in the Chilcotin and Mrs. Helen Barrett of the Skagit County Historical Society.

Some recommended reading:
*Bancroft's History of the Northwest Coast to 1793*
*The History of the Northern Interior of British Columbia* by A.G. Morice
The Journals of Alexander MacKenzie and Simon Fraser, respectively
*The Chilcotin War* by Mel Rothenburger
*Grass Beyond the Mountains* by Richard Hobson

# Preface
## The Beckoning Wilderness

There is a mystique about Cariboo Country that defies description; a sort of lure or magnetism that is unique to the wild and sprawling interior region of British Columbia, lying directly north of the state of Washington.

It is akin to the legend of Old Hasseyampa, who quenched his thirst from the river that bears his name, and—it is alleged—once retraced his steps over 1,000 miles of burning sands to again quaff from the waters that miraculously restored his youth, and thereafter never left the realm.

Old-timers, like pioneer rancher Bill Bliss of Willow Springs and Scotty Shields, the patriarch of Tatlayoko Valley, will tell you the lure of the big country is legendary and that it is profoundly potent on the high Chilcotin Plateau west of Fraser's river.

It has been called many things: Cariboo Fever; The Spirit of the North; The Call of the Bush. I came to a personal conclusion more than forty years ago that the lure of Cariboo, like the unorthodox spelling of its name and the historic disputes over its actual boundaries, easily becomes a happy aberration, a sort of nostalgic ailment pleasant to bear; a healthy love affair with an old frontier whose limits are mythical in regions of the mind.

Mildred and I first ventured into Cariboo Country, north of our old home in Washington State, during the early years of our marriage. The big clean regions of Canada's westernmost frontier quickly won our hearts.

We explored the hinterland during the 1930s and 1940s from Fraser's canyon, beyond old Fort Hope and the Brigade Trail, to the sage hills of Thompson River; from Lillooet's "Mile 0" on the historic gold route over Corson's Kingdom to the Bonaparte, the cow country beyond 100 Mile House to Quesnel Forkes and the placer camps of Barkerville; from Fort George to Kispiox, to Stuart Lake and old Fort St. James; and finally to the Blackwater River Road where MacKenzie pushed his perilous route to Bella Coola and the Pacific sea in 1793.

Our roamings in those young years were fired by a mutual love of wilderness and pioneer history. The West Chilcotin's appeal became an impelling force in our plans for retirement there, "some day." The plan became a sustaining dream as we followed a systematic program of saving to make fulfillment possible.

*Chilcotin Diary* is the product of more than forty years of wilderness adventure, recounted from the old diaries we kept. It will be obvious to many that while Mildred and I were both woodswise from years of following the mountain trails of the North Cascades, we were truly novice pilgrims when we challenged the wilds of the Chilcotin bush. We had much to learn.

Obviously the life we chose when we finally reached the age of retirement is not for everyone—and ours was admittedly unorthodox—however, if, in the following pages some degree of pleasurable reading is found by those who are able to follow our footsteps only in the printed word, the purpose of this narrative has best served its intended purpose.

W. D. J.
LITTLE EAGLE LAKE, 1987

# Introduction

## *Alexander MacKenzie, Front-runner of Empire*

Canadians, and especially British Columbians, are deeply indebted to a twenty-nine-year-old Scot who gave to Canada and the empire the vast area west of Quebec, without firing a shot in anger. To this young man, Alexander MacKenzie, Americans are also indebted. His exploit was a forerunner to the establishment of the 49th parallel as the longest unfortified border in the world. The colonial ancestors of these two nations were children of a common mother.

As this manuscript is completed, Canadians have celebrated the 200th anniversary of Alexander MacKenzie's famous walk across the top of the high Chilcotin Plateau in northcentral British Columbia. His long walk was in search of a suitable trade route for the Northwest Fur Co. and the Coastal Indians. We can envision MacKenzie standing on the banks of the white-water stream at a point approximately now known as Quesnel, puzzled by his lack of knowledge of the country that lay ahead, not knowing the name of the stream on which he stood. MacKenzie was with a Cree Indian guide who told him he thought this river was the Tocoutche Tesse, an Algonquin term which he believed meant "Columbia River."

This vast area west of the Rockies had not yet seen the incursion of Europeans that would follow in MacKenzie's wake. He faced a total wilderness occupied only by scattered nomadic tribes of Indians who roamed the land and fought with each other. A scattering of Europeans were in wind ships—British, American, Spanish and Russian—coasting up and down from Mexico to Russian Alaska, more concerned in their quest for the highly valuable fur of the sea otter than they were in looking for a landfall on which to hoist their flag proclaiming national possession. It could be said much of the North American continent was up for grabs 200 years ago: a region most European governments regarded as an unimportant howling wilderness.

Unsure of himself, MacKenzie, with two canoes, traveled a considerable distance down the stream to a point now known as Alexandra and sought information from Indians there.

The Indians at Alexandra told MacKenzie he should go back to his starting point and proceed west because the Indians in the Chilcotin Plateau, around the Blackwater River, were known to wear ornaments of copper in their noses and ears and this copper had to come from the Pacific Coast.

It would be twelve years before Simon Fraser would start from this same spot and descend the river through the vertical walls of Hell's Gate Canyon and determine that it flowed into the Strait of Georgia.

The river would thereafter be known by the name of Fraser River.

MacKenzie well knew the copper had originally come from the hulls of wind ships wrecked on the ocean's coast where the Indians had salvaged it. He was also told that the northern Indians had a trade route which they called the Glease Trail (meaning grease, from seal and candlefish oil rendered by the Coastal Indians and packed in skin bags to the interior for trading purposes). In later years, the Hudson's Bay Company would know that route as the Train Trail.

On May 9, 1793, MacKenzie, at the head of a nine-man matis crew, began his long walk to the coast. He left part of his entourage at the forks where they raised a high platform on jack pine poles and stored their two big river canoes, along with bags of pemmican and other provisions, so that they would have food on return for the winter.

The remainder of his men were to build cabins and other shelter. As MacKenzie walked westward to a little southwestward, following the Glease Trail, he must have been bewildered at times by the meandering of the Blackwater River from north to south and from east to west. He must have made repeated compass observations to maintain the course he wanted to follow.

At the western rim of the Chilcotin Plateau, which butts against the eastern ramparts of the Coast Range, they came to what we know as the precipice, which drops more than a mile to the floor of the Bella Coola valley in the heavily timbered mountainous area. Descending the mile-deep gorge of the Bella Coola, they entered the region of giant ancient forest and were conscious of the sudden change of atmosphere identified by the salt air of the distant Pacific. The air here embraced a dampness in sharp contrast to the arid atmosphere of the high plateau. On the Bella Coola, they encountered other Indians and observed the fact that his crew was being watched very closely. MacKenzie's small band was taking no chances of surprise attack from the Bella Coolas, who were said to be very savage. His men kept the powder dry and well covered in the pans of their flintlocks.

At a place we know as Bella Coola, MacKenzie bartered for the big canoe on which to proceed farther west and for some fresh fish to supplement the meager rations in their backpacks. As the bartering began, a group of warriors gathered about the canoe, their avaricious eyes roving over its contents. MacKenzie and his men consciously shifted the brass-bound gun butts of the muzzle-loading pistols in the waistbands of their buckskins. The sun shining brightly on those highly polished weapons was undoubtedly a sight to dampen any desire to attack or rob the strangers. Those big flintlock pistols were smooth-bores of approximately sixty caliber. The Indians well knew, from past experience with white men from the windjammers, these pistols could be quickly brought into action and the wide pattern of their buckshot could be counted on to maim or kill several men at close range.

MacKenzie, being an Easterner, could not understand the Chinook trade language of the Coastal Indians. The old man with whom he bargained for the fish and big canoe told him that to the westward lay the "Skookumchuk" (the big ocean); that it was sometimes "messachee" (very angry); that his canoe might go "killipie" (upset)—all white man be "memaloos" (dead). MacKenzie was at least perceptive enough to get the message and realize he'd have to go it alone with his small crew. What the old

Indian probably did not tell MacKenzie was that out there was the fierce Haida Indianss in their seagoing sail canoes, the Bella Bellas, and a little to the north the Tsimsians, with whom the Bella Coola tribe had warred for many centuries. MacKenzie and his men observed tidal water marks on the rocks of the more than 100-mile-long inlet, a sort of fjord in from the actual Pacific. As they proceeded west they repeatedly dipped their fingers into the water and tasted them to determine whether the water was salt.

Ultimately reaching a point which he considered the actual coast of the Pacific, MacKenzie beached his canoe and on the face of a rock painted his famous message: "By land from Canada, July 22, 1793." He signed his name: Alexander MacKenzie. The paint MacKenzie used was known as vermillion, a mixture of mercuric cinnabar. When he finished his lettering, he smeared the surface with a heavy coat of grease calculated to withstand weathering. I am told by people who have been there the message is still visible and I'm also informed that from time to time in the past 200 years some patriotic Canadians have repainted the message to guarantee its future visibility.

That night they hid their canoe, posted a "watch" and camped on the top of the rock, beginning their return trip before daylight.

The Bella Coola Indians followed MacKenzie's crew back to the foot of the precipice. The explorers climbed to the top of the plateau and proceeded east toward their starting point at Tocoutche Tesse. The soles of their moccasins were so thin, the Indians were forced to stuff prairie grass from the parklands into their moccasins to protect their feet. They arrived back at Tocoutche Tesse on August 24, 1793, having traveled well over 1,000 miles on foot. It would be another twelve years until Simon Fraser, John Stuart and Jules Quesnel would stand on the spot from whence MacKenzie began his famous cross-country march.

In Fraser's review of MacKenzie's journals, in which he described the vastness of the plateau, its beautiful grasslands and its parklike character, he said, "It so reminds me of the birthplace of my mother in the highlands of northern Scotland, we will name this entire area, from the Rockies to the Pacific and from

13

the Arctic south to what is known as the Oregon country, New Caledonia."

It remained New Caledonia for many years on maps of the British Empire in Canada. I have always regarded Alexander MacKenzie as the real front-runner as an explorer for the Empire. The French explorers, ahead of the British by nearly 100 years, lost their chance to acquire Canada for France. They had already explored far to the northwest including the Coppermine River near the border between Canada's Arctic and the north coast of Russian Alaska.

Hard pressed for funds, they sought help from the French government for financial assistance and were ignored. Finally, in desperation, they appealed to the British, and the British were not slow to respond. It was men like MacKenzie and Simon Fraser and Stuart, Quesnel, David Thompson and others, who secured for Canada this vast northern country, in obvious contrast to the bloody revolution of the American colonies in 1776.

A notable fact: at a still youthful age of only twenty-four years, MacKenzie had led an expedition of matis paddlers in birch bark canoes down the full length of the great river that bears his name from Great Slave Lake to the frozen rims of the Arctic Ocean. Only four years later found him standing ankle-deep on the shores of the Pacific to paint his famous message on the rock off Bella Coola.

I have made no attempt to be strictly historical. I lived for the better part of forty years in the wilderness of the Chilcotin Plateau and, during that time, maintained a daily diary which now fills a four-foot-long shelf in my den. In my journals I have endeavored to be honest, and if there are mistakes, which there are bound to be, they are errors of the hand and not the heart. I hope you'll like these stories, which include memoirs from my personal experiences among some of the original settlers of the country and a few essays dealing more personally with the happy years of my life with my wife Mildred, whose companionship over the period of sixty-six years was the inspiration for this work.

W. D. J.<br>WHIDBEY ISLAND

14

# An Old Map and Cariboo Fever

## *1936*

I came home from work one day to find Mildred on her knees, a tattered map of British Columbia spread on the kitchen floor, the happy gleam of discovery in her eyes, as she greeted me with: "Look here, Honey! This old map shows there's a road from a place called Williams Lake all the way out to Bella Coola! I'll bet we could drive to Bella Coola! You know how I wanted to go there and that cruise ship didn't go into Bella Coola."

Yes, I knew that. She had already visited the Queen Charlotte Islands and Bella Bella in pursuit of her studies on the pre-White culture of West Coast Indians. This was a project that had grown from a hobby to a concerted research effort.

I thought: "Well, here we go again!" as I followed her finger, tracing the old Chilcotin Road from Williams Lake westerly to Riske Creek, to Hanceville, to Alexis Creek, meandering on through Redstone and Chilanko Forks to Kleena Kleene and Anahim Lake. The line of the old trail that twisted through the Coast Range to Bella Coola appeared a little uncertain, as if the cartographer may have lacked some definite information in his final draft. But at any rate it "looked" like a road, all 300 miles of it.

So thus it came about on a September day of heavy rain and equinoxial turbulence we left our ancestral home on Lake Whatcom, near Bellingham, Washington, to head north into Cariboo Country, bound for Bella Coola.

We were late getting packed and on our way.

My wife has an excitable appetite. We seldom ever get underway on a back-country trip without being forced to stop and eat within hours of starting out. It was as we pulled into the village of Boston Bar on the old Cariboo Trail that she reminded me she was already hungry. A homemade, crudely painted sign with big letters that said "EAT" caught my eye and we pulled aside to a little shack to sample its fare. The interior was dimly lit by the pale glimmer of a single electric bulb hanging from the ceiling, its glow pulsing weakly with the "juice" of a noisily humming gas generator. The kitchen smells indicated the soup of the day was French onion so we climbed onto a couple of bar stools and ordered soup and coffee.

Our waitress was a very pretty young Indian girl; the cook, who smiled at us from the kitchen, an aged Chinese man. The soup, a generous helping, came in thick crockery bowls with big spoons and a plate of soda crackers: it looked good and smelled good. I reached for a cracker. It seemed to be moving. Mildred was about to help herself when I saw the source of the power that was moving the cracker and I restrained her hand. The "mover" was about three-eighths of an inch long with a white body and a dark head that wiggled happily in the dim light of the cafe. We drank our coffee and got out of there!

We only got to Lytton on our first day. Two days later, by way of Lillooet and Pavilion Lake, to Clinton and Williams Lake, we "gassed up" for our initial venture into the Chilcotin—destination Bella Coola, 308 miles west to the shores of the Pacific—hopefully!

Rain was still pelting us as we headed west on the Chilcotin road. When this old dirt road had last felt the blessing of a grader's blade would be anyone's guess. Mildred was clinging to a door handle as we crawled in second gear, jolting through bone-jarring chuck-holes that splashed mud from our wheels, blowing back to smear the windshield until the wipers became useless.

After more than an hour of this and we hadn't reached the twenty-five or so miles to cross the river, heading west from Williams Lake, Mildred's enthusiasm was as rain-soaked as the countryside. She finally stated emphatically, "So far as I'm concerned, you can turn around any time! I've had enough!"

But before I could respond to her, and I'll admit I was having misgivings, there wasn't any place to turn around. We had begun the long down-slope into the valley of Chimney Creek, the road suddenly becoming a very narrow series of curves and switchbacks little wider than a trail skirting the steep sides of the mountain. I promised Mildred I would find a place to turn and we would go back home. Pelted by rain and wind gusts boiling up from the gorge of Fraser's river, we drove on in second gear. If there was a place on this old mountain road wide enough to turn around, I had missed it. With Mildred still protesting and beginning to complain of a headache, we arrived at the high brink of the canyon and the approach to the old cable suspension bridge at the foot of Sheep Creek Hill.

I pulled to a stop on the lip of the gorge, one front wheel chocked against a boulder. A glance at the steep slope of the mountain and the narrow width of the road told me there was no chance here for a turn-around.

Ahead, a short distance below where we sat, old Sheep Creek bridge hung in its cables, the worn planks of its deck shining in the rain.

We rested a bit. And then I told Mildred we had no choice but to cross over. I again promised to turn our outfit around and head for home as soon as we possibly could. Feeling deep discouragement, I eased our heavily loaded car onto the span.

We crossed in second gear as the wind moaned a dismal refrain in cables that swayed, jerked, creaked and groaned in their turnbuckles, the deck undulating in its center like the contortions of a weary belly dancer. Mildred gripped the door handle in terror, her fear of high places had her staring wide-eyed at the opposite end of the bridge. She heaved a big sigh as we crawled from the span. The rear bumper of our Chevy was barely off the bridge when the front wheels turned upward into the first of more than three miles of switchbacks; a narrow, cliff-hanging road little wider than a trail the pioneers of Chilcotin ranch country had dug from the steep canyon walls.

Rain came as a deluge. Visibility was limited to the shortened length of the turns. Flood waters, draining down from the summit more than 2,000 feet above, swirled around the low inside curves, a noisy rush of mud, rocks and pebbles heading for the Fraser.

On the curve of a dizzy ledge Chilcotin's old-timers had aptly named Cape Horn, we caught a brief and final glimpse of the Fraser surging through the gorge below and a moment later turned our car into the dark density of old-growth timber that flanked the canyon of Sheep Creek Hill. Approximately half way up our climb to the summit, we were able to pull to a halt on a short but almost level spot and allow the Chevy's overheated engine to cool. Not wanting to dally in Sheep Creek's canyon, and conscious of the fact there was always the chance of meeting another vehicle on this narrow trail, we were soon on our way.

Our emergence from Sheep Creek Hill came with sudden surprise. The final upward switchback left the dark cover of timber to level off on the lip of the open Chilcotin Plateau, its grasslands sweeping away in startling immensity to distant horizons. In a sense of deep relief from the tense anxiety we had felt on that muddy rain and wind swept trail, we drew to a halt, amazed by the abrupt change in the landscape that spread before us. Then, almost as a climax to travail, the skies cleared. Sunshine, which we had not seen in two days, swept the earth with its sudden warmth. The sun of late September quickly drew veils of mist from the rain-soaked road.

On either side, as far as the eye could see, lay the natural parklands of the Interior, rich in the pine grass of wild meadows. On the high prairie a scatter of boulders, many of them huge, lay dotting the green of the ancient moraine that marks the wake of the dying centuries of the Ice Age. Open range here, old signs warned, for this was then, as now, a cattleman's paradise. White-faced Herefords, roaming these grasslands, eyed us with stolid indifference.

From a carton on the floor of the Chevy, Mildred withdrew a thermos of coffee and jam and peanut butter sandwiches. We sat here, for a time, ate our lunch and savored the newly felt warmth of the sun. It was when the clouds finally drifted from the Coast Range far to the west and sun drenched the snowfields and glaciers pocketing the distant summits that the renewed urge to move came. I turned to Mildred and asked: "Honey, do you still want to go back?" Her mouth was full of jam and peanut butter, but her eyes were smiling now. I felt the squeeze of her fingers on my arm and got the message that needed no words; I tromped on Chevy's starter and we were once more off and away, headed for those distant snowy peaks.

Near the crest of a long slope in the road above Riske Creek, we drew to a halt on a grassy knoll to again view and savor the beauty of the Plateau. In clearing skies the gently rolling grasslands were revealed in even greater expanse, an ever widening panorama of nature's finest talent.

Autumn's most colorful phase had already arrived in the high country. Clustered stands of whitebark aspen shimmered in the sun, their leaves a frenzy of copper and gold in the light breeze flowing in from the west. A myriad of lakes and ponds nestling in shallow valleys and low swales of the prairie shone like polished silver, mirrors to the friendly cotton of puffy clouds lazing in the blue of the sky.

The road from Sheep Creek west to Riske Creek and beyond, through the high meadows of the Plateau to Hanceville and Alexis Creek, took us through seventy-four miles of the 300-mile route to the Pacific. As we drove through Hanceville, we didn't realize this town would play an important part in our future explorations of the early history of the Chilcotin Plateau.

This was the best stretch of the old freight route we would encounter in the week to follow. Beyond Alexis Creek, where the road skirted Chilcotin River almost at its level, we ran into quagmire conditions that had become a threat to travel in any type of vehicle. Beyond Chilanko Forks much of the road varied from sand to stretches of boulders typical of the old moraine. We labored through the mud of Chilanko Slough, climbed to the rocky summit of Bear's Head Hill, plowed through gumbo at Burnt Corral and eventually reached Graham's ranch at Tatla Lake by slogging across the flooded flat where the Graham's winter hay crop was a maze of black, rain rotted shocks floating in the floodwater of Tatla Creek.

Alex Graham's diesel-powered "Cat" stood handily by at Tatla, prepared to rescue any vehicle that might get stuck in the gumbo of road spanning the soggy meadow. More by luck than the science of driving, we arrived late in the day at the lodge home of Bruce and Grace Kellogg on the rocky shores of One-Eye Lake and camped that night with the Kelloggs, 177 back-aching miles west of Williams Lake.

Though the day had turned encouragingly warm at the summit of Sheep Creek Hill, the road in low valleys of the Plateau was still soggy. The Kelloggs advised against any attempt to drive to Bella Coola, having received word of a massive earth and rock slide in the canyon of the Atnarko below the summit of the Coast Range.

Our maiden trip into Chilcotin country ended at One-Eye Lake, so named for old One-Eye himself, a chief of the nomadic Chilcotins whose wickiup stood among the shoreline pines. It was again raining as we turned homeward. I remember Bruce telling us, the day we arrived in sporadic September sunshine, "You know, this is the second day of summer!" What a summer!! Those ranchers lost all their hay shocks.

But despite the rain, wind, mud and the discomfort of chuck-holes on one of the worst roads we had ever traveled, the mystique of the Cariboo, the sprawling grasslands and the timbered wilderness of the West Chilcotin, had cast its spell. We went home exhilarated. We had "the fever" the old-timers will tell you is incurable. As in the legend of Hasseyampa, we would return again, and again, and again, and...eventually make it a final goal....

* * * * *

One of our earlier explorations of the Interior country had been a piggy-back trip in our old car, wheels blocked on the deck of a railroad flatcar for a wild ride from Lillooet to Shalalth. This was on the famous "PGE" which, officially, stood for Pacific Great Eastern, reputedly the most crooked railroad in the world, whose interior terminus—at that time—was Prince George. In the parlance of Cariboo, PGE was humorously interpreted as

"Prince George Eventually." There was a tolerant affection for the system's frequent struggle to maintain anything resembling a reliable time schedule on a line gouged through some of the most rugged mountain terrain of this hemisphere.

We left home in Bellingham right after work one summer day and drove all night through the canyons of the Fraser to arrive at the little town of Lillooet by train time at seven the following morning. The canyon road was a tortuous one through the twisting gorge beyond the old placer town of Yale. Lacking sleep, we rolled into Lillooet bleary-eyed and hungry. But there had been no time for breakfast. My watch indicated it was almost seven o'clock as we hurried across the river bridge and headed for the station. A grinning "brakey" waved us up the loading ramp and onto the flatcar, kicking some worn and splintered wood blocks against the wheels of our Chevy. In seconds, it seemed, we were all set for the piggy-back trip to Shalalth. I looked at my watch. It was now just a few minutes past seven. The PGE's new diesel engine, which had lately replaced the big mountain Mallets of the dying age of steam, was throbbing loud and steady as we anticipated the melodious clang of the engine bell and the jerk of drawbars that would start us over winding rails to Shalalth. This was a most beautiful day, sunny, the air clear and fresh. Steep-rising mountains on all sides were sharp against the blue of a cloudless Canadian sky.

At noon that warm and zestful day we were still sitting on the flatcar at Lillooet. The diesel was still idling noisily. But we hadn't turned a wheel. Somewhere up along the twisted route beyond Seton Lake a crew of gandy dancers was making repairs to a culvert washed out by a recent freshet.

Underway "eventually" soon after noon, the train made up of locomotive, mail car, a day coach and the flatcar on which we rode with some other vehicles, bucked and swayed along the drunken curves of Seton Lake and on toward Shalalth. This was the wildest hair-raising ride in my experience as the engineer poured on speed to make up time. I wondered about those loose blocks of wood serving as chocks against the wheels of our car, but hesitated to crawl out of my seat for a closer inspection for

21

fear of being catapulted into Seton Lake. I looked at the "brakey" riding our flatcar and all the encouragement I drew was a big grin. The blackness of Seton Lake, bordered by the near vertical slopes of the Mission Mountains, dropped off to deep and unknown depths at the very edge of a rough railbed blasted from solid granite. The run to the old Indian village of Shalalth, where once the packtrains following the Harrison-Seton route to Cariboo passed with their heavy loads of miners' supplies, ended within about an hour of our starting. Here our smiling brakeman kicked away the wheel blocks and waved us down-ramp to the foot of the dusty switchback road that began at once to zigzag up and over the Mission Range. We were already climbing the sharp pitches of the narrow road as the PGE rolled and jerked on westerly, the raucous disharmony of its air whistle wailing among the hills.

Even with the shortened time caused by the morning delay, we visited some of the oldest hard-rock mining country of British Columbia. From the Lower Fraser near Lillooet, an old horse trail traverses some high mountain meadows. We sought information of the route. It was our plan to make the trip with our horses, at a later time. The trail, we learned, goes by way of Gun Lake, the Taseko Lakes and Nemiah Valley to reach the vicinity of Alexis Creek and Redstone on the Chilcotin River. Long followed as a trade route of the interior Indians, it was still in occasional use. From the summit of Mission Mountain, we viewed in spellbound wonder the seemingly endless reaches of the Coastal snowfields, high meadows and deep, rugged valleys.

Lacking, at that time, any other road for the return to Lillooet, we eased our car down the switchbacks late in the day to again board the flatcar at Shalalth on the PGE's return run. The trip back was a reversal of the wild ride coming out. We again clung to door handles while the flatcar pitched and careened over the crooked miles to Lillooet as if trying to shake our perched car from the open deck.

The narrow grades and sharp curves of the Fraser Canyon highway seemed tame as we drove homeward the following day. On a subsequent return to Lillooet we traversed a narrow cliff-skirting road up the Bridge River and the Yallacom, to the rich gold diggings of Gold Bridge and Bralorne.

By now we were admittedly scouting for a spot on which to build a cabin home for our anticipated retirement, though that happy day was still several years in our future. On the Yallacom, an old rancher named Christy had us about convinced we should locate in his valley. We went back to Lillooet to inquire, at the Provincial Government House, how to go about acquiring a bit of Crown Land. But the office was closed for the day and no one seemed to know the whereabouts of the agent. So we went into a little cafe near the depot, operated by a Greek who was said to be an old-timer in Lillooet and well-versed in such matters as Crown Land. We ate our dinner there and talked to the Greek. "It's easy like nothing at all," he assured us. "You jus' go out, fin' wat you want and drive a stick in the groun'—pum-pum-pum! (Beating his fist on the counter to demonstrate.) An' then it's yours!"

Actually, we would learn in time it was almost—but not quite that easy.

\* \* \* \* \*

In successive years of "looking around," our backcountry roaming took us into the higher, mountainous margins of the Chilcotin Plateau, to the wild region embracing Chilko Lake, Choelquoit (Big Eagle) Lake, the alpine grass of the Potato Mountains, and west of there, the Tatlayoko Valley. Also Bluff Lake and the West Branch, which drains the glacial region northeast of Mt. Waddington to join the Homathko, flowing into the Pacific at Bute Inlet; the crystal waters of Charlotte Lake, and the valley of the Klinniklinni, "down in the hole," where wild hay stood high as a horse's belly.

Relying on the inadequacy of an outdated government map, we followed many leads and suggestions. Everywhere we traveled through the Cariboo and Chilcotin country we were impressed by the outgoing friendliness of the isolated Interior ranchers. There was no pretense among these people. Their welcoming attitude was plainly sincere and warm. It would be

23

"Come in and rest awhile," or "Would you like some tea?" We spent many pleasant hours with these people. Such urgings to stop and rest at these remote homes were, I thought, a possible inheritance of the natural friendly way of the families of southern states which I had known, to "Come in and set a spell." Many of the early settlers on this Plateau were, in fact, migrants from the States, and the old spirit of pioneer hospitality had not been lost.

Our initial venture off the beaten track of the Chilcotin Road was a fifty-eight-mile crawl to Chilko Lake—an overland trip in second and first gear that consumed nine jolting hours over a road that could be described as little better than a trail. It was, actually, an old route worn into rocks and glacial scrabble by the wagons of Indian families traveling to Chilko for the annual harvest of spawning sockeye salmon at Henry's Crossing. As such, this old road had enjoyed the benefits of few attempts by white men to make it better than it had been for many forgotten years.

The long hours we spent tooling our old vehicle among the thick pines crowding the narrow, twisting way to Chilko included time out to salvage a rock-battered exhaust muffler with a length of haywire, and to examine the uncertain condition of a shaky pole bridge spanning a stream swollen and wild with the white water of glacial melt. At the bridge approach, on poles that sagged under the weight of our car, someone, who evidently knew by experience, had nailed up a piece of cardboard on which we read the pencilled words: "Bridge rough but safe." Mildred was skeptical and chose to get out of the car and walk over.

I took courage from the sign, shifted into low, and began nursing our machine slowly over the span. The steering gear jerked madly in my hands as the wheels jolted over the pole deck and I felt that strange sensation that afflicts the senses while walking the top rail of a high fence. There were no reassuring guardrails and the bridge timbers jiggled and shook their worst at the center of the span above the racing crest of the mountain stream.

Mildred had hurried down the stony bank of the creek to take a picture. I heard her yell and caught an eye-corner glimpse of her headlong tumble into the edge of the stream. She made an exceptional landing, on her knees and elbows in the icy water, awkwardly but effectively holding her camera in both hands, inches above the swift current. She saved the camera at the expense of skinned elbows and painfully bruised knees. Wet and chilled, she managed to take the picture despite the tumble. I sat in the car in the middle of the span for the "shot." In this one I was not smiling. I was laughing, while my wife demanded I shut my big mouth and sit still.

Three hours later at Chilko Lake a woman rushed out of a sod-roofed log cabin to greet our arrival. Bug-eyed, incredulous, she asked: "Did you drive in here?" It must have been obvious that we had. She added, "The only outsiders we see fly in from the Coast."

# "This Is It!"

In September of 1954, the greatest adventure of our married life was dawning. It was the beginning of a love affair with the Chilcotin that lasted until forty years later when physical infirmities caught up with us and dictated a change in our life-style. At this time we had no awareness of the ultimate change. We spent that span of time in complete happiness with our love for a north region where nature makes all the rules by which you live.

It was late September. Early frosts had already triggered the arrival of brilliant autumn as we again headed north through Fraser's canyon into Cariboo. The reds of sumac among the arid bluffs of Thompson River, the rich cinnamon brown and dense greens of the ponderosas above the old cowtown of Clinton gradually merged with the gold of aspens in the interior grass country. As we rolled on beyond 100 Mile House on the historic freight route of the old North Road we felt the increasing sharpness of the air.

Bumping westward from Williams Lake, we crawled down the rough winding dirt road to the Fraser crossing. There was a return of the original feeling of uncertainty as we again eased onto the worn wooden planks of the old cable suspension bridge. It creaked and groaned as we crossed above the muddy turbulence of the river at the foot of Sheep Creek Hill.

In low gear we lugged up the dizzy switchbacks to the deck of the Chilcotin Plateau. From this, the eastern rim of the high country, the amazing spread of parklands again lay before us—undulating miles of wild grass dotted with a myriad of lakes, pine ridges and aspen groves that shimmered in the prairie breezes. Far westward the peaks of the Coast Range stood dimly along the horizon. Again the exhilarating feeling of being on top of the world! In her silence I knew that Mildred was aware of it too.

We moved on westward. Our vehicle now seemed to respond more willingly, having survived the long climb up from the river. We wound past miles of log and pine pole fences of old ranches, some of which date back to the closing years of the gold rush to Barkerville. In our rearview mirror the dense, dun-colored dust of a roadbed that had baked under weeks of hot sun followed us as a continuously swirling cloud. The dust found its way into eyes, noses, ears and everything we carried in the back seat including sleeping bags, camp gear and grub. We were a study in yellow when we rolled to a jolting stop at Chilanko Forks to refill our near-empty gas tank, seven hours out of Williams Lake. We had come 114 jarring miles.

At that time, the little store at Chilanko Forks was the business of Curly (Pat) Swaile and his pretty, young wife Dolores, a friendly outgoing couple. She set out cups of coffee and huge slices of homemade apple pie for us as we rested and visited. I made the inquiries usually asked by Interior travelers, "How's the road on west?" and drew the standard Chilcotin answer: "A little rough!"

Having mentioned we were looking for some available Crown Land, preferably on a lake, Curly suggested we take a look at Little Eagle, which he described to us as "real pretty, blue as a robin's egg, with a lot of little bays and islands." He went on to picture the natural beauties of Little Eagle as equal to anything to be seen at Banff or Lake Louise. Mildred and I were really interested by the time Dolores was refilling our coffee cups for the third time. I was enthusiastically proclaiming her the champion of all Canadian pie makers when a rancher named Satre came in. Told we were looking for Little Eagle Lake but didn't know where to turn off to find it, Satre said, "Just follow me, I'm going on that way. I'll show you where the turnoff is."

We did just that, choking on the dust from Satre's truck to follow him west of Chilanko. An hour and twenty-seven miles later Satre stopped and walked back to us. Pointing to a dim trace of old wagon tracks twisting into the dense bush, he said, "Little

Eagle Lake is back in there about four miles. The road's rough, not much better than a trail, but it's rock solid and safe. Just take it easy and you'll be okay." He turned back to his truck and his "So-long" waving arm was lost in the dust as he headed on west rattling over the stony road.

We were at once in low gear, crawling jerkily, bumping over and around boulders of the pioneer trail.

At half the distance in, we came into the reddened dead foliage of seedling pines where fire had raced across the moraine leaving acres of death in the young forest. The scene of so much devastation was disheartening. But around another curve in the trail we were beyond the burn and once more in the cool shade of densely standing lodge poles. Mounting a sharp rise that crested on a rocky ridge and sent us easing down a long slope, we were aware of a cool freshness of the air and realized we were nearing water. Minutes later, still moving at a crawl, our dusty car rolled through an arbor of green overhanging limbs of close-standing pines to emerge into the grass of a wild meadow studded with blue asters, sloping to the white sandy shore of a blue-green bay.

"Umm!" I heard Mildred exclaim softly.

There lay Little Eagle, its startlingly bright turquoise depths a placid mirror reflecting the puffs of cumulus clouds and the 9,000 foot crests of the Niuts whose wild and shattered summits arced across the skyline, snowfields and the blue ice of old glaciers gleaming in the hot September sun.

Along the near shore, open slopes bordered by aspens and cottonwoods already gold in the wake of recent frosts shimmered in the heat of afternoon sun. At the water's edge the dark red of willow, golden birch and the buffy browns of scrub alder marked the curves of the meandering beachline.

A profound silence lay over this peaceful landscape, broken finally by the clear and haunting call of a loon whose solitary movement trailed slowly widening ripples where the big bird cruised over the smooth face of the bay.

Spellbound by the tranquility of this place and the rarity of wilderness beauty, I heard Mildred say, barely above a whisper, "This is it."

"Yes, I guess it is." I agreed, keeping my voice low. And we both knew then, without need of words to emphasize our feelings, this was really no guess. We had found what we were searching for after years of roaming the backlands of Cariboo!

To our southeast—possibly a mile—the far shore was darkened by the thick spires of tall spruces, their slender spikes rising above the gold of the aspens. The spruce forest, interwoven with the paler yellow-green of lodgepole pines, stretched back and upward to become the dark bulk of Splinter Mountain.

The Niuts are a spur of the main chain of the Coast Range which include 13,260-foot Mount Waddington. The sheer and broken crags of the Coastal Range farther west and northwest dominate more than 100 miles of visible horizon. We felt the immensity of sky and mountains here. In this vast panorama of wild grandeur, the timbered hills fell away northward beyond clear vision to become mere obscure and hazy forms on the far horizon.

We were anxious to explore.

The profusion of wilderness magnificence that greeted our arrival was exhilarating. The weariness of heat, dust and long hours of driving over bone-jarring roads fell away, to be forgotten as we walked Little Eagle's shoreline and the autumn woods. Warm sun brewed a heady fragrance of evergreens and drying meadow grass. Yellowing clumps of soapolallie were thick among the gray trunks of aspens where grouse flushed ahead of our approach. Frost-nipped wild rose bushes made startling patches of flaming color.

Nature had created a natural park here and she had been most generous. The chirking of fat pine squirrels racing among the spruces in lightning-fast leaps from tree to tree, and the drumming of grouse, told of the abundance of food and security they had found here.

We came into an old burn. Blackened trunks of fire-killed trees lay criss-crossed where they had fallen many years ago. Here the young lodgepole seedlings were rising in their characteristic bushy density to reclaim the land with a new living color. Among them we followed well worn trails where moose had passed to other aspen and willow groves along the borders of the lake. The droppings along these trails told not only of moose, but of deer and wild horses that patronized the rich nourishment to be found in these parklands.

As we walked onto a rounded promontory we came to look across the jade green waters of a narrow channel to a small island lying about 300 feet offshore. Against a background of blue sky, its tall spires of dark spruces, bright yellow cottonwoods and golden aspens cast their bright reflection onto the clear depths of the channel.

The island was alive with birds and their clear twitterings came to us, accented by the sharp knocking of sapsuckers and woodpeckers at work on the decay of old snags standing starkly gray among the living trees.

We began speculating on the possibility of this island becoming a sanctuary, forever preserved for the protection of birds and other wildlife. It was while enjoying our first sight of the island and its many birds that Mildred and I concluded our cabin should be built among the trees on this promontory where we stood, if the land were open to settlement.

From the vantage point here our view also took in the wider, deeper expanses of Little Eagle to the east, the far hills surrounding it a mixture of greens in varying shades bordering the red scars of old forest fires. Ragged swatches of the yellow and gold of autumn-turned aspen groves formed a staggering patchwork on the slopes of the hills. To the south and southwest the ice and high snowfields of the Niuts lay sharp and clear against the sky.

Following a day of walking, in which we explored several miles of lakefront, we decided to make a fast trip south to Government House in Clinton to learn whether this land might be available; and if so, to secure the application notices we would need for posting—"Staking our claim"—in the Chilcotin. It was about 250 miles back to Clinton.

Near dusk we returned to the meadow.

We pitched our two-man mountain tent in the ripening grass and long after our night fire had become a dull red of dying embers we lay talking in our sleeping bags. It seemed strange that such a place still existed, unspoiled, untenanted by humankind.

We dozed off in peaceful, satisfying sleep.

Our hours of sleep that first night were suddenly shattered by a blustery south wind and pelting rain that drummed on the canvas of our tent. We roused out, hurriedly pulled a big protecting tarp over our light shelter and secured it with ropes and rocks. We were somewhat dampened returning to our sleeping bags but were soon warm and comfortable again, finally dropping off to sleep while the rain continued its hammering above our heads.

Dawn came with new snow on the Niuts and an urgency to get going!

We once more walked over the area we had chosen, returning to camp, hurriedly stowed our gear and headed out, realizing the season was late, our own available vacation time fast expiring, the distance great and the road exceedingly rough. Failing now, the impending snows of winter would block us out until another year.

There was the temptation to rush, to push our vehicle beyond the ten to fifteen miles an hour the pot-holed road dictated. The overnight mantle of new snow on the Niuts gave us an added spur. By dark we arrived at Chilanko store and that night we remained with Pat and Dolores Swaile, enjoying the warm comfort of a sod-roofed log cabin. We were again on the road early, with a quart of good Canadian coffee in our thermos prepared by Dolores to supplement the sandwiches we would consume on the way to Clinton. We did just that, driving nonstop to get the rough

31

miles behind us, even drank our coffee from cups half-filled to avoid sloshing as we bounced and banged over the rutted road.

That day we traversed the remaining miles from Chilanko to Williams Lake in five hours. This was excellent speed. At Williams Lake we were back on an improved highway again and made better time on its blacktop south to Clinton. At Government House we learned, happily, that we could apply for the desired land at Little Eagle; that the island was, in fact, an established sanctuary. We obtained the application forms we would need to post and advertize, ate a quick lunch in the historic old Clinton Hotel and were headed north, again bound for the lake, before the engine in our car had time to cool.

After two full days and nearly 500 miles of steady driving, we were again parked in the little meadow at the west end of our lake, prepared to stake a homesite. Looking back, it occurs to me that one remarkable feature of the entire wild ride out to Clinton and back was not one of our old tires blew!

That Mildred was never one to dally is borne out by our diary entry for September 28, 1954, in which, after recounting the long and jolting hours of the return trip, she wrote:

"Back to Little Eagle. Arrived about 3:00 p.m. Road slow account of rain, mud, and very rough. Made camp again, same spot where we camped Wed. Gathered wood for campfire—made tent secure for threatening bad weather. Temp. 36 degrees (F.) tonite, overcast. More fresh snow on Coast Mts. We again hiked north shore of Lk late today, made preliminary pace-off of land lines. Looks very good. Turned in 9:00 p.m., tired from long drive...."

We were awakened by the heat of early sun pouring into the open face of our tent. I raised onto elbows for a look around, sleepy eyes blinking in the dazzling brilliance of sun on the flat surface of the lake. The pine grass in the little meadow was white with frost. Beyond the rise of forested hills of the Homathko Valley, the snow peaks and ice-bound saddles of the range were sharply outlined against the intense blue of the morning sky. Another fresh coat of snow had been added during the night.

Under the warmth of our big double sleeping bag I pulled on

woolen socks before rolling out to dress. The quick crackle of a dry pine cooking fire and the sweet smell of its smoke were a pleasant prelude to a hearty breakfast for healthy appetites.

Carrying a shovel and camp ax, our light packsacks stuffed with extra wool shirts, peanut butter sandwiches, chocolate bars, an orange apiece, compass and surveyor's chain, we headed through a mile of autumn woods on the business of staking our claim to a homesite in the Chilcotin. This was our big day.

Walking the shorelines of the narrow channel separating the mainland from the island, we were again on the promontory which embraced about fifteen acres with sandy bays on both of its flanks. The lay of land here was ideal for our purpose, with a fairly good supply of slender northern spruces closely available for cabin logs. After studying the shape of waterfront trees, which indicated by the slant of their crowns the prevailing winds here were from the southwest, we selected the site of our future cabin in a spot calculated to give us the best available protection, relying on a stand of spruces for a windbreak.

The location was ideal for other reasons. The island, where we heard bird song any time we stopped to listen, lay in a direct view from the spot where Mildred said we should have some big windows. Beyond the west end of the island the full sweep of the Niuts would be included in our view.

Enchanting bays with their white sand bottoms flanked both sides of the point of land where we planned our cabin. The greater bulk of the lake stretched off to our east, its extreme limits an obscure dark line at the foot of steep hills. From the sloping contours of distant headlands it was quite obvious even from where we first viewed it, Eagle's eastern waters were deeper. We saw them as dark areas of near jade green in contrast to the turquoise blue of the lake near its shallower west end.

In a stand of old spruces, their crowns bowed with the weight of huge clusters of ripening cones, we came upon the weathered gray poles of slim lodgepole pines that in time past had served the Chilcotins as a horse corral, and nearby the rotting square of logs which had stood as a wall for a tent. The brittle dry heads of squawfish, old rib cages and the scattered bleached bones of deer and moose bore mute evidence of the Indians' harvests of winter meat, in some earlier time.

I was sure we could resurrect the old corral with the reinforcement of a few new poles and visualized its future use as a good holding pen for our own two saddle horses when the time should come to bring them north. On this same warm day we also discovered, a short distance east of the site chosen for our cabin, a little meadow of possibly half an acre that would lend itself as a good location for a stable. The meadow was almost completely surrounded by a golden ring of aspens and could readily be fenced in such a way our horses could drink from the edge of the lake.

From our cabin site we chained off the acreage we wanted. Under the rules of the Land Act in force at the time, we could each claim five acres. Each tract would be limited to five chains or 330 lineal feet of lake frontage, by ten chains or 660 lineal feet of depth extending at right angles to the frontage, thus comprising five acres more or less.

Following the letter of the act, which was explicit in a typically British style of wording (leaving nothing for conjecture), we ran our lines north, east, south and west to point of beginning, allowing twenty-four degrees by the needle, west of north, for declination in this latitude.

With an ax we cut and squared green aspen posts on which to

attach our location notices. The Act said these posts shall be at least four feet above ground; they shall be hewed square for two feet down from the top, each face of the squared section to be not less than four inches wide. They shall be set facing the lake, with all obscuring brush or other growth removed to assure a clear view of the posted notices.

The attached notices were titled "Declaration of Intention to Apply for the Purchase of Crown Land in the Province of British Columbia, Canada."

Long before we arrived at the post setting phase of our efforts, however, we walked, chained and rewalked the shoreline at least a dozen times, my wife in particular. In the heat of the day I finally pooped out and took refuge in some shade while Mildred continued. It seemed to me she was forever trying to stretch our statutory lot limits to include "just this little clump of pines" or "just enough to take in this big old spruce." But a 100-foot surveyor's chain will not stretch. Consequently there was a lot of back-tracking that day, to select, finally, the best nature had to offer. For here, her offerings were bountiful and difficult to discard, even when faced with a final choosing limited by the cold, uncompromising length of the steel tape.

Exact copies of the notices as posted must be submitted to the nearest newspaper of general circulation. This would be Al Hardy's *Lillooet-Bridge River News*, a weekly nearly 300 miles to our south. Also required was publication in the official *British Columbia Gazette*, a government recording at the provincial capital Victoria. Following publication over a period of six weekly issues of the newspaper and the *Gazette*, a provincial inspector would look over the land under question and if he saw fit we would have approval to apply for purchase—or rejection if he didn't. We might lose out for any of several other reasons, including an improperly posted notice, or a protest from the Cariboo Cattlemen's Association. This was—and is—an organization of ranchers which is perhaps best known by the long record of its protests against the government's policies of land alienation to new settlers. If we cleared that hurdle, we might buy the land outright at so much per acre, when and if properly

35

surveyed by an accredited engineer, and then would be given four years in which to make minimal improvements. These improvements also had to be approved by a government representative, following which title would be issued as a Crown Land Grant.

The day we set our location posts was one of those truly typical of a Chilcotin September. So calm, so tranquil, that while standing quietly to gaze upon the autumn scene about us the silence could be heard. In setting our posts—one at each of the southwesterly corners of the tracts bordering the lake shore—I was digging among sand and boulders to sink a post hole, when we both became startled by the sound of what we thought were gunshots a mile or more away on the south shore. We had thought we were the only two people in this wilderness, but surmised then it might be Indians after winter meat as there was considerable moose sign around the lake.

We paused to listen, then I resumed digging. There were more shots and again we stopped to listen. The sharp sounds ceased. Experimentally, I jabbed the steel of my shovel down among the boulders and we realized that we were hearing the reports only with my action. The "shots" were simply the sharp clear echoes from the shovel rebounding from the mountainside of the south shore nearly a mile away. I struck a rock a ringing whack with the shovel and got back a ringing musical echo from the distant hills. And as we laughed in the enjoyment of our surprise, the long-drawn wail of a loon came to our ears from far up the lake, as if to protest the fractious racket of our invasion.

Somewhat laboriously—for we had no other tool—I carved the name "Jenkins" and "S.W. Corner" with my hunting knife on the proper face of our location post.

* * * * *

Goldenrod, somewhat out of blossom, was still thick along the shoreline. Numerous other plants now with seed pods, some familiar, many unfamiliar, stirred our interest. Under the spruces we walked on the deep, springy carpet of many years' accumulation, where squirrels had dropped the thin brown scales of spruce cones in their diligent quest of the small black seeds which are the chief source of their food. Some of the cone scales were in heaps to a depth of more than a foot under the low branches, the discard of many years. Overhead, in several of the tall spruces, great blobs of dried grasses and twigs appeared to be nests as well. Limbs on the sunny south sides of the trees were dotted with mushrooms spread out for curing in the sun.

We returned to our camp in the meadow by bright moonlight, flushing several grouse in the willow thickets near the shore. We prepared our supper after dark that night and later crawled, well satisfied, into our sleeping bags. Nightfall had come on the heels of a red and gold sunset that turned the new snow on the Niuts to coral pink.

On the following day, September 30, we hiked our land lines again, made a further and final check of the setting of our location posts and then regretfully broke camp to start homeward that afternoon. My fingers were lame and stiff from lettering on posts with the hunting knife. Getting away from Little Eagle too late in the day to be sure of reaching Williams Lake before midnight, we stopped for the night at the Willow Springs Ranch of Bill and Irene Bliss on the Chilcotin River, a little east of Redstone. We bunked warm in a small cabin they maintained for the use of occasional hunters. The Blisses are pioneer Chilcotin ranchers, and Bill is a very lucky man as Mrs. Bliss is one of the best cooks north of the 49th parallel, has one of the finest gardens seen anywhere on the plateau and maintains a home that exudes such warmth and friendliness you can feel it just driving by their flower-banked log house on a summer day.

The next day we were again heading south to the routine of gainful employment. But this was a satisfying means to an end, now, and we would be returning soon. We had staked our claim to the future, richest years of our lives.

# The Wilderness Road

Months of hope and anxiety ended for us with a June letter from the provincial land office in Victoria, informing us our applications for purchase had been approved.

In early July we were again headed north. With us were Floyd and Ruthella Cyr and their seventeen-year-old son Gary, friends of long standing and all "outdoors people" with whom we had enjoyed many a camp-out. This was to be their introduction to our Eagle Lake and Chilcotin, and from that time on they have been as in love with it as we have, sharing with us many of its pleasures. The two vehicles were heavily loaded with camping gear, ours also carried our new seventeen-foot aluminum canoe strapped on top.

On this trip I learned one of my early lessons in what not to do in the northern bush and the experience cost me the pain of several cracked ribs. En route we were camping overnight at Beaver Dam Lake in the southern Cariboo. In stretching up a new canvas tarp for a shelter I chose an aspen about six inches in diameter on which to secure one end of the ridge rope. To get the rope high enough for head clearance, I shinnied up about five feet and made the mistake of throwing my leg and weight onto a lower limb—the brittle wood quickly snapped out of its socket-like joint. I landed flat on my back on the rocks we had piled up to shield our campfire, the breath knocked out of me. By next day my ribs were agonizingly painful, eased somewhat when Mildred strapped me up with two-inch wide adhesive tape from our first aid kit.

With both Floyd and Gary along, I was relieved of driving and managed quite well despite the discomfort.

During the following week, my ribs being too sore for more strenuous action, we trolled in the deep bays of Little Eagle, hopeful of taking some of the big rainbows Curly Swaile had told us about. We eventually tried "everything in the book" as a lure without so much as a strike. It was then I began to realize that Curly's remarks about the indifference of the lake's rainbows to the lure of artificial baits were well-founded.

Little Eagle is known for its big rainbows. They run to six and seven pounds, and are first cousins to the steelheads of the Chilcotin River. But Eagle's rainbows are fat and lazy, the result of the natural bounty of the lake, which is richly populated with varieties of insects and other native foods.

We saw the fat rainbows frequently in the clear depths shaded by the canoe bottom. Floyd remarked once that he thought he saw one as long as his arm actually sneering at his favorite gear—a Colorado spinner and a fat nightcrawler. Finally we drove thirty-five miles west to Clearwater, a lake with no reputation for other than a tangle of weed beds, and there we filled our limits and ate rainbows up to fifteen inches.

This is not to say the rainbows in our lake are never taken. (In years since, Floyd has fulfilled his ambition here.) They are caught on occasion, but generally only through the exercise of great patience and a willingness to endure long periods of disappointment. Little Eagle's big rainbows are a fisherman's challenge.

During this vacation trip we widened our acquaintance with the Chilcotin Plateau and many of its lakes by showing the Cyrs some of our favored discoveries. Under expert tutoring from Floyd, I was becoming a slightly rabid fisherman, particularly addicted to a preference for spinning gear and light tackle which, at the instant of strike from a hungry rainbow, telegraphs an electrifying thrill to the angler. Mildred also became infected. Our spinning rods and tackle box are now carried with the camping gear. Nightcrawlers, brought into the Interior from the lower Fraser country, were preserved in a large kettle of damp woods moss.

The nightcrawlers, we also learned, could be kept fat and healthy over long periods of time by an occasional very light feeding of cornmeal and by keeping the moss dampened and cool.

This was the year the fabulous fishing at Nimpo Lake to our north became hot news among sport fishermen in the States and the old Chilcotin Road was a solid streak of choking dust as an invasion of American anglers poured into the back country. We saw car licenses from several different states, all apparently heading for Nimpo.

We were glad Eagle Lake was not considered "hot" as the stampede of eager fishermen brought nothing to the peace of the wilderness that we were interested in. While a majority of them, both Canadian and Americans, were definitely appreciative of the clean beauty of the Plateau and burned or buried their garbage and left clean camps, there were those whose contribution of beer cans, blown-out tires and other abandoned trash did nothing to enhance the beauty of the bush. This was also a year of thoughtless invasion of the winter emergency cabins the Provincial Department of Highways kept stocked with food and fuel at strategic intervals along the lonely 300-mile route between Williams Lake and Bella Coola. These were the tight little one-room cabins, provisioned and left unlocked, that stood as mute signals of warmth and shelter, havens of security for snowplow crews stalled by deep winter drifts, or anyone else who might be the victim of breakdown, long miles from available help.

We were happy to be by-passed at Little Eagle.

Initial experience with our new aluminum canoe quickly convinced us an outboard motor was not to our liking. We had brought with us our son Will's light-weight five-horsepower motor. The canoe not being designed for a transom attachment, the motor was hung from a bracket clamped to the stern gunwale on the port side. Despite the fact the motor weighed less than fifteen pounds, the power and thrust of its propeller was so strong the canoe shot forward with unexpected speed. The least shift in the angle of the propeller sent the canoe into a quick curving run; any sudden push or pull on the steering lever resulted in fast, wide circles. It was difficult to idle down to a slow cruising speed, or to hold an even course.

I think we gave it a fair trial. Mildred, Floyd, Ruthella and Gary made one trip to the south shore. Returning, they got caught in a strong westerly that churned the lake to a froth. The outboard motor had been stalling that day and, rather than risk more trouble in open water, they beached the canoe and walked the two miles around the west end of the lake to reach camp. We recovered the canoe in calm weather the following day.

Mildred readily admitted she was likely the cause of their walking home as she was terrified of rough water. We could get her into the canoe only when there was absolute calm. On more than one excursion she had made us pull ashore to wait for a breeze to subside.

Floyd, Gary and I worked on the motor, trying to familiarize ourselves with its sudden acceleration and its eccentricities. After cleaning the spark plug, adjusting the "gap" in the firing space and nursing the choke for half an hour, the motor suddenly took off with such a burst of speed I nearly fell out of the canoe.

When I complained to Mildred that our new canoe was jumping around like a wounded jackrabbit, she simply confirmed what I knew she felt, saying, "Take the darned motor off and leave it off! I don't like it anyway—it stinks up the air and makes too much noise."

Happy to be included in opposition to any device that tended to disturb the solitude of Little Eagle or pollute the purity of the air we were privileged to breathe, I took the motor off and from that day on—with few exceptions—we have relied on our paddles for power, with complete satisfaction.

We learned the honest reliability of our canoe. Proper handling was an ability acquired only through use and experience. On this trip we did have good use of the canoe, but without the attached motor. It took us where the fishing was excellent, however, with only two or three of us in the canoe at one time, realizing the proper capacity. Mildred begged off every time she could, for she still was timid of being on the water.

While the Cyrs were with us, when we weren't fishing or otherwise traveling, we searched out a suitable route for a mile of road to our cabin site. This meant scouting out possible grades through the aspen, spruce and pines between the Old Tatlayoko Road, a little north of the wild meadow where we were camping, and our cabin site to the east.

We spread out, five abreast but at intervals of about 100 feet, always within shouting distance and walked slowly westward through the woods until we emerged on the old wagon trail. In this manner the best grades were discovered; low gullies, large rocks and thick clumps of trees or other major obstacles were called out among us as we walked and thus would be avoided when the final route for clearing by ax and saw was decided upon. The result was an excellent grade in dry weather, following a gradual hogback, or ridge, from east to west, which is also a good winter road when snow lies deep over the land.

Building road in the thinly timbered areas of the Chilcotin presents only minor problems as compared to those one would face in a similar task among the old growth of giant conifers and dense underbrush of the wet Coastal belt. The Plateau climate is semi-arid; annual precipitation is a scant fifteen to seventeen inches a year and cutting out a road, such as the one Mildred and I eventually built, is frequently accomplished rather quickly with the aid of a chain saw, severing the stumps flush to the ground. Two "good men" can open up a mile of road in three or four days in areas favored by occasional grassy glades.

During construction of our log house, in which we hired some help, a rough truck trail was slashed out hurriedly to make access easier from the Old Tatlayoko Road. The location was not to our liking, however, because it passed through some low and troublesome dips and hollows and, at one point, a sharp, steep pitch with a difficult curve at the bottom of the grade. Invariably, we dragged bottom getting in with a heavily loaded truck—the way we usually traveled. We planned to abandon that section and ultimately did. The new grade was a trifle longer but followed a very gradual slope and was quite smooth as compared to the original route.

I recollect the satisfaction we felt in laying out the final mile. Especially now do we enjoy a section which skirts the open crown of an ancient moraine. Here the pines are more scattering

and here the snow disappears early as sunshine warms the gently sloping hillside. This section is also favored by many birds, attracted by the early warmth and bare ground. Here we often see black cap and mountain chickadees, juncos, nuthatches, hairy woodpeckers, swallows, grouse and an occasional flock of Bohemian waxwings.

In summer and early fall the slope is dotted with mats of a very small, low-growing blueberries. The fruit is exceedingly sweet, especially after a frost, and well worth the effort to pick if you can beat the birds and bears to them.

From this open hillside we get our very first sweeping view of the blue-green waters of the lake, together with the full panorama of the many glaciered Coast Range and the deep valleys stretching south to Tatlayoko. From here we also glimpse the peaks that surround Bluff Lake. It is also our final viewpoint when going out, as this old moraine is quickly swallowed from sight by thick stands of pine.

At the western end of the moraine are a number of pines favored by the birds for nesting. There are some old snags, dead for many years as the result of fire, where the woodpeckers have had annual good foraging for grubs. Among these blackened snags, the swallows and other small birds contend for the right to occupy the woodpecker holes at nesting time. Even the yellowjacket wasps, which we could get along without, and the friendly bumblebees, favor the broad sunny slope.

The ridge is not on our land but we have come to call it "our ridge" as the result of the pleasures we have found there on summer days. One time, when Mildred and I had been woods-walking and missed an old game trail we counted on to bring us out to the lake shore, we sat down to rest and take our bearings. Relaxing on a grassy mound dotted with the crimson blooms of Indian paintbrush, we pondered in which way lay our camp. As we sat there and speculated, a glimpse of the ridge of the old moraine came unexpectedly to us through an opening in the pines. A tall blackened snag—one we had built our road around rather than cut it down because we thought it grotesquely beautiful—caught our eye. So we headed for the ridge, guided by the shiny black satin of the fire-charred pine and were soon back to our cabin.

It is strange how a piece of wild landscape can attach itself to one's affections. Not once, but on several occasions, on leaving Little Eagle Lake in our car, and in later years in our pickup trucks, we have slowed to a halt on the open ridge, there to take one last look at the sapphire depths of the lake and the sweep of snow-capped mountains beyond. As a rule, Mildred packs a size-able lunch of sandwiches and fills a quart thermos with coffee when we leave camp, as the drive to Williams Lake and the Cariboo Highway would usually take from six to seven hours, and sometimes longer. We always went well prepared. The ridge is less than ten minutes driving time from the cabin, but we stop here, and not infrequently we remain to eat our lunch before going on; the reason for that being we get all ready to go, then we want to take one more look around to stamp its beauty in our memories. It's always so beautiful we dread leaving and sort of begin dragging our feet. It seems it invariably works out that the day we get set to go "Outside" turns out to be a day we just can't forget. I don't know how many times it has happened this way for us. So, by the time we actually drive off, a good part of the day is already gone. The number of pictures we have taken from this ridge would fill a large box.

"Aren't we the nuts!" Mildred will say. "Here we are less than half a mile from camp, and already it's lunch time!"

"It depends on how you look at it," I say.

We may be sort of crazy but we're having a lot of fun being that way. And besides that, we seldom know the time of day any more. We have quit watching the clock in more ways than one.

Today our log home stands on the promontory in the shoreline facing the snowy peaks of the Niut Range and Coastal Sierra, and our big windows take in a scene of natural grandeur unrivaled. We are within easy seeing distance of Little Eagle's four islands. The larger one "out front" beyond The Narrows, we named Bird Island. Another, a little to our southwest, we named Goose Island. As many as five honker pairs use it annually to bring off their young. A third is Loon Island, a low-lying hogback with one part nearly awash, where loons nest at water's edge and are thus able to belly-slide into the lake with one push from their webbed feet. The fourth we named Coyote Island, for a pair of sly coyotes. But that is another story.

# We Asked For It!

Around Little Eagle Lake, and especially along our north shore, wintering moose moved down from the high country to browse on the plentiful hardwoods. The hooshum berry bushes are thick here, too, and these all combined as excellent forage. Several bulls and cows made their beds in deep drifts close to our cabin while others took up quarters on Bird Island. We bothered none of them and they came to regard us with a casual, almost intimate tolerance. There was more than three tons of available fresh meat standing around out there, or sleeping in the drifts, if we ever needed it. But we never did to the point of drawing a bead. Some of Chilcotin's old-timers seemed to think we were foolish to pass up so much meat on the hoof around our door, but we never felt the urge to kill.

In mid-January, we noticed in The Narrows, a maze of tracks criss-crossing the snow crust to converge at a roughened and dark area of the frozen surface. Watching from our window we soon discovered the dark spot was water percolating up through the ice from a hot spring and the animals had been coming there to drink during the night.

On the morning of the twenty-seventh, after an overnight temperature of 30 degrees Fahrenheit, we noticed another water hole had opened in the ice about twenty-five feet off-shore. We laid some boards on the ice out to the wet spot to examine it. I stood on the boards to sweep and dig the crusty snow away from the hole. A thin flow of water spread outward to saturate the surrounding crust. The hole appeared to be approximately round and eighteen or twenty inches in diameter in the crust, while the opening in the underlying ice was possibly six to eight inches wide. Looking down into this hole, we could see the sandy bottom of Eagle Lake and the movement of fine sand in the water percolating upward from below. I stuck the handle of the broom into the hole and found water to a depth of about three and a half feet. Mildred took some snapshots of our discovery. Days of melting snow for water had come to an end. I enlarged the hole so water could be dipped with a bucket.

Within a week several additional spring holes opened in the surface. Now we understood the pattern of animal tracks seen earlier. The channel of The Narrows between our foreshore and Bird Island was an area of warm springs.

We were elated by our good fortune. We drove pine poles into the lake bottom to mark the location of several of the springs. The following summer we would build our log canoe landing with its outer end at the very edge of a bubbling spring, and here, in future winters, dipping buckets for fresh water would be a simple matter.

In February, large flocks of mountain and blackcap chickadees came to feed and hover in the trees around our cabin. We were often awakened in early mornings by the rapid tapping of their bills on the frozen feed board outside our window. We spread corn meal, rolled oats and all available crumbs on the boards. We often sat at our table, scant inches from the hungry birds, and they soon developed a manner of acknowledging our presence and our offerings of food, by a fearless willingness for intimate association.

In time, if we were a little late to the table, the chickadees had a way of showing impatience. Hopping along the edges of the sash, close to the glass, they cocked their heads inquisitively and eyed us closely. Their every move seemed to be urging us to hurry with the business of breakfast.

The chickadees were joined by Canada jays and hairy woodpeckers, who came in boldly to gobble scraps of bacon fat, much of which the jays carried off to private caches in the forest.

This winter we discovered that squirrels are not strictly vegetarians. They came to gnaw on bacon rinds, often quarreled over them with the jays and woodpeckers, and worked endlessly to pull the rinds from the nails that held them to the boards and trees.

The extreme cold of early February caused the chickadees to fluff their feathers. They often sat in our feeder window squatting low over their feet for the added warmth of their tiny bodies. Water was no problem for our chickadees. They got all they needed simply by flying up under the cabin eaves to land—often head down—on the suspended spikes of icicles where they drank from the drip produced by cabin warmth.

As days of below zero weather continued, we gave up starting our truck motor to keep the pickup in running condition. We brought the truck's two batteries into the cabin to prevent freezing and draped the hood with a large canvas tarpaulin. Every day now we snowshoed out to the summit of the Old Tatlayoko Road, packing down the winter trail. We were frequently out on our webs until dusk and sometimes our trips back to the cabin were made in the cold brightness of early moonlight. In time Mildred and I graduated from the clumsy, stumbling phase of our snowshoe education. As the soreness of leg muscles gave way to a toughened endurance, we became more proficient in ability to swing along on our webs at a steady rhythmic pace. Our treks over deep drifts that began in the futile effort to keep our road open, became a routine chore of pleasure.

I think that among my fondest memories of our first winter on the Plateau are recollections of moonlight among the aspens, their long shadows cast upon the milky whiteness of the snow, the soft, gentle crunch of our snowshoes the only sound in a world of silent wilderness. There would be the sweet pungence of pine smoke from the banked fire in our heater as we returned to our cabin woods on these quiet nights. A late meal was immediately satisfying to our healthy appetites. And to crawl into the snug warmth of our bunk was to fall into instant and profound sleep. No sleeping pills needed here.

Early one morning as we were preparing for a snowshoe trip along the north ridge, we were startled by the barking of a dog. A big red Chesapeak came bounding through the pines. It came loping joyfully up to Mildred and me, plainly happy to see us. While we speculated on who the dog could possibly belong to, we heard the rumble of a motor. A moment later a B.C. Forest

Service truck—a heavy four-wheel drive that sat high on wide chain-clad tires—came pushing through, quite unhindered by the depth of snow that had proved such a bane to our light pickup. In it were four young men of the Service, who explained they had come to the north ridge to lay out the lines of a wood lot granted to us on an application we had made during late fall.

When introductions had gone around, we were told they would be through running our wood lot lines by about four o'clock. They suggested if we wanted to get out to Tatla we could follow with our pickup, taking advantage of the tracks of their heavy vehicle. Also, if we had difficulty, they could help us. That sounded good to us.

We visited over coffee and after the young fellows left, we prepared to act on this opportunity to go out for mail and groceries. Since it would be late when we arrived there, we prepared for an overnight stay at Tatla.

Immediately, we placed a Coleman camp stove under the engine block of our pickup to heat the oil in its crank case. About three o'clock, I returned the warmed batteries to the truck and the motor fired into action at a touch on the starter.

As we headed out, expecting to join the crew of young foresters at the junction of our trail and the Old Tatlayoko Road, we were immediately conscious of a difficulty we had not foreseen. The chain-equipped Forest Service vehicle had a much wider wheel base than our light pickup. In our snowshoeing, Mildred and I had tamped down the tracks our own truck had made, and these were now parallel ridges of solid ice and compact snow.

My efforts to follow in the tracks of either our own truck or those of the foresters' machine caused constant wallowing and skidding, the steering wheel at times jerked from my grasp by the contortions of those frozen tracks. We managed, however, to reach the junction with a lot of swerving from rut to rut. We found the forest crew waiting for us. They piloted us out and eventually all arrived at Tatla.

At the post office and store we collected accumulated mail and newspapers. We also stocked up on some needed groceries. There had been a spitting of fine snow all day, as if to warn of more to come. We should have returned to our cabin on Eagle then, while our truck tracks in the new snow were still of some value to our chance for a return. Instead, we decided to remain overnight at Tatla and head out the following morning.

We enjoyed a hot meal with Fred and Betty Linder and spent that night in the old pioneer ranch home known as "the Big House" of the Graham Ranch. It was after midnight when we had gone through our accumulation of mail from home. Before I blew out the light of the coal oil lamp I checked the weather from our bedroom window. It was still snowing finely but steadily. We settled under the warmth of Hudson's Bay blankets and a soft down comforter with misgivings about what to expect in the way of weather by daylight.

With a husky ranch-style breakfast of bacon, eggs, hot cakes and coffee under our belts, we headed for Eagle Lake in the morning. It was nineteen degrees above zero Fahrenheit. The three to four inches of snow that had fallen during the night was of no particular problem on the six miles of plowed out Chilcotin Road we traveled. But, the moment we turned onto the old wagon trail that winds the final four miles through heavy stands of pine to Eagle Lake, we knew we were in trouble.

Where the Forest Service power wagon and our own truck had plowed and wallowed through yesterday's drifts, at times merging with the older tracks of Ross Wilson's cattle truck, here now was a tangle of wheel ruts, hard-crusted, and overlaid with several inches of new snow. We shifted immediately into low gear and soon found that we were able to make only about 200 to

300 feet of headway before the snow rolled up into a solid mass over our front bumper and radiator. Then we were forced to stop and dig away the accumulation before going ahead again for another short distance.

As we alternately pushed ahead, stopped, dug out and pushed ahead again, we became aware that as we progressed farther into the jack pines the drifts were becoming deeper. Also, our speedometer was registering mileage we were not actually making as our drive wheels, although well shackled with chains, were spinning uselessly much of the time. At our present rate of slow headway, this day was going to become night long before we reached our cabin.

At times we were barely inching forward. Despite the severe cold, we were wet with sweat and fast becoming weary from tension as well as the constant digging. Getting in and out of the pickup cab to shovel snow, we became soaked to our hips from wallowing into the drifts. At some time around the middle of the day we sat in the cab with the heater full blast to ward off the chill of our soaked clothing, ate a couple of candy bars and drank a thermos of coffee. The exertion was beginning to tell on both of us. At times, when we rammed into the drifts, we found it difficult to swing the cab doors open, then to haul out shovels and flounder forward to a point where we could attack snow piled high against front bumper and radiator. Worst of all was the shoveling where the snow had balled up beneath the front axle and under the engine block. The heat of the engine caused melt which gradually froze into an ever thickening mass of ice under the front system of the truck, and there it could not be reached with a shovel.

Wearily we fought on as the day waned, reluctant to admit defeat. The drifts were much deeper as we struggled toward the summit; the weight of shovel and snow steadily grew heavier to our aching arms. We became aware that after each dig-out to clear the front wheels and bumper our gain in headway was steadily less. The packed and frozen snow under the engine block dragged heavily, opposing each attempt to buck through a new drift.

Finally, in a last futile try in a deeply buried open glade among some seedling pines, we just sort of slid sideways into a smother of snow and came to the halt we knew was final. We had plowed into a king-sized drift that stretched for more than 100 feet ahead and beyond this one we could see still another rise—and deeper snow. Daylight was fading into the dusk of an early winter night. We were too tired to talk but we both knew what we had to do.

We were two miles from our cabin. I threw a big canvas tarp over the hood of the truck, then pulled out our snowshoes while Mildred packed the perishable groceries into two light packsacks. Without wasting further energy by talking, we strapped on our snowshoes, swung the packs onto our backs and were on the trail heading for camp as dusk settled over the Plateau. We kept moving to keep warm. Actually, we both agreed later, putting on our snowshoes and getting some leg action had been a relief after those hours of back-bending digging in the drifts.

My five-foot trail shoes with their north-country webbing (for dry snow) made a good track, sinking only to the depth of the rim. Mildred came along on her smaller bear paws without too much difficulty. Making fair headway though weary, our cold, snow-soaked clothing was soon warmed by walking. We paused now and then for a breather, then pushed on again, aware of the danger of our extreme weariness and the need to keep moving. It was six o'clock and black dark when we came into our clearing. Our cache of pitch pine and dry split wood soon had a fire crackling in the heater and in a few minutes the kettle was singing. We were again warm, sheltered and comfortable, though extremely tired. We had covered a distance of only eleven miles since early morning.

My old diary reveals it was ten degrees above zero at 10:00 P.M. It was then bright moonlight and the tall spruces that circle our clearing stood with tops bent under the shrouds of new snow. We found the tracks of our pet squirrel on the window sills and doorstep where it had come looking for the creatures who had been putting out sunflower seeds and peanut butter every day until this day.

Our registering thermometer indicated four degrees below zero at daylight, which is usually the coldest hour of the day in winter. The barometer stood at 29.26 and was falling. We had slept in a little, still bone tired from yesterday's battle with the drifts. But the appearance of a hairy woodpecker in our window feeder, and a hungry squirrel on hind legs with forepaws and little black snout against the windowpane, obviously looking for us, coaxed us out of our warm bunk. The moment Mildred's feet touched the cabin floor the squirrel began racing wildly back and forth on the window sill in great excitement. Mildred settled him down with a wad of peanut butter. We fastened fresh bacon rinds to the trunks of several trees. The woodpeckers and Canada jays were quick to move in.

I swept out our path to the lake and water-hole. Ice was now approximately twenty inches thick and daily growing thicker. I found that a big, wide bristle barn broom, the push-broom type, made a path in light dry snow faster than by shoveling. I swept the big broom back and forth and, sideways, and soon had a good clear path the near 200 feet from cabin to water-hole.

This day we christened our new cast-iron Dutch oven. Mildred prepared our evening meal with a roast of beef, potatoes, dry onions, carrots and celery from our hoarded stock. We were well fed and relaxed, reading by lamplight, when the silence of the night was suddenly shattered by thumping, a muffled whining at the door, then a voice called out, "Anybody home?" How well we knew that voice!

We opened the door to a big redbone hound and her bluetick running mate, tails whipping joyously, and right behind them shuffling through the snow with full and heavy back-packs came our younger son, Chuck, and his wife Wilma. We stood in the flood of lamplight in our doorway, hounds dashing and leaping around us, as they came stomping in. It was nine o'clock. They had been on the road from Williams Lake since early morning, then had been unable to push their truck more than a quarter mile onto the lake road. As Mildred and I had done the previous day, they left their vehicle, filled their packs, and hiked in the remaining three and a half miles. They were tired and hungry. It didn't take long to have hot coffee and a good supper prepared for them. We made room on the floor for their sleeping bags. The hounds we sheltered that night in an old umbrella tent, warmly banked with snow.

We talked out all the news and recent happenings on the Outside until well after midnight. It was twelve degrees above zero, clear, calm, the blue-black sky scintillating with starfire, one of the most beautiful nights we could recall, made the more enjoyable because two of our kids had joined us.

Next day Chuck and Wilma hiked back to their truck and brought in packloads of food and clothing.

The sudden appearance of the trail hounds, Hoecake, a big female redbone, and Jezzabelle, a slim, whippetlike bluetick, had evidently inspired our pet squirrel with the decision to lie low. We saw no more of it for several days.

Snow lay to a depth above our knees with the temperature at fourteen degrees. Chuck's supply of feed for his hounds was low and he decided to snowshoe out to his truck to get more from a fifty-pound sack he had left in the pickup. Our seven-foot toboggan was still in our own truck two miles from camp and, taking the toboggan with them as they passed, it was used to haul in the dog feed and other supplies.

Gauging our time to meet Chuck and Wilma coming in, Mildred and I left camp on our snowshoes at about three o'clock in the afternoon. We met them with a heavy load on the toboggan, Hoecake in the lead, pulling in an improvised rope harness. The big redbone was hauling the load with apparently little effort, as if she had always done it. On the toboggan was feed for the hounds, extra provisions, Chuck's cased five-string banjo and Wilma's guitar. We were all back in camp by dark. The last mile had been a little rough and I got into harness with Hoecake, pulling on a rope, while Chuck pushed from the rear on a jack pine gee-pole lashed to the load.

All attempts to use the young bluetick, "Jezzy," as a sled dog had been futile. While old Hoecake plodded along patiently pulling the heavily loaded toboggan and showing a willing heart for work, Jezzabelle would have no part of it. We tried her in the harness several times only to see her go wild and unruly in the traces. After she was taken out of the line she would run and dash about and jump on top of the load to ride if she got the chance, mouth spread in a joyous grin.

That night the rhythm of country music filled the winter air as the beat of banjo and guitar drifted over Little Eagle. We played and sang past midnight and I think the coyotes must have enjoyed it too because they joined us, whooping it up at moon-rise. The big northern owls bass fiddled with their deep-throated hooting while grouse drummed loudly among the jack pines. The wilderness of Little Eagle Lake had never heard "a combo" quite like the concert we held this night.

With two trucks stalled in deep drifts all transport in the immediate vicinity of Little Eagle was reduced to the use of snowshoes, the toboggan and back packs. Snow continued to fall, soon became thigh deep over all but the packed down stretches of old snowshoe trails. To leave those trails, any attempt at travel, even on the webs, demanded such an expenditure of physical effort to break a new trail, the notion was quickly aban-doned. We were snowbound.

Wilma surprised us when she brought out a dressed chicken from a foam box in which the bird had been kept fresh. Her chicken casserole, biscuits hot from the oven, green beans and home-frozen strawberries were mighty tasty.

This seemed a good time to take care of some neglected chores around camp, including the installation of windows in the cabin's two doors. Taking advantage of the narrow grooves in the edges of some tongue-and-groove pine boards, we sawed pieces to make frames and inserted panes of glass Mildred and I had brought in from Williams Lake. We soon had good windows in both doors to replace the plastic sheets which had served as panes until now.

Among the items we brought in with us that year was a telescope with which we expected to do a lot of star gazing. I don't recall the maximum power of our tripod telescope but it was plenty skookum; in fact, it was so strong it was hard on my sensitive eyes and I soon lost my enthusiasm for it.

We had the tube set up and working when Chuck and Wilma arrived and spent several evenings drawing a bead on a big glittering star that flared brilliantly in the night sky to our east. I think this one turned out to be Jupiter because there were four small moons around it, constantly shifting their relative positions. Sometimes one of the moons would duck around behind the big flasher and then we would see only three of them for a time.

I soon discovered that the highly technical phrasing of my new handbook, "Reading the Stars Made Easy," was beyond the limits of my ability to understand. I got tired of watching the little moons shifting around their big brother and found I was getting more enjoyment with less eye strain just looking at the craters on the moon with my inexpensive binoculars and wondering who would be the first to hike up there among the crags and craters, so plainly visible.

Not so my wife, who has long been famous for unlimited enthusiasms. This old Jupiter and some others too numerous to mention, really sparked Mildred as an amateur astronomer. In fact, that winter, Mildred would hop out of bed at two or three in the morning if the stars were particularly bright and spend an hour at the scope, exclaiming over every new change apparent in the heavens and demanding that I get up and look. This sort of thing seemed to occur when the heater fire was very low at the coldest hour before dawn and on one of those nights I really made her mad when I refused to get up with the thermometer at forty below zero. On this night, Jupiter was at such a high angle that Mildred had to open the cabin door to elevate the telescope for a shot above the tops of the trees. It was soon as cold inside the cabin as it was outside. To get the high angle sight on her goal, she had to put a pillow on the floor and get down on her knees in order to put her eye to the eye-piece. There she was, in her nightgown with a pair of heavy wool socks on her feet, a blanket around her shoulders and a woolen head-scarf tied under her chin.

In Chuck and Wilma, Mildred had a pair of more sympathetic recruits who were ready and willing to suffer extreme cold for the privilege of looking at the stars. Night after night they gathered around the big tube to look and speculate and exclaim. I'll have to admit, here, that I was then usually deep in my bunk because they were star gazing from the open doorway. When this was going on, all the blessings that radiated from our cast iron heater were drifting out the door and ice was forming in the water buckets.

Then one night, there was such a display in the Chilcotin sky that the scope couldn't pick it all up from the cabin door. It had to be moved outside at about midnight in order to get the full benefit of the high-angled spectacle. It was twenty below zero, a dead calm, brilliantly sparkling night of unsurpassed beauty. I awakened to some thumping of boots and scraping of chairs. Then I heard Mildred exclaiming over something that had changed in the heavens and my curiosity drew me out of the bunk.

There they were out there in the snow—Mildred, Wilma and Chuck, with the telescope set up in a frozen drift, its lenses trained heavenward. My wife and daughter-in-law were in their flannel nightgowns, tucked into heavy woolen trousers, their big winter coats, heads swathed in scarves. The women were excited and exclaiming over the beauty of the stars, taking turns squinting into the eyepiece of the scope. My son, meanwhile, was hopping around and flailing his arms against the bitter cold penetrating the weave and warp of his only protection, a suit of trap-door long johns and a pair of rubber shoe pacs.

In the eerie moonlight the shadows cast over the snow by this unusual scene were accompanied by the wild moaning of the ice in Little Eagle, the hoarse hooting of the big owls among the spruces and the staccato drumming of grouse in the near cabin woods. Overhead, Jupiter blazed in its fierce red fire and the heavens blinked in the diamond dust of the Milky Way. I gave up, dressed and joined the crazy party. From that night on, I too became a member of the late stargazing company.

As the nights grew colder, we made a sort of canvas igloo for Chuck's hounds, smaller than the old umbrella tent and, therefore, much warmer. We spread a canvas tarpaulin over two sawhorses, on which we first laid some boards to carry the weight of snow, then banked the whole enclosure until it was practically buried except for a small opening through which the hounds could crawl in or out. A bale of dry hay Chuck had purchased in Williams Lake made a cozy nest for Hoecake and Jezzy, a pair of short-haired hounds in a cold long-hair country.

We chopped a hole through the lake ice and put down a baited hook, held near bottom by a lead sinker. But the big rainbows that inhabit the depths of Little Eagle disdained the bait. There are some beautiful trout in our lake, but they are hard to come by, probably because natural feed—principally freshwater shrimps—are so plentiful. Our rainbows are never hungry. We have taken them with trolling and spinning gear only on a few rare occasions. Thus Little Eagle does not enjoy the reputation of being a "hot" trout lake, as compared to others in the Chilcotin.

To ward off cabin fever we made daily treks on snowshoes, following our old pack trail along the north ridge and usually out to our snowbound trucks. And one day, despite the fluffy softness that allowed our webs to sink deeply, Chuck and I made a slow, three-mile circuit of the lodgepole forest north and east of our cabin. We came across the tracks of two Canada lynxes but restrained the eager hounds. Moose tracks we noted in random criss-crossings throughout the woods. As we swung back to the cabin late in the afternoon, we came across such a maze of tracks and overnight beds of the big animals among the willows of the north shore that the area resembled a well-trampled stockyard.

From an open glade in the pines of the north ridge we had seen the white sweep of snow dust racing across the face of the lake as the result of a sudden brisk westerly wind. On return to camp, we found that much of the powder snow that had fallen on a recent night had been blown from The Narrows, leaving a long track of frozen crust above the old ice.

Chuck was quick to try out some ice skates but found the crust too rough for the blades. It was then we began thinking in terms of ice boats rather than skates and our seven-foot toboggan seemed to have possibilities. The wind was light but promising.

The idea became father to the act. While Chuck searched out a suitable pine pole for a mast, I fastened an open tomato can to the deck of the toboggan with some wood screws. We stepped the butt of the sapling mast into the tomato can and braced it with light cord. A four-by-six-foot rectangle of plastic tarp made the sail. In less than an hour we were out on the frozen surface of Little Eagle sailing the toboggan before the wind.

Mildred and Wilma, not as yet convinced of the safety of the ice in the area of the hot springs, stood watch from the edge of the lake. At their feet lay fifty feet of half-inch rope carefully coiled, one end attached to a slim pine pole which could be pushed over the ice for the rescue of the boaters in event of a break-through. Fortunately the rope and pole were never put to use.

We had some good rides. You had to stand with feet braced, or sit down and steady the mast firmly gripped in both hands to hold the sail into the wind, but it worked. This rig would not tack, however, and we wore either snowshoes or ice creepers for secure footing while towing the toboggan back against the wind after a wild ride. You could sail in one direction only—with the wind at your back—and paid for the privilege by returning on foot with sail furled.

It was fun and it sharpened appetites. Once I tried standing up, holding the mast with one hand, feet braced for a fast ride while Mildred took some footage with her movie camera. Everything went fine until the toboggan hit a pressure hump that sent me cartwheeling while the toboggan raced off unmanned.

Eventually a safe sailing route was determined and Wilma joined us in trips on the toboggan. Mildred refused, saying she didn't mind being called "chicken." Even the hounds took part, running joyously along with the toboggan, Jezzy jumping on to ride whenever she had the chance.

Our pet squirrel finally returned, coming somewhat timidly to the feeding board in the window, after an absence of several days. Apparently hunger had overcome fear of Chuck's two big hounds. The squirrel's nervous actions indicated the little animal's awareness of the dogs' presence. Its approach was by way of a high and safe route through the limbs of spruce trees in the cabin woods, the cabin roof and finally the underside of the eaves and the log walls, to the feeding board. But now there was no dashing away across the snow to bury sunflower seeds. The squirrel contented itself to remain on the high safety of the feeding board, stuffing greedily on seeds and peanut butter until its belly began to drag. Then it dashed away to the dark security of its nest deep in the tiers of our winter woodpile.

Chuck's birthday, February 13, dawned at four degrees below zero, probably the coldest anniversary he had ever had. Mildred and Wilma combined to cook his birthday dinner, complete with a "Happy Birthday Chuck" inscribed on the cake icing. He had jokingly said he was three years old, so on the table were three turquoise candles on a copper tray. As we enjoyed our dinner, the window sill at our elbows was alive with Canada jays and mountain and blackcap chickadees.

During the evening, Chuck's banjo and Wilma's guitar rounded out our day with old-time ballads from the deep south, spirituals and blue-grass music. I even got out my mouth organ and joined them. We turned in at midnight with the mercury at twenty degrees and the moon hazy behind clouds. There was the feel of more snow in the air.

That the evening of music was, or was not, the inspiration for my dreams I shall never know, but that night my slumbering subconsciousness drifted back to boyhood on a timber claim in Washington's Skagit River foothills. There, at the age of sixteen, I had labored at the building of my mother's cabin. Some young fellows of a family by the name of Lee had been hired to help raise the log walls. They were all musicians of the banjo and fiddle variety and one or two of the Lees were constantly making music as the logs went up. So it got to be said the Jenkins cabin had been "fiddled up" by the Lee boys. It was a very good cabin. More than half a century later I was hearing the same brand of string melody in a snowbound cabin on the high plateau of the wild Chilcotin. I pondered the strange attraction, the sympathetic appeal that music has for mankind and the fact that life had not changed much for me, after all.

Next morning—Sunday, and Valentine's Day—seven degrees above zero. Wilma wakened us early to look at a beautiful, strange bird feeding on hooshum berries not far from the window. It was not quite a stranger to Mildred and me, for we saw it was a lovely pine grosbeak. We told the kids about two birds that had flown against our window the previous fall and we all wondered if this might be the same one that had survived.

We were out early for another toboggan sail ride but there was no wind. It was one of those days of dead calm typical of Chilcotin winter. Since we couldn't go sailing, we spent the time improving on our improvised ice boat. We rigged a plastic sail with a pulley in the top of the mast and a nylon line to raise and lower it. We were hopeful of more fun on the ice.

Mildred walked out on the dike to enjoy the sparkling sunlight play on frost crystals and when she came back she said she heard the wind coming. Chuck went out to listen and he called back, "It sounds more like a motor somewhere off in the distance." We all listened intently, but out here in all the great expanse of silence we often hear our own heartbeat and mistake it for a distant motor. None of us was sure then.

"Maybe it's the snowplow," someone suggested.

"No, can't be...this is Sunday," another corrected. And so went the speculations.

It wasn't long until the sound increased in volume and we were more sure of it as we hurried to the lake shore to listen. Then we heard a distant metallic clang as if metal had struck a boulder. Now we felt certain the snowplow was on its way. Excitement spread among us. Jezzabelle, the sensitive hound, ran out to the lake shore to listen also, excitedly ran back past the cabin and out on the snowshoe trail toward the oncoming sound, then back again to where Hoecake was snoozing in the warm sun. She nosed her mate as if to tell her the news. Hoecake roused, listened, sniffed the air and joined Jezzy in running about excitedly. Chuck lit a cigarette, then laughed, calling our attention to how his hands were shaking and he was pacing back and forth beside his toboggan-sailboat. Wilma had gone immediately to put on a fresh pot of coffee and was preparing something to eat.

Mildred went for her cameras. To tell the truth, I'm not sure what I was doing, but it was music to my ears to hear the rattling, clanging, banging and purring of that big diesel. Down our roadway among the aspens it came, a big red monster of a grasshopper-looking machine, slowly pushing a high rolling wave of snow diagonally off its wide blade. We were no longer snowbound!

"What a beautiful Valentine! And red, too!" Wilma exclaimed.

When Trevor Lauton jumped down from the cab of that big red Galeon grader he was all but greeted with kisses! He had cleared five miles of road from the Chilcotin junction to our cabin. Though he worked for the Provincial Department of Highways and this was supposed to be his day off, Lauton had plowed out our road, knowing we were isolated. We noticed a big bruise on his forehead, which he explained had happened when the grader banged into a boulder in the road, throwing his head against the frame of the cab. That must have been the noise we heard.

Mildred took some pictures for our records and Wilma said, "Come on in, the coffee's ready. You can help us finish Chuck's birthday cake." She had a spread of food on the table. And a joyful mood filled the one-room cabin as we all visited while stowing away Wilma's food...there seemed to be a lifting away of the tension that had been with us for many days. The road was open and passable, at least for the present.

That afternoon Chuck rode out with Lauton in the big grader to bring his parked truck in to camp. At the same time, Mildred, Wilma and I, with the hounds, hiked out to where our truck was stalled on the Old Tatlayoko Road and dug it out of the drift. Wilma went on ahead to meet Chuck. We all drove back to camp.

The kids began to make plans for their camp-out in the Tatlayoko Valley, to go cougar hunting, now that they felt sure we could get out if an emergency arose.

Our diary for February 15 recounts that on this day Chuck got out his slingshot for some target practice. (He has been an expert with this weapon from childhood days...though this is not what

62

he uses when cougar hunting!) But he had not brought in a supply of the old wheel bearings which he customarily uses for ammunition. No pebbles available here, under nearly two feet of snow. Not to be deterred, he gathered a quantity of solidly frozen moose droppings. He complained later that owing to their peculiar shape, they all flew in a curve. "Can't hit a darned thing with 'em."

# Lost Dogs

On February 17, while snow still lay deeply over the Plateau, Chuck and Wilma loaded their hounds into their pickup with camp gear and provisions for their annual midwinter cougar hunt and drove down into the Jameson Basin, about thirty-five miles south of Eagle Lake.

The basin lies at the foot of the western slope of the Potato Mountains, a spur of the Coast Range bordering Tatlayoko Lake. The lake itself, about fourteen miles in length and a mile across at its widest, stretches north and south along one rim of the basin's shoreline. The basin was (until the loggers got into it) forested with old-growth Douglas fir and here, in the depths of the big conifers, Chuck and Wilma made their winter camp. This is deer country and, by that token, it is also cougar country. It is known for its wolves and for the grizzlies that feed on the wild potatoes in the high meadows above the basin and make their winter dens on the snowy slopes of the surrounding high country.

Our kids had been gone a week when Mildred and I decided to join them for a day's visit. We drove out to Tatla post office, picked up the weekly mail, filled the truck tank and an extra "Jerry" can with gas, assembled a few groceries and headed for Tatlayoko Lake. We made the twenty-five mile run from Tatla without having to put on chains as the road crew had recently plowed the route, but found ice conditions severe in Jameson Basin. Where a recent thaw had spread melt-water over the earth surface, another freezeup had turned the entire area to a sheet of glare ice. Here it was almost impossible to walk without ice creepers strapped to one's shoes. This was particularly true in the shaded areas among the big firs, although the more open hillsides were largely bare and easy going.

The hunters had pitched their 12-by-14-foot wall tent in a big

Will at Jenkins Way where it turns off from the old Tatlayoko Road. November, 1983.

Old Sheep Creek Bridge, built in 1902. One of the last over-land cattle drives can be seen coming down the road of Sheep Creek Hill.

The new bridge opened in 1977.

Loading on to the train at Seton, on the way to Eagle Lake. August, 1955.

Eagle Lake and its lovely mountain backdrop. September, 1959.

A hazy day at the coffee bar in Alexis Creek. July, 1955.

Winter could come early at the Eagle Lake camp. October, 1958.

The Department of Public Works' emergency cabin, number 3, at Burnt Corral. September, 1955.

Will and Wallie slabbing wall logs for cabin number two. September, 1960.

Chuck and the hounds on the hill above Clearwater Lake in Anahim District. November, 1954.

Will with Hoecake, a red bonehound. Hoecake proved to be a good Huskey. Six hundred pounds of winter supplies on a toboggan moved quite easliy with the assistance of a gee pole. Eagle Lake, winter 1965.

The post office at Kleena Kleene. October, 1954.

The old roadhouse at Hat Creek. November, 1957.

Lee's General Store in Hanceville, on the way to Eagle Lake. May, 1958.

Another view of the original Lee's store. It is used for storage now. May, 1961.

The wedding picture of Tom Hance and Eleanor Verdier.

*Photo: Irene Bliss*

Historical memorial in Hanceville Cemetary.

*Photo: Irene Bliss*

George Turner in failing health in the 1950s.

*Photo: Joy Graham*

George Turner and Mrs. Grace Kellogg at One-eye Lake. 1950.

Sitkum Memmoloos, daughter of Chief One-eye and wife of George Turner.

*Photo: Joy Graham*

A couple of Chilcotin Natives during a cattle drive. 1955.

Members of the Alexis Creek Indian Band. The fellow in the middle is Felix Lulua, now living in Neamiah Valley. 1947.

*Photo: Joy Graham*

Women of the Alexis Creek Indian Band. The woman on the left is Emily Lulua. 1947.

*Photo: Joy Graham*

A Russell fence on the Chilcotin Road. 1969.

A variation of the Russell fence. Anahim Lake, 1993.

A Bennett wagon at Redstone.

An old gas pump at Bliss Ranch, Willow Springs.

Indian fish-drying rack at Bridge River and Fraser River junction. August, 1955.

Stampede time at Williams Lake. July, 1956.

An old picturesque ranch on Jesmond Road. 1957.

Bill, Will and Irene at the Bliss Ranch in Willow Springs. 1993.

grove of old-growth firs. The tent was banked with snow around its bottom edges and a Yukon stove with pipe wired to an upright pole kept the interior snugly warm. Sleeping bags were spread on a bed of fir boughs.

We called the usual "Anybody home here?" as we pulled into the grove and when Wilma emerged from the tent we knew at once there was trouble in Jameson Basin. Chuck was nowhere in sight. And then we got the story from Wilma: the hounds were gone, probably lost. Chuck was somewhere up along the high rims of the basin looking for his dogs. He had been searching since very early morning. As Wilma spoke, the high tenor of Chuck's calling horn came faintly to our ears from a ridge far to the south.

Early that morning, Hoecake and Jezzabelle had jumped a hot track, probably a cougar, within a few hundred feet of the tent. Wilma said the noise of bawling hounds was so close and excited that she felt sure the dogs would be barking "treed" momentarily and she had listened to hear the crack of Chuck's rifle. Then, suddenly, the hounds were bawling not "treed" but "trail," (which you have to be a houndsman to understand) and in a few minutes were completely out of hearing. It was as if their voices had been shut off rather than fading away in the distance.

Wilma had been baking bread and pies and this accounted for her being in camp when we arrived. Otherwise she would have been with Chuck. As we visited over fresh coffee, Chuck came in from a six-hour tramp along the high rim of the basin. It was plain to see he was deeply concerned for his dogs. The way they had gone out of hearing just wasn't usual. In snow well up above timberline he had come across the big splayed footprints of wolves...headed south. There appeared to have been three or four in the band. Hoecake and Jezzabelle, probably exhausted from hours of running, would be no match for a pack of hungry wolves and Chuck had heard that wolves will lead dogs off, so he had plenty to worry him.

In the afternoon, Chuck and I went back up on the rim to timberline. Here, on a high ridge, thinly grown with a scattering of wind-twisted conifers, we could view miles of the open basin with our binoculars. We built a small fire under a sheltering tree where he had recently cached two pairs of snowshoes for future use in the deeper snow above timberline. We ate some candy bars and I remained at the fire to watch and listen while Chuck tramped in a wide circle out along the rim to the south. I frequently heard his calling horn, the long drawn, high thin wails of the horn echoing against the 9,000-foot crags of the Niuts on the far west shore of Tatlayoko Lake.

He came back late in the day and it was dusk, fast becoming night, when we returned to the tent. He confided in me that night that he was almost sure the wolves had killed his hounds. He had found wolf tracks again, far to the south.

While Chuck and I had been up on the rim, and as soon as Wilma's bread was finished baking, she and Mildred had walked out through the lower reaches of the basin. There the old-growth timber was so huge and dense it was like walking through a darkened cathedral. Wilma carried her rifle as Chuck had admonished her to do, for he had observed grizzly sign in the deep woods and he told her she must never venture away from camp without being armed. Mildred said afterward that she had felt perfectly safe with Wilma but did admit she "kept both ears and both eyes very open!" They had found no tracks of the hounds.

After a camp supper by lantern light, there was only quiet talk and no music that night, for all were listening for a bawl or a scratching to say the hounds had returned. Several times one or another would suddenly say, "Listen!" and all ears would strain to catch any sound. Sometimes we would hurry outside the tent, the better to listen, or peer into the darkness. But only the occasional night sound of an owl hooting in the deep woods or a grebe's cry on the lake could be heard.

The following morning we all resumed the search. But this time, Wilma, Mildred and I climbed to the high rim while Chuck swung farther south. Again we spent some time on the open knoll where any sound from the lower country would reach us and we could see a great distance. For a time, Mildred and I stayed at the "snowshoe tree" while Wilma hiked out north on a timbered spur of the rim "for a look and a listen" in an area not yet fully checked. She came back with no encouragement. Then we all climbed higher until we were into snow to our hips and the going became too tough for Mildred and me. We all turned back. During the afternoon my "trick" right knee gave out and an old lameness from an injury made walking very painful.

We were back to the tent about 4:30 P.M. but Chuck was still out somewhere far to the south. As we sat and rested with our coffee, a long, faint wail came to our ears. We all heard it and immediately listened intently. I thought it was the voice of a loon out on Tatlayoko. Then we realized, without saying so, that we were not certain it was a loon. I could see by the look in Wilma's eyes that she was not convinced. The women were quickly out of the tent and heading for the shore of the lake. There was a loon far out on the water. Mildred and Wilma stood and listened for several minutes. Here at the edge of the water any sounds back in the basin or high on the hillsides, especially the bawl of a hound or the wail of a calling horn, could be more readily heard and the direction of its source determined.

We discussed the possibility that Chuck might be calling for help. Wilma, thoroughly familiar with the area, suggested a place a short distance from their camp, where an opening in the timber would afford a more thorough checking. Shortly, the women prepared to hike south on an old trail threading the basin floor. This trail led gradually upward to some of the open slopes of the Potato Mountains. Here there would be more visibility in the remaining daylight and they might be able to see Chuck, in case he needed help. Wilma and Mildred were still not convinced the wailing they had heard was not the bawling of a hound.

To add to Wilma's worry, she had discovered their light .22-caliber rifle under the sleeping bags and was immediately afraid that Chuck had gone off unarmed. As it later developed, she need not have worried. He was carrying my old thirty-forty carbine which I had earlier insisted he should include in his equipment when they had left for a district known for its big bears.

The women took binoculars and a couple of candy bars. Mildred carried a flashlight and Wilma picked up and loaded her old 30-30 Winchester. My lameness was acute now and I remained in camp.

It was getting dusk when the women reached an area where they could view a wide expanse of the basin's hillsides with the glasses. Afterward, they told of seeing many deer browsing on the open slopes. They remained at this place, constantly listening and combing the hillsides for any sign of Chuck or the hounds. Finally, when it was becoming too dark to see, they started back to camp. About half way they met Chuck...he had come down by another trail, but he had seen them high above, so walked to meet them. The hounds were still missing.

He had tramped all day and was exhausted. He had crossed and recrossed the mountainside from the rim of the basin far above snowline and on southward. He had gone past the snowshoe tree in our absence and picked up a pair of snowshoes to travel high into the drifts, hoping for a sound or track to lead him to his dogs. No sign of them...only more wolf tracks to add to his worry and discouragement.

While waiting for the others to return I had prepared a good hot meal for all of us and it was waiting when they came back. We ate half-heartedly, more for the nourishment than any pleasure in eating. We were a sad company that night.

Chuck said to me later, "I expect to find my dogs have been killed by wolves. I found wolf tracks again today, heading south out of the basin. There were at least four in the pack and the tracks of two of them were huge. I can't give up, now, until I know what has happened to my hounds. I'll search farther south tomorrow. Maybe I'll find the answer...somewhere."

Mildred and I concluded there was nothing to be gained by our remaining longer in Jameson Basin and prepared to return to Eagle Lake the following morning. The Tatlayoko Valley is approximately 1,000 feet lower in elevation than Little Eagle and spring comes earlier down there. In fact, midday sunshine hours were already thawing the valley road into a muddy quagmire. It was necessary now to travel only during early morning, taking advantage of a temporarily hard surface created by overnight freezing. As a rule now, the road was too soft for truck travel after nine o'clock in the morning.

We had left our pickup on a stretch of high, well-drained ground, to avoid the probability of getting stuck in the event of a sudden general thaw. We said our good-byes to a couple of sorrowful hunters. Chuck and Wilma planned to remain in the basin at least a few more days and continue the search, but were already convinced there was little chance the dogs were still alive.

As soon as we drove out of the deep shade of timber in Jameson Basin to enter the more open glades of the Homathko River Valley, we realized the morning sun had already done its work. The road was a meandering streak of wet muck dotted with watery chuckholes. There were long stretches of road completely submerged in the yellow soup of the morning's thaw. On the occasional slopes, where the water had a better chance to drain from the roadway, the driver's choice was confined to a maze of deep and contorted soggy ruts. We had learned from experience that it was better to follow the ruts as these usually offered the best traction, but at times we wondered if we were going to make it. We wallowed through, often hub deep, to finally climb onto the more solid ground of the Plateau.

We were home by two o'clock. Our registering thermometer had dropped to a low of six degrees below zero at some time during our absence. The recorded high for the same period had been forty-seven degrees above zero.

We found ourselves listening for the bawl of hounds, even at this far distance from the basin. The lost dogs were constantly on our minds and we were often drawn to the lake shore, to listen time and again, despite the fact we both well knew the distance dispelled any chance of hearing them. We did, however, consider the possibility they might have tried to return to Eagle Lake on their own.

Chuck and Wilma had continued their search after we left the valley. The long days of climbing onto the high ridges of the basin, of calling and listening, had been followed by nights of near physical exhaustion and despair. Then, late on the fifth night

85

while lying in silent wakefulness, they heard faint whimpering and the scratch of claws on frozen ground. Hurrying out, they saw the young Jezzabelle staggering toward the tent, limping painfully on raw and bloody feet. Beyond Jezzy a little distance came the older Hoecake, wobbling on legs barely able to sustain her weight. Obviously both dogs were near collapse. Seeing Chuck, Hoecake fell and lay, unable to get to her feet. Chuck ran to her and carried the big redbone into the tent where Wilma was already caring for the younger "Jezzy."

The hounds lay limply and exhausted as Chuck bathed the bloody abraded pads of their feet in a solution of warm water and epsom salts. Their sides were gaunt, their ribs bony ridges under tight skin, loins sunken from hunger. Chuck had to lift them into their beds in the straw-padded bottom of the pickup canopy and for two days the hounds did little more than sleep and lick the worn pads of their feet. They could not walk; did not have the strength to rise to their feet. It was three days following their return before they were again able to stand to eat.

We would never know the real sequence of events that had transpired in the days the hounds had roamed the rugged country surrounding Jameson Basin, or how many miles they had traveled; whether there had been an encounter with wolves or, for that matter, why the dogs had left the basin in the first place. Chuck was of the opinion his hounds had simply refused to quit the trail of a cougar. "Probably an old cat that knew about dogs," he said, "and had led them on a long, wild run many miles from camp." Whatever happened, Hoecake and Jezzabelle had quite obviously stuck together; had begun the long, hungry trek back to camp after days of futile running over crusted snow that wore the pads from their feet.

If they could have filled us in on their adventure it would undoubtedly have been quite a story.

# A $900 Hole and Breakup

By the March 8, breakup was well advanced. Frequently, the overnight temperature still fell below freezing level, but daylight hours were definitely warmer, generally in the forties. A widening area of bare roof was now exposed around the base of the chimney, the roof was dripping and sun warmed icicles fell from the eaves, breaking with the sound of shattered glass.

The smell of earth had returned as bare patches widened under the trees. Out on the moraine in front of our cabin the snow was gone, wild onions were up and pungent in the sun. The red-green sheen of new willow sprouts stood up vividly along the shoreline. There were big pans of melt water standing on the lake ice. And as this ice thinned, the jade green of Little Eagle's depth was reflected by the warming sunlight.

We were soon to learn what gambling with the hazards of breakup can do. Chuck and I felled several large spruces we considered dangerously close to our cabin and we celebrated Mildred's birthday on the fifteenth with a chicken dinner; Wilma turning out another beautiful birthday cake.

On a trip out to Tatla for mail on the eighteenth, I contacted Leo Fowler, who was then repairing ruts and holes in the Chilcotin Road with big loads of gravel and boulders. We wanted a load of fill dirt for a low spot between our cabins. Fowler said he would bring it in if the road remained frozen, but would not risk getting stuck if the temperature rose above thirty-two degrees and there was danger of sudden softening.

There is one stretch of about 500 feet where the Old Tatlayoko Road traverses a flat area, known to flood to a depth of a foot or more during spring thaws. So far we had experienced no trouble in this section as the road was a solid sheet of ice. On our way out to Tatla early that day we drove over the ice with

87

misgivings, but it held. On our return, however, the ice gave way under our truck when we were about in the middle of it. By some miracle—how or why we'll never know—we thrashed on through to higher ground beyond the flat, but there were moments of lurching wildly, the truck shuddering, then leaping ahead again. We fully expected to become stalled runningboard deep in mud, shattered ice and water, but succeeded in getting through.

Moving more easily on higher, solid ground, I recall we had some conversation about warming temperatures and expressed the hope that Fowler would be smart enough not to attempt to come in with a big truck load of fill dirt.

As we were eating dinner that evening, in walked a bareheaded young man who said he was Doug Fraser, a truck driver for Leo Fowler. "My truck and a load of dirt I had for you is sunk in a big puddle about half way in here," he explained. "I thought maybe you might have a tractor or something to pull me out."

We assured him we had nothing but half-ton pickups. We fed Fraser, then Chuck and I drove back with him in my pickup to where the Fowler truck, a huge one with an estimated ten-cubic-yard load, was sunk in the middle of the big water hole. It was in the exact spot where our lighter vehicle had wallowed through earlier that afternoon. Completely surrounded by muddy water and ice, the rear wheels had gone out of sight in the muck. Fraser said he was sure Fowler would come looking for him when he failed to show up at their headquarters at Tatla and thought he probably wouldn't have to wait much longer.

As darkness settled, Chuck and I gathered dead, dry pine and built a good-sized warming fire. The night was going to be cold and it might be a long one.

Fowler and two of his pit crew showed up in a pickup at about 9:00 P.M., and got stuck in the mud before they quite reached the big truck. The five of us got him out and turned around onto solid road again. Fowler, after sizing up the problem, then drove back to Tatla to get his diesel-powered front-end loader and some cable chokers.

Returning about 10:00 P.M., the bin of the stalled dumptruck was raised and the load of fill dirt and gravel dumped to get rid of the weight. Then the chokers were attached to the front of the truck and the loader gave a mighty heave. The chokers snapped under the strain. In the short struggle, the area all around the sunken truck had become a quagmire of gumbo mud, ice, old snow water and rocks. The night was a moonless black. Light from our fire helped only a little, along with the headlights.

Then I noticed Fowler moving around with a very dim flashlight as if searching for something.

"Lose something?" I asked.

"Yeah!" he replied. "Lost my damned billfold with $900 in it...my payroll for the crew!"

I walked back on the road where our pickup was parked and got out a gas lantern, returned, and Chuck and I joined Fowler and his crew looking for the lost wallet. We searched, slogging around in the jumble of sloppy mud and ice as thoroughly as darkness would permit, but without success. Finally, as time was passing, Fowler sent his two crewmen back to Tatla to get some heavy logging chains to replace the broken cables, while Chuck and I continued the search with Fowler and Doug Fraser.

The crewmen were back again by eleven o'clock.

"We found your wallet," one of them said, handing it to Fowler. "It was under your pillow in the bunkhouse..right where you left the damned thing."

Fowler grinned and commented, "You know, that's the second time I've done that!"

Near midnight the chains had been attached and with a surge of power the diesel loader hauled the big dump truck from its bed of mud. It came up and out, a dripping behemoth of mud-plastered steel and in slow, but steady, movement rolled to high ground beyond the quagmire.

Fowler and his crew prepared departure.

I felt keenly responsible for Fowler's misfortune on this freezing night. I said, "Mister Fowler, I want to pay you for your trouble."

His answer was, "Hell, man, you don't owe me anything. I didn't deliver," and turned and walked away.

My fill dirt, what hadn't sunk out of sight, lay in a monumental heap. We call the place "The $900 Hole," and still get a laugh over the soggy adventure. But looking back on that night of mud, ice and water and the bitter cold of six degrees below zero, I recall there was nothing funny about it at the time.

March 21, spring had arrived, our landscape was suddenly white with new snow, but this snowfall disappeared in a few hours of warm sunshine.

By the twenty-fifth our registering thermometer was pushing up into the warmer sixties. The earth about us had become a sponge. Puddles formed in low spots during the sunny days but the frozen earth below refused to absorb the top melt. It lay suspended. Wherever we walked, the ground trembled like jelly under our feet and any movement caused water to seep to the surface.

Chuck and Wilma wanted to go back to the Tatlayoko Valley for a little more hunting before leaving for home in Washington. Their departure for the basin was followed by a blinding snowstorm during which we heard the cries of honkers winging over Eagle Lake. Since, apparently, Chuck and Wilma had made it out without getting stuck, Mildred and I decided to try it. We wanted to go to Tatla.

When we arrived at the $900 Hole we found a note left by Chuck in the cleff of a split limb stuck in the roadbed. It warned us to take the detour and head straight for another stick he had set up at the north end of the mud hole and to watch out for broken young jack pines as a dangerous menace to our radiator.

We succeeded in making another gumbo-plagued trip to Tatla for needed supplies, including a 100-pound bottle of rock-gas for cooking. We had wallowed through the softening detour around the $900 Hole, where water stood runningboard deep and the big puddle was wider than ever.

The day following our return from Tatla we saw a large flock of Bohemian waxwings feeding through the jack pines and regarded their appearance as a sure harbinger of approaching fair weather. Geese continued to appear, their arrival proclaimed by noisy gaggling as they settled on the ice.

On the last day of March, Mildred and I walked out along our truck road to sample the stability of the roadbed. Water was running everywhere, draining the snow melt from the wooded areas where shade had held onto winter. Now the rising temperatures ruled. Water stood in every small depression and overflowed into others, seeking a way to the lake. Two streams of water ran in the ruts of our road. The earth was still soggy...a fair warning. We knew we would be in for trouble if we tried to drive out again.

In the days that followed we walked the lake ice, close to shore, ever mindful of its weakening condition. There was open water in The Ponds at the west end of Little Eagle and we hiked there to observe the movement of newly arrived waterfowl and songbirds.

Realizing the extreme sponginess of our truck trail along the north ridge, we posted a sign at its junction with the Old Tatlayoko Road, warning of the danger of getting stuck that lay ahead. The words: "Do not drive beyond this point" were calculated to stop anyone who might be lucky enough to get that far. Actually, the sign was inspired by our hope that we could prevent the trail being used while the earth was still mushy, thus uselessly chewing up the roadbed.

When Chuck and Wilma returned from Tatlayoko Lake on April 10, they left their truck at the north end of the $900 Hole, mired to the hubs. They had to walk the remaining distance to our cabin.

It had been a rough day for travel. Heading north out of Tatlayoko Valley they wallowed, skidded and churned through heavy mud and water. Stuck twice within a mile of their abandoned camp, they had laboriously jacked up the truck to free the wheels. A little farther north the help of a rancher and his tractor was required to pull out of a pothole where the truck had sunk to the runningboards.

The Chilcotin Road, east of Tatla, was not much better although this section lies over higher ground of the Plateau. Nearing the Eagle Lake junction, they met the Tatla school teacher, a man named Jukes. He was walking toward Tatla and was mud spattered to his knees. Early that morning, he had driven about forty miles east to the Puntzi air base to obtain medicine for his ailing wife. Jukes had gotten stuck near Chilanko, left his truck, walked on to Puntzi, got the medicine and phoned back to Tatla for help. Fred Linder, in his own pickup, started from Tatla for Chilanko to rescue Jukes. On the return trip, Fred's truck sank into a pothole near Burnt Corral. Now Jukes was walking the last seven miles back to Tatla with the medicine for Mrs. Jukes. Fred Linder was staying with his stuck truck until help could arrive.

Cautiously, Chuck turned his truck around and drove the weary school teacher on to Tatla. The assistance of the Forest Service and a power wagon capable of negotiating the muddy Chilcotin Road was obtained to rescue Fred Linder. Chuck and Wilma finally got on their own way again, but on turning into the old wagon road to Eagle Lake, sank axle deep, for the fourth time that day, in another mudhole. They could hear the Forest Service four-wheel-drive coming up the long hill from Burnt Corral, where Linder had just been pulled out of the muck. Chuck ran back to the main road and flagged them down. The Forest Service fellows stopped long enough to haul Chuck's pickup out of its latest bed of mud. But at Leo Fowler's $900 Hole the cougar hunters called it a day, and they began walking the last two miles to our cabin when their truck bogged down to the level of its box in the same area where Fowler's bad luck had occurred. They came in, mud plastered and weary at dusk, packboards loaded with grub and sleeping bags. Too tired to eat, they fed the hounds and crawled into bed, completely exhausted.

Tatlayoko Lake, a huge body of water whose depths were said never to have been determined, had remained open all winter. During the cougar hunters' campout in Jameson Basin they had used our light eight-foot pram to reach the west shore of the lake when the weather was calm. Now the little skiff was lashed to the top of Chuck's truck, at the edge of the $900 Hole.

Hiking back to the stalled vehicle for a sack of hound feed and other supplies, Chuck pulled the pram from the top of the canopy, piled in the dog feed, the oars, a Yukon campstove and several lengths of pipe. With packboards on their backs, Chuck and Wilma drew towing ropes over their shoulders and began dragging the skiff over the snow and old ice still coating the old wagon road to Eagle. But at the end of a mile they came onto a stretch of road which had become bared by the sun. Not wanting to damage the hull by further dragging over rocks and bare earth, they parked the pram among jack pines at the side of the road, where it could be picked up and loaded on one of our trucks when the road again became passable.

Mildred and I hiked out over the north ridge to meet them that day and at the junction of our side road relieved them of part of their packs.

Following their arrival, Chuck revealed he had received a letter at Tatla from the district ranger of the Mt. Baker National Forest in Washington advising he would be expected to report for work in about ten days. He began to worry about ever getting out of the Chilcotin mud. There was no way to answer the ranger's letter in our present predicament. By this time breakup was a full and complete condition over the entire Plateau and all vehicular traffic was at a virtual standstill. The bottom had simply gone out of most of the roads.

The next morning we all hiked out to the $900 Hole to see if there was any chance of liberating Chuck's pickup.

We dug down and got a jack under the rear bumper, working in muddy water. When we tried to lever it up, the jack sank on down out of sight and we had to dig it out. The jack was useless. We went into the woods with an ax and cut some pine poles. We chopped out a pry pole about fourteen feet long. Then using a shorter, heavy chunk as a "deadman" behind the rear bumper, inserted the long pole over the chunk and under the bumper. Wilma, Mildred, Chuck and I got out on the end of the pole. Our combined leverage raised the rear-end of the truck. It came out of the muck with a loud sucking noise and Chuck quickly thrust another heavy timber under the bumper to keep it from settling back. We re-set the pole and raised it a bit and pushed more chunks under. In this manner we finally cribbed up the truck until we could see the wheels again and there we left it for the time being. We still had to get it onto drier ground and turned around.

We dug some trenches off the side of the road to let the water out of the hole. We hoped that might help but it didn't drain much.

The $900 Hole was now a small lake where only the tops of seedling pines stuck out of the water. The run-off of fast-melting snow on a broad slope to the east was pouring into The Hole like a permanent stream and just where the Old Tatlayoko roadbed lay under this flood was anyone's guess. We trenched some more and tried to veer the water from going into The Hole but had little success.

Since Chuck and Wilma would, of necessity, be leaving us soon—if they could get out to the main road—they were worried for our safety, isolated as we now were. Their chances out beyond the $900 Hole were better than ours here at the lake. Now Chuck wanted to concentrate on getting our truck out also.

Next morning we warmed up the Ford, well before putting it into gear, to try our road. At first it seemed we were going to make it...a happy surprise. Then the wheels began to spin and the next moment we were hub deep on a gentle slope about 600 feet from the cabin. After one or two more tries, each time sinking a little deeper, we gave it up and all hiked out to Chuck's pickup to see if we could get it turned around and headed out.

By dusk that day we had moved it out of four bog holes for a distance of less than fifty feet. Once we thought we had it made as Chuck drove out onto a higher, more solid looking edge of the road to make his turn around. One foot too far and down it went. Chuck got out to take a look. Down on his knees, peering underneath, he said, mournfully, "It's down on the frame again! I could just cry!" Then we all started laughing at ourselves for being in such a predicament. We built a fire, made coffee and rested a bit while we ate some sandwiches.

After some more prying, jacking and pine-pole cribbing, we managed to get the truck back on the roadbed and turned around. Now, at least, it was headed in the right direction. A few more days of drying weather and we felt sure Chuck and Wilma could be on their way south.

On the eighteenth—Easter Sunday—we again decided to see what we could do with our own pickup. The ground seemed solid. Very carefully we jacked up the sunken rear wheels and placed planks in position for a lengthwise track. Only a few feet to good ground, we thought. After warming up the motor, Chuck got in to make the try. He gave it the gas and the planks sailed straight out behind the truck and down it went into the soupy mud. A little more strategy. We attached a set of blocks and tackle to the front axle, using a third block to gain the extra power of a luff. Wilma, Mildred and I hauled mightily on the running end of the tackle while Chuck urged the truck ahead in low gear. In five or six attempts we moved about fifty feet. We had gained some higher ground, but there the wheels again stirred up another mess of soupy muck that floated even boulders. We gave it up after pushing a couple of planks under the wheels and went back to camp.

My diary for that April recounts that on the twenty-fifth we gave it another try. The ruts beneath the wheels seemed fairly dry. Our chances looked good. The motor roared willingly at the turn of the ignition key. I shifted into low and we began to move quite easily down a gentle slope. At the bottom of the grade we turned into a low damp grove of aspens and soon felt the wheels spinning in the black muck.

As we began to lose headway, Chuck yelled, "Step on it!" and I gave the motor all the gas the foot lever would produce. We plowed across the dark depression in the aspen grove, momentarily lurched forward as the drive wheels found traction on a gravelly stretch. Our hopes of getting out soared. The truck seemed to be gathering headway on a section that appeared well drained and dry. Then, suddenly, it died when we hit another hidden soft spot, muddy water gushing up around spinning tires and we sank to a dead stop.

Again we jacked up the truck and again we shoved planks beneath the wheels and dug trenches to drain off the water. Then we gave it up as a futile struggle and returned to the cabin. We were still marooned, but somehow we found the ability to laugh. That evening as we stood watching a fiery sunset lacing among the high snow peaks of the Coast Range, Mildred redeemed our spirits when she said, "Well, anyway, this is the most beautiful place in the world to be stuck!"

Next day we all hiked out to The Hole to check on conditions. This time Chuck had the little chain saw strapped to his packboard. He insisted on cutting a stock of short pine poles to serve as puncheon, to be laid down across the softer places when we might try to get our truck out later. As yet it was out of the question.

The road beyond Chuck's truck was drying and his chances looked more promising. They prepared to leave us.

On the twenty-sixth, a beautiful warm day, we all walked out to the $900 Hole and said some reluctant good-byes. We watched as their mud-splattered truck rolled successfully through the last mud hole within our vision and disappeared among the pines. They had been sad to leave us, knowing our own chances of getting up and over the north ridge were nil at the time. But Mildred and I urged them to go. Chuck's employment was important to them. He had finally agreed to leave us on our promises to make no further struggles to move our truck until we were positive the big thaw had ended and the earth dried.

Mildred and I remained at the scene of their departure until the sound of their motor dimmed and faded. When they did not return in half an hour we concluded they had reached the Chilcotin Road and were finally on their way east to Williams Lake and the Cariboo Highway stretching south to the Border.

We walked back to the cabin in silent moodiness. We were already lonesome for our kids. And we had learned—the hard way—that to contest with breakup in the wild Chilcotin was to challenge a law of nature that had not been laid down for the convenience of impatient mankind.

# The Cougar Marsh

While we were impatient for spring and had been fighting the relentless forces of breakup, usually without more than temporary success, the wildlife at Little Eagle was taking the convulsive weather in stride. March and April would be remembered for a series of sporadic rain showers by day which frequently became wet snow by night and mornings when fog lay around us as an all enveloping shroud.

Around our cabin we fed birds and squirrels yearround and included the chipmunks when they came from hibernation in spring. One squirrel, a precocious little beggar we named Alvin after a squirrel cousin of radio fame, had become tamed to the point of accepting sunflower seeds and wads of peanut butter from Mildred's fingers. During April, Alvin developed a nervous cageyness. He became very excitable, often screaming loudly as he raced from ground to tree tops. Our cabin stood in approximate center of his range, which he defended against all squirrel intruders except one female we called Sissy. She was large, fat and pugnacious and would actually stand toe to toe with Alvin, slapping his face and biting when he attempted to drive her away. Then one day we saw Alvin frolicking about in high leaps, acting sort of silly, and soon Alvin and Sissy had disappeared. It was that time of year again.

Then there was also Snoozy—in the old cottonwood on the lake shore east of the cabin. We often visited him, but Snoozy never came to our cabin, as it was off his particular range.

The bird we have been in the habit of calling a blue jay and which is not a blue jay but in fact is Steller's jay, is not common around Eagle Lake. We have seen very few and they are scarce here probably because the pine and spruce habitat is not exactly to their liking. They show up occasionally, however. And unlike the blue jays we knew south of the border, they seem to have little fear of humans. In fact, once while camping in the little meadow at the west end of Eagle—long before we had built our cabin—four of these beautiful jays came into our camp and fed voraciously on bread and table scraps, right at our feet!

A "blue jay" showed up on our window feeding board one sunny day and continued as a regular guest well into March. It came in company with two Canada jays which, by their actions, showed every indication of being greatly upset and annoyed by the presence of the blue foreigner.

Jays as a species are noted for their greedy ways, one of which is to carry off the largest chunks of anything edible, first; then to hide or deposit the loot somewhere out of sight and immediately return for another mouthful. They will keep this up until a feeding board is completely cleaned, only occasionally pausing to gulp down a little (probably to sustain their energy) between flights. The smaller birds, blackcap and mountain chickadees, juncos, fox sparrows and others of lesser size, have little or no chance for feeding when the big marauders move in. In fact, we have observed only one bird of comparable size that takes no lip from the jays and that is the hairy woodpecker. This bird seems always ready and willing to do battle if the jays ask for it, and they generally don't. It has been our observation that the jays are unwilling to challenge the red-capped bird with the long

98

sharp bill that can drill holes with the speed of a machine gun on full automatic fire. The woodpecker is clumsy on its feet in any but a treeside position. It rears back awkwardly on its haunches in attempting to land on a flat feeding board. Usually, it winds up hanging with its backside over the ledge, feet firmly gripped to the outer edge, head level with the board. But regardless of how it lands, or where, the jays depart immediately, or at least give it plenty of room.

We noticed the obvious animosity between the Canada jays and Old Blue, as we immediately dubbed the Steller. They seemed ever anxious to be rid of him; would grab up hurried mouthfuls and fly off among the trees. But Blue was quick to follow. He was literally right on their tails as they took off. And when they returned you could be sure Blue would also be back within a minute or two. We often speculated that, during the brief moments that elapsed before he reappeared, he had probably robbed the Canadas of their food cache and secreted it somewhere as his own.

As the days passed, this threesome spent a lot of time perched in the trees close to the cabin, their keen eyes constantly watching for the appearance of someone coming out to replenish the feeding board. They would be swooping down to the board and choking on chunks of bread or suet, or whatever we put out, almost before our backs were turned. But always Old Blue—the foxy boy—would be watching his unhappy mates, taking note of their choice of food. Sometimes he would sit in an aspen that offered a good vantage point and we'd hear him softly chortling and singing to himself, a joyous kind of self-satisfied song. Then he would quickly swoop down to the board, hood feathers standing upright in defiant arrogance, seeming fully aware of his striking appearance. With his own mouth full, he waited for the Canadas to take off first so he could follow and spot their hideout.

On March 15, Redcap came in to feed on the board while Old Blue and the Canadas—all of them—were on the feeder. Old Blue's hackles came up full spread and he squared away at the hairy woodpecker. Redcap's response was immediate. He crouched for attack, tail feathers braced low on the feeding board, head and neck cocked sharply back, hair-triggered for a lightning series of jabs with his long pointed bill. Inches apart, woodpecker and Stellar jay eyed each other for a split second. Then Redcap gave a short hop forward, closing in—and Old Blue chickened out and flew away. This time the Canadas were the last to leave and you could almost recognize a note of joyful triumph in their ordinarily mournful call.

Old Blue did not come back.

Little Eagle was breaking up. Days and nights were filled with sharp whipping sounds and loud crashes as the ice began to release its grip. Soon more honkers were overhead, often in night flights in dense fog. Lying in bed and listening we often tried to estimate their numbers by the multiple garble of their voices. Days of hail and snow flurries continued intermittently with bright sunshine.

By the end of April there was more open water around the edges of the islands and mated geese were arriving in pairs. Around Goose Island, which is a favored nesting place, six pairs idled, hunkered down and sleeping, usually side by side, or afloat in the small areas of open water at the points of the island. Always they were in pairs which were usually somewhat separated. They seemed waiting for a certain time or condition known only to themselves. Then one day they would be heard talking quietly in the island underbrush, building nests lined with the down the goose would pluck from her own breast. Here the usual five to seven or more eggs would be laid. The elders would fly away during the day to some distant feeding meadow, later to return.

Mildred and I remained "truck bound," or rather, "truck stuck" at Eagle Lake while the earth was still in the soggy process of thawing. Any attempt to drive our vehicle would simply end, again, in being bogged down, so we just left it where it sat, on the rocky ground a little west of the cabin, to await the restoration of solid earth. But we were never idle, even during this, the only truly irksome time of the Chilcotin year.

We have often looked back on many of the daily activities of our life at Little Eagle during breakup, as among the most eventful and rewarding. I think this was true mainly because we were never much for cabin loafing, even in the severe weather of winter. Quite often I found myself witness to something called to my attention by my wife, for she has always been more observant of fine detail than I. Sometimes our mutual enjoyment of some small, unusual thing, such as the minute pattern of rock lichens, or the design of snowflakes caught in the mesh of cobwebs, would keep us outdoors, hours at a time even in subzero weather.

By May 1, the sharptails were strutting in their prenesting rituals on sun-warmed slopes above the Ponds. Here in the brown, withered pine grass, recently bared by melting snow, the courting rites of the sharptails could be heard in their deep-toned cooing as strutting males proclaimed their proud qualities to sleek and seemingly indifferent hens. The low sounds often drifted to our ears as the sun's early morning warmth spread over the wild meadows. At times the courting sounds of the sharptails seemed to have the quality of the soft deep notes of a bull fiddle heard at great distance. On these mornings we would resume our oft-repeated attempts to sneak quietly close to the knolls to witness the mating dances. In this we had not succeeded, chiefly because the knolls are open country and unobserved approach is virtually impossible.

Half an hour's walk from our cabin lies a broad grass and reed-filled marsh, covering perhaps as much as ten acres, with areas of shallow swampland around its borders and some black-looking deep water near its center. On three sides the marsh is surrounded by stands of young lodgepole pines with some aspens and a few small spruces. From this marsh the ground rises gradually to become the southern lower slope of Tatla Hill. Along the eastern rim of the

big wetland, the Old Tatlayoko Road ambles among the pines close to the swampy edge, but on a bit higher ground.

On the morning of May 1, we hiked to the marsh. In a muddy stretch of the old road, we noted the broad pug marks of a cougar. The tracks had been made by a sizable cat. I guessed them to be the pad prints of a heavy male. We made note of the spot as I wanted to come back here with our can of plaster of Paris and make some footprint casts. Then we walked on south and eventually entered the grassy slope at the north end of the big marsh. Here we had a favorite spot for watching. We could sit with our backs to a huge glacial boulder in full warmth of the sun.

Almost at our feet, muskrats swam in a narrow canal between rows of tall reeds, where last year's dead and browned stems of cattails and rushes were intermixed with the bright green of upcoming new shoots. The muskrats passed each other in the narrow slot without so much as a casual glance or other sign of recognition, each apparently intent upon its own business. Overhead three marsh hawks circled above a pair of ruddy ducks but made no attempt to attack while the drake strutted with his tail-fan in the air and swam in short circles around his mate, their heads bobbing to each other.

Blackbirds—redwings with crimson epaulets, and the yellowheads—fluttered to hold their swaying balance on the curved-over tips of the reeds, or flew out and back to new nesting spots, their warbled notes a joy to hear. There is surely something in the blackbirds' song that no other sound approaches on a May morning in the Chilcotin.

A pair of grebes raced over a short space of clear, open water in the deep center of the marsh, for a moment raised onto their tails as if about to go into the swift run of their courtship ritual, changed their minds and dropped back to their normal swimming posture.

While we sat there enjoying all this activity, there came to us a sudden and raucous sound unlike anything we had ever heard. It came from well out in the marsh. Its source was not revealed to us. It seemed to possess a waterfowl quality, we thought, but we were not able to account for it that day—although we heard it two or three times, briefly, and thereafter no more. It remained a mystery of the marsh for a long time until we later learned such calls are made by courting coots.

For some time we studied the marsh with binoculars. Mildred was sweeping the far shores with her glasses when I heard her exclaim in hushed disbelief: "I see a cougar!"

I turned quickly to look where her glasses were pointed, but saw nothing.

"You sure it was a cougar?" I asked, doubting.

"Yes," she declared, sounding a little short of breath. "I saw it walk out on a log and I thought it must be a deer. It stopped and looked our way. I saw its face, then when it turned back into the woods I saw that big, long tail and I knew it had to be a cougar!"

I had to accept that. If it swung a thick long tail it was a cougar, all right. In my shirt pocket was a game caller, a reed instrument that, when held in the teeth and blown, gives out with a wail like the cry of a wounded rabbit. I gave it a couple of toots and slid a shell ahead of the bolt in my old Springfield. We sat still for a short time and watched. The cat did not respond to the predator call. Finally we concluded it had probably seen us, anyway, and had slunk away at the sight of a natural enemy. After a few more minutes, I told Mildred to remain where she was seated, that I was going over on the old road for another look-around. Maybe I would find some new tracks suitable for making a cast. I swung around on the grassy slope to the spot where Mildred had seen the big cat. After a casual scouting of the road and seeing nothing of particular interest, I wearied of the business, grasped my rifle by its barrel and swung the butt stock up and back over my shoulder. Then I turned to go back and stood for a split second, face to face with the biggest cougar I had ever seen! I stood as if rooted! The cat had been coming to my call.

The cat stood motionless, its green-gold eyes holding me transfixed, and then it melted into the bush...what a beauty!

This is as good a place as I will ever find to confess I am no hunter; had no intention to shoot to kill. In fact, I carried the old

Springfield only because I had always felt the value of its protection but inwardly hoping the day would never come when I would feel compelled to use it.

Walking back along the road in late afternoon, we found more tracks. Mildred was watching both sides of the road, "Hoping," she said, "and yet a little scared I might see it again." We both kept a watchful eye on the woods. We found scratch marks and tracks where a cougar had urinated and then heaped up a mound of earth...which is their habit. The claw marks were plainly visible. As we examined the scratches, a pair of nearby crows were venting their raucous fury against a huge horned owl that had no stomach for battle with its black enemies and flew off hurriedly.

We were back in camp at six o'clock, the end of a nine-hour day of walking and watching.

Since that time we have always referred to the area as the Cougar Marsh. Also, I quit a bad habit of carrying my rifle backwards...with the butt over my shoulder!

# Our Horses Come North

Our two saddle horses had been farm pastured in Washington during our first winter on the Plateau. Except for some finishing touches the log stable was complete. Now we were ready to bring our horses north. Trigger, a black Morgan gelding, and Amber, a registered sorrel Arabian mare, were hauled up to the border on a warm June day. There, a Canadian veterinarian met our truck and trailer by appointment. Certificates attesting to the good health of both animals were presented and approved. The formalities completed, our horses were admitted as eligible livestock. At this time they were unbranded and, noting this fact, the inspector admonished us to apply for a British Columbia brand without delay if we expected to remain in the "wild horse" country of the Interior.

During the preceding fall, Mildred and I had applied for status as Landed Immigrants. We had completed our personal requirements, including health certificates. On our recent return to Washington we had assembled household and personal effects we expected to need at Little Eagle Lake. Thus our equipage this day, in addition to the double horse trailer, included our heavily loaded pickup and Chuck and Wilma bringing up the rear in their own truck crammed with such items as we had been unable to jam into the canopy of our Ford.

As all our papers were in proper order, bearing a liberal variety of bureaucratic stamps and seals, we were on our way in an hour with the smiling good wishes of the inspector.

Our horses and trailer were weighed and the color and sex of the unbranded animals recorded when we arrived at the Royal Canadian Mounted Police scale house near Hope. Here we were given a clearance certificate for the gelding and mare which we would submit to the provincial brands inspector at Williams

Lake before entering the Chilcotin. The inspector, in turn, would certify information concerning our horses to the Police at Alexis Creek, the last outpost on the Chilcotin Road seventy-four miles west of Williams Lake.

We left the scales, pulled heavily up the long hill north of Hope and, from the main street of the old mining town Yale, entered the mouth of Fraser Canyon. Here we left the last of the wide valley of the lower country and now skirted the dizzy brinks of the turbulent Fraser where the ancient river snakes through a 7,000-foot range in its search for the sea. We were back on the Cariboo Road, the roar of the frothing Fraser in our ears, our eyes drawn fleetingly from the rims of a road hung among granite cliffs to the overhang of high rock escarpments. A cooling breeze blew up the gorge from the Pacific, pushing scattered rafts of cottony cirrus clouds across the blue of the bright June sky.

Our horses were used to their trailer by the time we arrived in Southern Cariboo and made no fuss about their narrow confinement. We stopped for a few minutes about once an hour to allow Trigger and Amber to rest; to give them some reassuring pats and an occasional carrot. We made good time. An hour before dusk we came into the grass of an old pasture at 83 Mile House. Here a flowing stream wound through a dilapidated corral dating from the days of the horse freighters.

We put both horses in the corral and they drank deeply from the clear, cool stream. Nearby, but for many years in disuse and disrepair, stood the sagging log ruin of the old 83 Mile barn. During the wild 1860s, that witnessed the rush to the placers at Barkerville and other camps in Cariboo, as many as 100 horses had been barned at 83 Mile, then one of the several relay points on the long freight haul. We stopped here for the night.

As we roamed among the rows of parallel mangers, where the jerkline teams had rested and fed a century ago, the earth floor of the big barn gave up the musty odors of an era when men and beasts toiled over the rutted, dusty track from Mile "0" at Lillooet. In the mind's eye and the magic of imagination, I could detect the sweet smell of the big hay mow, the sweat of tired horses and hear the voices of a breed of men no longer known to

Canada. In the dark interior of the empty barn I stood in awareness of the vast difference of the times, past and present. Our own two horses had been trailered this day, in a matter of hours, over a stretch of miles the old-time freighters would have required more than a week to negotiate with full loads in high wheeled, creaking wagons.

We were up, breakfasted and on our way early the following morning. Rolling on through 100 Mile House and the grasslands of Lac La Hache, we arrived in Williams Lake before noon.

Having entered another jurisdiction of the Mounted Police, we again cleared our animals and proceeded westward on the first leg of the rough Chilcotin Road. Here we left the last mile of blacktop, over which we had sped with such ease for the first 320 miles from the border, to encounter one of the roughest roads in the British Columbia Interior. We were now on the final day-long haul to Little Eagle, where a new log stable and a pine pole corral awaited our horses.

Our speed was reduced to about fifteen miles an hour and frequently to a low-gear crawl. Our outfit jolted over old and rutted sections of road where the winds of early summer had blown away the cushion of yellow dust, leaving only the exposed tops of deeply imbedded boulders.

The day turned hot and we seldom felt the caress of a cooling breeze. We stopped frequently, especially if we could find a spot of shade. Slowly winding down to the Fraser crossing, we cautiously drove onto the old suspension bridge, keenly aware of its tendency to sway rhythmically along with its creaking and groaning as the great cables seemed to protest the exertion. After crossing the bridge, we immediately began the steep pull up the opposite wall of the canyon following the torturous switchbacks of Sheep Creek Hill. More than once we had to stop to cool our overheated motor, grinding in lowest gear to pull the trailer load of our two horses.

It was with a feeling of great relief that we again emerged from the last rough and twisting switchback to roll westward over the high Chilcotin Plateau. The myriad of lakes of the grassy parklands glinted like polished silver among groves of shimmering aspens as we spanned the rolling meadows of Beecher's Prairie, which seem to spread endlessly south, west and north. Bluebirds flashed vividly and the lilting melody of meadowlarks came pleasantly to our ears. We were once more experiencing the unique beauty of the high, open country west of Fraser's river.

The first jarring note of the day came as an explosion sharp as a rifle shot. A tire on our pickup blew out on the long slope dropping down to Riske Creek, thirty-two miles west of Williams Lake. We replaced the blown tire with one of the two mounted spares we carried; we were thankful the tire failure had occurred in comparatively open, level country, rather than somewhere back along the steep switchbacks of Sheep Creek Hill.

We rumbled on, through Hance's Timber to drop down the long grade to Lee's, then at Alexis Creek headquarters of the Mounted Police stopped to file our final report on the unbranded horses. An hour later we blew another tire on the Ford and now we mounted our only remaining spare with more than fifty miles of rough road still to be covered before we would arrive at Little Eagle.

With two useless flat tires, we were on the last of our good rubber many miles from any source of repair or replacement. Though we had been driving slowly, often in second gear, we reduced our speed further to ease the shock of the road. Over a distance of more than ninety miles we had met but one other vehicle that day. In it was Bob Elliott and his family, from Tatlayoko, en route to Williams Lake. We visited briefly during this meeting with old friends and Elliott offered us his one and only spare tire, which we declined.

By 10:00 P.M. on June 25,. we came onto the north ridge, a mile from camp. There being a good open area among some pines, we backed the horse trailer into a level spot and unhooked from the truck. Here we unloaded the horses and Chuck and I walked them to the old Indian corral near the cabin with the aid of flashlights while Mildred and Wilma followed with the trucks.

The horses had stood the trip well. They quickly scented the sweet pine grass and wild vetch growing among the lodgepoles and aspens and began reaching eagerly for their first taste of the rich, wild forage. We had been sixteen hours on the road this hot and troublesome day.

As we entered the corral the rapid thunder of hoofs thrashed through the woods. We recognized the sound as the commotion of a feral band of range horses. Despite the burst of excited action among the running animals, our own horses paid little attention, and seemed content to stand and browse as Chuck and I speculated on the probable number in the band. We were not immediately aware, then, of the trouble this roving herd would cause us in the months to follow our arrival at Little Eagle.

We watered and corralled Trigger and Amber. Bone weary with 490 hard miles behind us, we crawled into our sleeping bags at midnight. In the cabin, nothing had been disturbed in our absence.

Next morning we put bells and hobbles on the horses and turned them loose.

After sleeping late, we chose this day following arrival to rest. On Mildred's suggestion we visited the Ponds west of Eagle Lake. Chuck and I covered the mile of open water between our cabin and the outlet to the Ponds in the canoe while Mildred and Wilma walked through the woods for some bird-looking, accompanied by Chuck's two hounds. We met at the meadow where Mildred and I had first camped years previous to this day and together strolled on to the Ponds. They were at a stage of low water and almost devoid of waterfowl. We saw no ducks nor geese. There were several mud hens. We were gratified to see a few bright bluebirds among the aspens clustering the meadows along the north shore of the Ponds.

While walking, Chuck discovered the hoof prints of a young colt. We saw nothing of yesterday's wild horses. While Chuck and I paddled back to camp, Mildred and Wilma had been attracted by horse bells on the north ridge. They feared our horses were wandering. They hurried up to the ridge and met Amber on the truck road. The little mare, alone, came trotting up to Mildred, whickering, acting bewildered by her strange surroundings. Mildred gave a call for Trigger and the gelding answered with a whinny and came charging up the ridge road. Both animals seemed glad to see the women and stayed close to them as they all walked back to camp, Trigger and Amber breaking into a fast gallop as they neared the cabin. They ran straight for the corral, their bells jangling loudly. Trigger had broken one of his hobble chains while running.

On the twenty-seventh, Chuck and Wilma said good-bye and returned south with the empty horse trailer.

The horses seemed to recognize the new stable for what it was and promptly moved into its generous shade on hot days.

For a time we kept our stock hobbled but removed the restraints when they showed an inclination to remain close to camp. We let them roam the near grasslands wearing halters and bells. This method of keeping track of them in this fenceless region worked quite well for a time. And they usually came to our call.

Temperatures were in the high 80s as Mildred and I worked to complete a couple of box stalls and mangers in the new stable. The horses were frequently in the shade of the stable lean-to as we worked and we enjoyed their companionship. We had raised both horses from colthood and they were affectionate pets. As flies became a problem, we sprayed them. The gelding, Trigger, who had never approved of being curried or brushed, gradually discovered the fly spray's benefits and stood with nostrils flared and twitching as I applied the smelly insect repellent. Amber, always a gentle little mare, was never a problem in this respect and she loved to be brushed.

Daily, it seemed, the horses drifted to more the distant wild meadows beyond Eagle Lake. It was this tendency—probably because grass around our camp was getting short—that inspired us to use a police whistle to call them in for graining. The idea proved a good one. They soon caught on to the fact there was a feeding of oats waiting if they responded to the whistle. A long shrill blast or two would bring them full gallop among the aspens, hoofs pounding as they raced for camp.

# Horse Heaven

July grew hot, frequently sultry. On some of the sweltering days, when Little Eagle lay flat and placid, devoid of summer's usual westerly breezes, our horses stood shaded by the corral spruces, disinclined to leave the pen though the open gate.

On these days we favored our big canoe. On Bird Island, Mildred gathered sharply scented mint and some wild blue violets for pressing. On the island we also found thin slabs of granite, piled some at the water's edge, to be boated across The Narrows to our cabin later. They would make excellent flagstones.

We paddled into the narrow lagoon that cuts into the south shore, and found sunny seclusion so tempting we shed our clothes and swam in the sun-warmed waters of the little bay. The bottom here was soft white sand. We flushed great schools of sucker fish from the reed beds and Mildred stood in the canoe to take movies of them as they streaked beneath the light aluminum hull.

Off a point of land near the entrance to the lagoon we drifted silently within inches of a drowsing toad and Mildred added a photograph of the fat, pulsing sleeper to her collection. At Goose Island a bed of pink-red water buckwheat spread its vivid color in July. The kind we found here and in The Ponds is a species of knotweed that identifies with low wetlands and shallows and it is a favorite food of most waterfowls. Our ponds beyond the outlet of Little Eagle become so thickly mantled with the bright blossoms in midsummer the surfaces resemble wide spreads of pink velvet carpeting.

One evening, following a particularly warm day, I rode Amber over the mile of our camp road, out to its junction with the Old Tatlayoko Road and back. I wanted Mildred to ride and

thought it wise to give the mare a workout first, as days of idleness had made the Arabian a little hot under the saddle, though she had never bucked. The two-mile ride was uneventful and on return to the cabin I handed the mare over to Mildred.

My wife had not been riding much and I cautioned her to keep a close rein. Then I mounted Trigger and we headed out over an old trail Mildred and I had hiked on evening walks before our horses came north. Amber immediately began a quick-step and balked a bit, throwing up her head. Mildred dismounted and I examined the cinch, thinking maybe it was too tight. There was nothing wrong with the cinch and the saddle blanket was perfectly clean and smooth. Mildred remounted and the mare at once began to fidget nervously. My wife again got off, insisting there must be something under Amber's saddle causing irritation. I removed both saddle and blanket, examined them closely. There was nothing under the saddle but a round fat back, slightly wet with sweat. As I examined the riding gear on the ground, Amber pushed her head against Mildred, nudging and rubbing the cheeks of her bridle as a sign she wanted it removed.

I re-saddled for the third time in a matter of minutes and Mildred once more mounted her pet. Amber's fractious conduct was immediately resumed and when Mildred said, "I'm getting off!" I realized Amber was surely putting one over on my wife. The "something" under Amber's light saddle was simply an overabundance of hot Arabian fire. The mare, grown independent as the result of weeks of free roaming the wild meadows, had become convinced she need only make a determined show of resistance to the saddle to avoid being ridden.

We traded horses then, Mildred stepped up on Trigger and I climbed into Amber's saddle, pushing her at once into a fast walk and holding her to the pace until she lathered and the hot sweat rolled from her flanks. We were back in camp at dusk. The fire still smoldered under Amber's saddle but it had been dampened a little, at least temporarily.

We held both horses on dry hay and water for several days to work the green feed out of their stomachs. I rode Amber and let Trigger loaf. The mare would go quickly into the swift floating gait of her breed with flaxen tail arched and proud. Her neck and flanks lathered quickly as the sweat came out. In the few days trail riding she had leveled off and given up notions about bucking, though I never rode her with slack reins.

This was the one occasion when I was tempted to replace the gentle snaffle bit Amber had always worn with a port bar and curb strap, but gave it up as unnecessary. We discovered years ago that horses are not born with hard mouths. They became hard-mouthed as the result of the use of severe bits employed in the mistaken notion that such bits are aids to control. Mildred and I "gentle broke" both of our horses. They wore plain bar bits in summer and rubber bits in winter. Trigger's bridle was also equipped with a leather chin strap but it was never worn snug. I don't think either of our horses were ever suspicious of us or of the riding equipment we used, as there was never any rearing or show of resentment when saddles and bridles were brought out.

Hoofs hardened in the dry climate of the Plateau and trimmings were flinty under the fairing knife. The gritty glacial soil quickly wore down the toes and little rasping was necessary to keep the hoofs healthy. I think we spent more time grooming and petting our horses than we ever spent riding.

Trigger was twenty-seven years old when we brought him north and had long since gotten over being spooked. But sometime during their lazy grazing among the wild meadows up here, I think Amber must have been badly frightened by a bear. While riding, I noticed the mare's ears snap quickly forward, felt her shoulder muscles tighten at the sight of an old fire-blackened stump among the young green pines. Once, on rounding a bend in the trail where a black stump came unexpectedly into view, she shied off in a sidewise jump so quickly we nearly parted company.

The influence of breeding became apparent in the dispositions of our horses, once they had been permitted to run free on the open range. Trigger's sire was Black Prince, a registered Morgan stallion owned originally by the United States Army. Uncle Sam's cavalry remount agency had placed Black Prince at service in astern Washington, where Trigger was produced as a cross between the Prince and a range mare of good but unregistered lineage. Trigger had shown inclinations toward a wild waywardness since colthood, whereas Amber, of straight Arabian forebears, had always leaned toward people, rather than the wilds. She would often come up to us for attention when Trigger was openly disposed to avoid our approach. At times, after a day of searching and listening for their bells, it would be Amber that finally came to our calling while Trigger hung back, not wanting to follow.

That Trigger was reverting to the wild nature of his range-roaming mother became more apparent each time we hiked out among the scattered meadows to check on the whereabouts of the horses, or to bring them back to camp. Our chief worry at this time was the fact they were still unbranded. Our application to the provincial government for our own brand awaited official approval in a region where the mark of a hot iron is still accepted as the only proof of ownership.

One day, after the horses had failed to return the evening before, we could no longer hear their bells. With saddles, bridles, feed oats and carrots in the canopy of the pickup, we went looking for the wanderers. South of the outlet of Eagle Lake, we came on their tracks in the dust of the road, heading toward Tatlayoko Valley.

We had no difficulty identifying their hoof prints, particularly Amber's. As a filly she had sustained an injury to the outer wall of her left forefoot, which resulted in a slight bulging growth in the rim of the wall. This growth, while of no serious consequence, required occasional rasping to maintain a trim hoof. If left unattended for two or three weeks, it would develop a bulge that was readily recognized in her footprint.

Following the prints in the dusty road, we stopped the motor now and again to listen and whistle when the tracks led off among the pines. Continuing farther along we would pick them up again where the horses had come back onto the roadway. Then we lost the prints and there was no sound of tinkling bells. Our anxiety increased as we drove on southward.

Rounding a bend and onto a rise, the pine woods opened to reveal a small valley, rimmed by dense timber on the far side, some aspen trees and an open meadow. In the meadow lay a lovely small lake, ruffled by dabbling waterfowl. Ready with binoculars, we spotted our two horses knee-deep in lush wild grass on the far shore. They saw us about the same time and Trigger immediately plunged off into the woods, Amber following, their halter bells clanging loudly. They appeared to be heading for the valley road to our south.

Our hunch proved correct for we caught up with them in about a mile. Again, Trigger raced off among the pines but as Mildred called to Amber, the mare looked back and appeared hesitant about following the gelding. Finally, after catching up with them a third time and much calling and gentle-voiced coaxing, Amber turned and came walking up to Mildred, her favorite human. Trigger, however, refused to come out of the woods. A moment later he bolted away among the pines, but when he saw Amber was not following he stopped and looked back with impatient tail thrashing and a throaty, grumbling nicker. He came back a few steps, then stood off like a black blob among the trees, silent and unmoving, but ready to crash off and away. Black dynamite! His actions belied his twenty-seven years.

Mildred slipped a lead rope into the ring of Amber's halter. After considerable petting and handfuls of feed oats and carrots, she stood calmly while I saddled her. No amount of coaxing would entice Trigger. If we made a few steps toward him with

Old Corral

the oats can he took off at a gallop but stopped when we made no further advances. We decided he would give up if we left him. I rode ahead on Amber, Mildred following with the pickup, heading for camp and the home corral. In a few moments a black fury came crashing out of the pines as Trigger discovered he was being abandoned. Then, with head down, ears laid back, underlip flapping and feet shuffling in the dust, he followed us in a deep sulk. Old Trigger was definitely mad and pouting but was not about to be left alone.

Amber's only reaction to being saddled again was to shy at

almost every fire-blackened stump we passed, and finally to balk against fording the shallow creek at the outlet of Eagle Lake. She had crossed this small knee-deep stream numerous times in the past month of her free roaming. But not this day. Not wearing spurs, which might have been more persuasive than my smooth boot heels, I got out of the saddle and led her across the ford.

We corralled both horses that night.

Early in August, we received the provincial government's approval of our J/J horse brand and had an iron made up by the blacksmith at Tatla. One evening, young Roy Graham and Johnny Perjue came out from Tatla and branded our horses.

We had dreaded the ordeal but knew it was essential in this open range country. Mildred and I both thought it would probably be necessary to throw the horses but Roy, an experienced young rancher, assured us it was easier to brand them standing and no trouble at all. We heated the new iron in an open fire. Johnny held Trigger by the halter and Roy gave a quick and solid thrust with the hot iron to the right shoulder, which was the brand position assigned to us. The gelding flinched but stood until Johnny turned him loose. Trigger's only reaction to the searing iron was to turn his head sidewise, give the burn a quick sniff, then start grazing on the pine grass where he had been standing. Amber was branded a moment later in the same manner. Our horses now wore the Jenkins mark—J/J—which had been duly registered and we felt our animals were at least securely identified.

Then I walked to the cabin and told Mildred, "You can come out now. It's all over and Amber won't be a bit mad at you!"

By early September we noticed the complete absence of fruit on the hooshum (soapolallie) bushes which are usually loaded at this season; also that the conifers, lodgepole pines, as well as the spruces and Douglas firs, were devoid of cones. This was a strange coincidence and the lack of bush fruit and tree seed, which appeared to be general over the Plateau, portended serious problems for our winter birds and squirrels. The varied thrushes (winter robins) and pine grosbeaks would find their winter forage meager. The squirrels would fare a little better, as there had been a bumper crop of mushrooms and great quantities of these were now being sun dried where the squirrels had spread them out on the boughs of the trees.

Our diary for September 14 relates: "The first snow of fall came today, to a depth of three-quarters of an inch," and on the following day, "We put out extra feed for birds (bread and seeds). A fox sparrow, crown sparrows, juncos, a lone robin redbreast, all feeding on a bare spot of ground under some low spruce boughs. Kinglets, Audubon warblers and a nuthatch all here today. Alvin is busy turning over his drying mushrooms. During a recent shower he moved a lot of them in closer to the tree trunk, where they were sheltered. Now he's putting them out to the sun again. A hawk swooped in to seize a small bird on our window sill but flew off without success after striking the window a jarring blow. Out on our road, a bear has dragged a twenty-foot rotten pine log out of the bushes and into the road, where it was rolled over and over in the bear's search for grubs. We had to move the log off the road to get by with the truck."

Cooler days of early fall were reminders of winter to come and we gave more thought to our woodpile. A mile up the lake an old-growth Douglas fir with heavy red bark had been uprooted by wind. The tree, about four feet in diameter at the butt, lay almost parallel to the shoreline. We decided here lay our winter wood—if we could get it to camp. Our big canoe, our light skiff with outboard motor and chain saw solved the problem.

We canoed up the lake with ax, maul and wedges, chain saw and a bottle of gas, and went to work on the big windfall. More than forty blocks of fir heater wood, fat with pitch, and nearly a cord of heavy bark came out of the tree in the next two days. We loaded the canoe to the gunwales and towed it behind the skiff, also loaded, and powered with our little trolling motor. Seven trips in this manner delivered the entire tree to camp, and the blocks, when split and piled together with the bark, made a stack four feet high and more than forty feet long. We were soon well prepared for a siege of cold weather.

Autumn coloring came to the countryside and every trip with the boat and canoe, loaded with wood, was a breathtaking experience of beauty. The shoreline hardwoods vivid in bright yellow, apricot and flaming reds edged the deeper woods of dark evergreens...the setting for the precious jewel that is Little Eagle Lake. This is our favorite time of year.

The approach of colder weather brought in some big northern wood rats and a pair of them moved into a pile of boards stored against the side of the cabin. These animals are destructive, messy, and soon make their presence known by their foul odor. Unless eliminated, the route of their movements is soon marked by stinking trails of urine and scat, which they seem to leave with promiscuous abandon as they prowl everywhere about the cabin.

In our country they have a reputation of being hard to trap, supposedly possessing some sixth sense in the detection of mechanical snares. We found two methods to produce fair results. One was to place a small trap inside a length of stovepipe laid flat in a corner. The big rats have a propensity for dashing into dark holes and the stovepipe seems to attract them. Another system is to place a food bait of some sort in the bottom of a shallow box and cover it with shredded paper, through which they will dig to reach the bait. A trap in such cover is sometimes effective.

I saw one of them loping along at the foot of the cabin wall one day, grabbed my shotgun and gave it a charge of number eight chilled shot just as it ran in front of a quart can of varnish that had not been opened. I got the rat all right, but put about half the charge through a four-dollar can of varnish. Mildred, who dislikes shooting, had a few things to say about that.

Toward the latter part of September the horses had not come in nor had we heard their bells for several days. Our anxiety was increased by the fact a wild band had been seen near The Ponds. We decided we had better look to our animals. Mildred, her mother Mary, who was visiting us this fall, and I took off in the truck. We checked the meadows around The Ponds, then soon picked up their tracks in the soft dirt of the Old Tatlayoko Road, Amber's left forefoot print giving us the clue. We trailed them to the same meadow with the small lake, near the foot of Splinter Mountain's north slope.

The horses must have had a contented feeling about this spot, for here they were, Trigger lying on his back, well-stuffed belly turned to the sun. Nearby stood Amber, head down and dozing in deep grass, her only movement an occasional flick of her ears and a swish of flaxen tail against the black flies that pestered her. On our approach, Trigger rolled and lurched to his feet, lazily considering whether he should take to the woods, and might have except for the fact that Mildred called and waved the carrots at him. He decided they looked pretty good. Trigger's halter and bell were gone. Amber still had her halter but no bell. They were rolling fat. We gave them the last of our carrots and a handful of oats apiece, some petting and gentle talk. Trigger finished his tidbits and walked to the edge of the water and began nipping off the tender shoots of grass. Amber stood around for more petting. We left them where they had been found, in a lush paradise of feed, water, sun and shade, and in company of several kinds of waterfowl. We envied them and we started calling this beauty spot the Horse Heaven Meadow. As we walked away, Amber came part way along the meadow with us, then hesitated, looking back at Trigger, then at us, undecided. A few more pats and we told her to go back with Trig. She stood, watching, as we returned to the truck.

In a few days they came home, nosed around for their handout of oats, accepted the offering, sniffed around their corral, licked the salt block and wandered off again.

About a week later they came in around 7:15 one morning, Amber well in the lead. She came directly to the cabin door, walking purposefully, and peered through the glass. Trigger was some distance behind her, plodding along. He came to stand near the door. Observing him for a few minutes, Mildred said, "I believe Trigger is not feeling well."

I dismissed her remark by suggesting he was just lazy and full of food. The horses were around the doorway, persistent for attention, Amber all but putting her head inside the door. After a bit Mildred again insisted that Trigger was not feeling himself. "He acts so dopey and his eyes are dull. He seems very warm."

I was about to say it was because he had been running, when

I noticed he was "hiccupping" and appeared sweaty. After consulting our horse book we thought he had what some horsemen call the "Thumps," which are a sort of hiccups, probably the result of too much green swamp grass. He did have a temperature and diarrhea. Trigger was ill, for sure.

We put him in the corral, covered with a warm blanket, and gave him some chopped carrots and warmed water. Next day his thumps were gone and he seemed not as feverish, but he was racked with diarrhea. I drove out to Tatla to see about medicine. There was no medicine at the store, nor a veterinarian nearer than Williams Lake. But Mrs. Eleanor Graham, a rancher's young wife who grew up in the Chilcotin and who I was sure knew about such things, came out to our place, took a look at my sick gelding and said it appeared to be "swamp fever."

She loaded up a syringe with penicillin and gave old Trigger a shot in the chest. Then she reached inside his mouth, pulled his tongue out about eight inches, inserted the neck of a bottle containing a quart of epsom salts solution and poured it down his gullet. He had refused his oats but begged for carrots. By evening the following day he was much improved and had cleaned up his oats. Some eggnog and dry hay soon had him back to normal. When he came on thundering hoofs at our whistle for oats, we all laughed in happy realization that Trig was again his old spirited self.

While Trigger was ill Amber would not leave him for more than a few minutes. She would stand near our door anxiously, then nervously go back to check on her companion, going to him where he was lying down, sniffing around his neck, then coming back to us again. It was obvious that Amber was concerned for Trigger. As his strength revived and he was again ready to roam, both horses returned to the wild meadows, but we often opened our cabin door to find them standing there, ready to beg for a tidbit. They seldom stayed away more than a day as the colder nights approached.

November arrived with an early warning of winter. Southwesterly winds and temperatures in the high 40s were soon followed by a two-inch fall of snow that became a glazed crust. The mercury dropped below freezing levels. A fringe of icicles formed a shining crystal curtain along the low edges of the cabin eaves. There was a flurry of activity among birds that came to feed on the window ledge where we spread seeds and nailed down strips of bacon rind.

Our horses, fat on wild meadow grass, came in for their treats of cured hay and carrots. We now felt these occasional rewards would discourage any notion they might get about wandering out of the country. So far, our system seemed to be working.

Due to the crusty condition of the new snow we were unable to sweep a clear space for bird feeding under the trees. We had about twenty pounds of commercial wild bird seeds and scattered quantities over the snow. Canada jays, pine grosbeaks, blackcap and mountain chickadees, and redbreast robins appeared in steadily increasing numbers. Then suddenly the robins were gone, apparently in migration.

We removed the highway treads from the rear wheels of our pickup and replaced them with a set of new mud-grip tires, sure they were going to be needed. And into the canopy of the truck, stashed two pairs of snowshoes against the chance we might need them at almost any time from now on.

We used our pickup to haul in loads of two-foot heater wood, which we had cut and piled to season while clearing the route of our new road during August. Early in November we resumed our road work in the hope of completing the last half-mile of the relocation before winter.

Flurries of snow were sporadic. In one section of our road where Chuck had helped us by cutting up a mass of windfalls three years previously, we made several piles and burned those not suitable for heater wood. In another area, where seedling pines and young aspens were particularly thick, we spent long hours grubbing them out by the roots, alternately tending our fires and sawing up whatever wood was of heating stove value. We worked hard, ate hearty meals and slept like loggers. As the job progressed farther from camp we packed lunch and a thermos of hot coffee. We doled out a carton of Mackintosh apples from the Okanagan country at the rate of two a day, to be included in our lunch, usually eaten in the warm cab of our pickup. We saved the sweet cores and peelings for the horses and they would be waiting for us at the cabin, expecting the treat as we came in at dusk. We were frequently met by the horses out on the road, if they seemed to feel we were overdue with the apple cores. They also got onto the fact that bird seed is edible grain and we had a hard time keeping the bird feeding boards in our windows supplied.

We tried putting the seeds out on the boards after dark, in the hope the birds would find food waiting for them at daylight. But the horses soon got onto that too. We would be reading by lamplight long after full darkness, to be startled by the whites of Trigger's eyes in the inky black outside the window, his thick red tongue sweeping the boards, and Amber nipping at his neck and crowding to get in before the seeds were all gone. She seldom got more than a smidgen or two.

We finally solved the problem by scattering the seeds under some piles of logs which were stacked a few inches above the ground level. The birds could now reach the seeds under a low roof of logs.

One night in the first week of November a flock of swans settled on the lake. We heard their cackling but could only guess at their number. At daylight they were noisy again and we counted seven—two huge, beautiful white adult birds and five cignets whose immaturity was evident by their characteristic gray feathering and red bills. This day several rafts of buffleheads and fourteen Canada geese came to settle on the lake, the geese wheeling low and their white bellies turning pale green in the reflected light of the lake.

We continued our road work. The ground was now frozen. One old pine stump—a rather large one—stood in the middle of the road and we had to dig it out. The task required about two hours of picking out frozen clay and rocks and chopping off roots before the stump could be rolled clear. We had just finished filling the hole with clods of frozen earth when Trigger and Amber came up on the ridge to join us. Trigger sniffed the newly disturbed earth, which covered a spot about five feet in diameter, and promptly buckled his knees and took a roll, got up, shook himself and flicked his ears. Trigger was always ready for a roll and we frequently saw him down on his back in the snow, pitching from side to side. But like most horses he preferred fresh earth for a wallow even if it was frozen.

On November 10, our truck speedometer showed us we had made three-tenths of a mile of passable new road. The temperature idled around twenty-eight to thirty-one degrees. There were about three inches of snow on the ground and snow flurries were hitting us almost every day. By mid-November we had cut our way almost to the summit of the north ridge to join the section of old road we would still use. The temperature was twelve degrees to fifteen degrees above at daylight now, accumulated snow depth was about five inches. The earth was freezing so we had to pry out the windfalls and other down stuff to get it into piles for burning.

One morning, in the white softness of snow, Mildred discovered the broad tracks of a cougar where the big cat had trailed us as we returned to the cabin at dusk the previous evening. The front pad marks were about four inches broad and the imprint of the cougar's tail drag was plainly visible. Somewhere along the line of its thinking the cougar had changed its mind about following us and veered off among the pines. Nearby, the deeply impressed tracks of two moose, a cow and a bull, crossed our new road heading for the willow thickets along the lake shore. As we speculated on the probable size and weight of the bull, a wedge of honkers flew over, heading toward Tatlayoko. We counted an even forty of the beautiful big Canada geese flying so low the laminations of individual wing and tail feathers were clearly visible.

Although the snow was powdery dry, our cotton work gloves became soaked and wore out in a day or two. I think we must have gone through at least a dozen pairs of gloves on the last few days of road work.

Most of the young trees to be cleared from our road were from two to four or five inches in diameter at ground level and stood to a height of about seven to ten feet. They would make beautiful Christmas trees. They were thickly limbed and so densely growing a moose would be invisible among them at a distance of forty feet.

As we worked up onto the north ridge where the pines were small but standing in a dense thicket, we learned a new technique for their removal which proved quite efficient. We discovered that in this shallow, gravelly soil, the lodgepole seldom puts down a vertical or tap root. Instead, it seems to be their habit to send out, as seedlings, from five to seven small lateral root runners that fan out like the points of a star just under the gritty surface soil. I learned this after wearing out a sevendollar double-bitted ax, chopping off roots of young pines. Our newly discovered method for complete removal of the pines, roots and all, included the use of a miner's pick. We drove one point of the pick under each of the lateral roots, and by applying a foot to the opposite pick point, using it as a lever, and rearing back on the pick handle, the roots either came completely out of the soil, or snapped off. They are both tender and brittle in the young trees. Thus we worked around the base of the pines, levering out the small brace roots one at a time. Then, with both of us using our weight, a couple of rocking heaves on the trunk of the pine would snap it out of the ground. Mildred and I got so expert at this business we were soon popping out the young pines at the rate of one every three or four minutes. I called my 110-pound wife "Mighty Milly" and we had a lot of fun building road, even when the mercury dropped to zero. The horses continued to call on us most days about apple core time. If they didn't show up during the day they would be at camp when we came in at dusk, around four o'clock, and stick their noses right into the cab of the old pickup, well knowing we had probably saved our apple cores for them to eat.

On November 23, new ice closed The Narrows between our cabin and Bird Island. It was ten degrees Fahrenheit above zero. East of the island, where the deeper part of the lake was still open, a brisk easterly wind whipped strong waves against the raw edge of the thin pan ice, causing it to buckle and curl back against the main body of the pan. The movement made a pleasant tin-

125

kling sound. By evening there was a thin sheet of ice over the entire west end of the lake from Bird Island to the outlet.

We drove our truck out to the Chilcotin Road to break trail in five inches of new snow. Our tires with their heavy lug treads proved to be excellent snow grippers and we cut a sharply defined track. As the nights grew colder, we brought our two truck batteries into the warmth of the cabin to guard against freezing.

Thanksgiving Day—November 25—dawned at two degrees above zero, with brilliant sunshine and the air about us glinting with millions of frost crystals adrift on light variable breezes. This day we had to break ice in the lake so our horses could drink. We placed three kerosene lamps and a barn lantern under the engine of the truck and covered the hood with a large tarpaulin. Thus warmed for about three hours, the engine started readily and we drove to Tatla for mail and groceries. On return we sat down to a rather lonesome Thanksgiving dinner. We missed our family. Mildred had prepared roast chicken and dressing, with all the fixings. Letters from our family and others we read and re-read that evening and, admittedly, we were a little lonely.

We continued to work on our new road and finally finished cleaning out the last of the pines by November 29. We eliminated a steep hill that had caused us trouble in the past. It was ten degrees above zero the day we finished the job in seven inches of snow. Little Eagle was groaning in spasms of newly formed ice. We were groaning a little ourselves that night, from tired backs and sore muscles. But it was a good feeling to know we had completed the connecting link of our truck road.

By previous arrangement, Ross Wilson came in the evening of December 4 to truck our horses out to Chilanko Forks. He would keep them for us while Mildred and I would go Outside for Christmas with our family.

More snow blanketed the Plateau but government plows were keeping the Chilcotin Road open for winter travel. Our own four miles of road in to the lake, however, was now barely passable, and Ross' big diesel powered cattle truck was wallowing when it arrived at our cabin.

We had no ramp for loading the horses into the high bed of

the big truck. We finally devised a method, utilizing several bales of hay and some planks to lay a sloping ramp up to the open tailgate. The planks were bouncy and Ross and I both had misgivings, sure that Trigger would spook and refuse to go up the ramp. Strangely, Amber followed quite willingly when I led her up the planks and almost before I had her halter secured to the headboards of the stock rack, Trigger came plunging up and into the truck, snorting wildly. He stomped right up to the side of the little mare in a belligerent attitude of determination not to be left behind!

Mildred and I drove out four days later, to return in the New Year.

# Winter Takes Its Toll

## *1964*

An unexpected blizzard gripped the Pacific Northwest during Christmas week. By New Year's Day the cold front sweeping down from the Canadian Shield had driven the mercury to new lows. Fraser Canyon was clogged by avalanching snow and roads north of the border were blocked by deep drifts.

Unable to return to the peaceful wilderness of Little Eagle under existing conditions, we vented our frustrations somewhat by the purchase of a silver poodle puppy. When we finally headed north again on February 9, Vevette, a black-eyed silk-soft bundle of affection, snuggled between us as a happy third member of our company. Chuck and Wilma and their hounds came with us, planning another cougar hunt in Jameson Basin.

At Chilanko, after two days on tire chains and alternately driving through snow showers and the sparkling cold of the sunny Interior, we were saddened to learn from Ross Wilson that our twenty-eight-year-old gelding, Trigger, was dead. The Morgan had succumbed to a heart attack, dropping dead in his tracks midway through an evening feed of oats. Sorrowfully, we arranged for the return of Amber to the lake. She would be a lonely little mare, but she was due to foal in early April and we wanted her on the home range for that event.

Misfortune seemed to dog us that day. As we turned into the last mile of our road along the north ridge, we encountered a heavily drifted area where the older snow had crusted. My attempt to break through a drift in compound low gear ended abruptly when the cluster gears in the Ford's rear end let go with a loud snap and all forward motion stopped. A huge pillow of snow lay rolled against the front bumper. Chuck and Wilma came to a halt behind us. We concluded it would be unwise to risk Chuck's truck against the drift. On snowshoes, and under pack-

128

boards with such provisions as we could carry, we trudged the final mile to the cabin. Vevette was alternately carried in Wilma's arms or lunging through the snow in an effort to keep up with Chuck's long-legged hounds.

Except for the evidence mice usually leave to indicate their presence in wilderness cabins, nothing had been disturbed. Little Eagle lay deeply frozen and silent, more than two feet of ice shielding its clear depths. There had been some wind—probably during the recent blizzard—to pile snow in deep folds against the cabin walls and over the roof. The tall spruces and the lodgepole pines drooped heavily and there was a virgin whiteness among the naked aspens. A tangle of moose tracks punctured the white mantle among the lake shore willows and The Narrows had been repeatedly crossed by moose bedding at night on Bird Island. Our registering thermometer had set its plug on a maximum of fifty-two degrees below zero at sometime in our absence.

It was good to be home.

By moonlight that night, Chuck and Wilma took our seven-foot toboggan and returned to the trucks. They loaded about 100 pounds of supplies on the toboggan and were back to the cabin by ten o'clock.

The following morning Chuck and I drove out to Tatla where we made arrangements with Jack Butler to tow my disabled vehicle to the Graham ranch shop. On our return, we again loaded the toboggan with about 150 pounds of supplies. This time Chuck made up a better harness for the big redbone hound, using one of Amber's leather halters. Hoecake pulled the load with a steady plodding willingness and I helped with a pulling rope while Chuck pushed and steered with a gee pole. As she had previously, Jezzabelle loped and frolicked around her mate and had to be restrained from attempts to jump on the load and ride.

On February 13, Chuck's birthday, we made a third trip. The sled load amounted to about 200 pounds, which moved over the frozen snow with remarkable ease.

Butler hauled my truck to the shop. With a minimum of delay enforced by distance, he secured a set of gears from a supplier in

Williams Lake, and in a few days the Ford was back in running order.

Within the week of our arrival, the deep rumble of the provincial road grader was again heard as a welcome assurance of release from the drifts. Trevor Lauton plowed our road to the cabin door and we soon had both trucks parked in the clearing. During the ten days that Chuck and Wilma remained with us before heading for Jameson Basin, we cut ice with the chain saw. As yet we had no ice house, but improvised an effective storage by building a crib of pine and covering the ice blocks with the scales of spruce cones from squirrel middens beneath the trees. Over the duff from the spruce cones we spread newspapers and a tarpaulin. The ice stored in this manner lasted well into the following July.

Also during this time Chuck built an ice boat, using one-by-eight-inch boards for the frame and some old skis for the runners. The sail he fashioned from a piece of light canvas, the mast from a slender pole. Then, for several days, the new boat sat on the lake ice waiting for a favorable wind; but, in this, we were disappointed by the dead-calm of the sunny days that followed completion of the boat. It seldom moved more than a few feet on the vagrant breezes that blew in from the west.

When the cougar hunters finally took their leave, Mildred and I turned to some odd jobs around the cabin. These included the building of more book shelves and a kitchen cupboard, a new kitchen table, a wardrobe and a gaucho-type bunk that opened to a full width bed.

Occasionally, Chuck and Wilma drove up from Jameson Basin to visit us. By March 19, the first indications of breakup were evident. The overnight lows were generally around twenty-five degrees to twenty-seven degrees above zero; daytime highs ranged to forty and fifty degrees and on the twenty-eighth to fifty-six degrees at midday. Large pools of melt were standing on the surface of the lake ice, the ruts in our truck road had become rivulets. Robins, juncos, blackcap and mountain chickadees came into our woods in steadily increasing numbers to join the ever-present Canada jays. We increased our bird feeding, putting out larger quantities of seeds and yellow corn meal. Alvin the squirrel became an incessant beggar in our windows, often with forepaws braced and nose flattened against the glass to observe our indoor movements.

Beneath a plastic tarp that Mildred had spread over her small green garden in the fall, we discovered fresh shoots of young onions, lettuce, chard and parsley, which had survived under the warm insulation of deep snow.

In the woods the bronze buds of soapolallie bushes were bright on winter naked stems. In the dense profusion of these bushes among the groves of silvery barked aspens, there was promise of a bountiful crop of their fruits, the red berries relished as "hooshum" by the Chilcotins.

Along the sun-drenched north shore of Little Eagle the mid-day warmth was intensely reflected by the thick borders of tall spruces. Here the old snow was first to melt and the new sprouts of young willows stood in thick green clusters. We were boiling our drinking water now but could not entirely eliminate the taste of vegetation that drained into the lake with each day's thawing.

Though still deeply frozen, the Chilcotin roads were becoming surface soft during the daytime warmth and any who used them knew their chances of getting through to wherever they were headed grew slimmer as the breakup continued.

A zigzag crack opened one morning in the ice of The Narrows and gradually widened to an irregular, sun-shimmering streak between our foreshore and Bird Island.

Ross Wilson brought Amber back to us shortly following our return. The dirt floor in the little mare's stable became soggy from the draining slope on which the building stands. We moved her to our old Indian corral. There she was somewhat more exposed to the occasional breezes from the lake but at least the ground under the big conifers was bare and dry.

On March 30, we awakened to the cooing of sharptail grouse on the bare knolls at the west end of the lake, the deep melody of their throaty mating song coming to us on the still air at day-break. We dressed hurriedly, carried our coffee pot and cups out to the canoe landing to listen, and stood in sparkling frost as a blazing sunrise spread its early warmth over the lake. We searched the knolls with binoculars for a sight of the crooning sharptails but could not see them. The overnight low had been an even thirty-two degrees. As we listened to the "chicken song" of the sharptails, the drumming of ruffed grouse became incessant in our cabin woods and the spruces along the sun-warmed lake shore were alive with twittering chickadees. From an overnight bed in a thicket of junipers on Goose Island, a pair of lean and leggy coyotes emerged in a slanting trot to cross the lake ice, angling away with suspicious backward glances toward Mildred and me. They appeared gaunt and hungry. In the top of a spruce beneath which the coyotes had slept, a bald eagle sat stonily upright, only its head moving in quick jerks as the bird turned its eyes from side to side, watching for whatever the morning might offer in the way of food. Soon the eagle was joined by another, probably its mate, and the pair flew off in a bee-line for the south shore. It was as if, by prearrangement, they had a definite objective somewhere on the slopes of Splinter Mountain. We watched them until they became two black and white specks and finally disappeared in the blur of distant timber.

Taking advantage of the thaw, which by now had loosened and heaved up the ground around some big boulders in our road, we used a pick, a heavy steel crowbar and a shovel to dig out and remove some of the troublesome stones. We got rid of quite a number in this manner. Some we were barely able to roll off of the road when they were finally pried out of the ground.

On the last day of March the song of robins was heard. As we stepped out of the cabin the redbreasts were flashing among the trees and we counted more than thirty, which we took to be a migration. The robins ate sparingly of the wild bird seed we scattered on bare spots beneath the trees but probed and scratched hungrily for the few bugs that could be found in the newly thawed earth. The robins soon left us, but we were thrilled by the arrival of three geese which settled for a brief rest on the ice before moving off south toward the open water of Tatlayoko Lake. Mildred's review of our diary revealed geese had arrived on Little Eagle a week earlier in the previous year. We could expect them in increasing numbers at any time now and found ourselves listening for their familiar cries. We were feeling the urgency of spring. Mildred started outside fires daily, burning chips and other woods trash in small piles raked up where the earth was now bared by the sun. Chickadees and tree swallows quarreled over nests Chuck and I built from short sections of old aspen trunks in which woodpeckers had bored deep holes many years in the past.

In the warming days many more juncos appeared. Fox sparrows, ruby and golden crowned kinglets, robins and a lone grackle came to the feeding ground by the cabin, to join the chickadees and Canada jays. Flickers were observed flying back and forth across The Narrows to Bird Island. The overall number of birds increased daily. And now the certain-sure harbinger of spring—mosquitos!

On April 5, the mercury stood at sixty-seven degrees at three o'clock in the afternoon. Open water was widening around Bird and Goose Islands. Geese were arriving, crowding for swimming space and filling the air with their gaggling. A large flock of mallards settled in The Ponds and we had again seen the brilliant flash of bluebirds in the adjoining wild meadows.

Chuck and Wilma came in from Jameson Basin to remain with us briefly before returning to their home in Washington. Their hunt had been successful. On this trip up from the Tatlayoko country they left their truck at Ed Schuk's ranch and covered the remaining seven miles to our cabin on horses obtained from Schuk, as the Old Tatlayoko Road south of Little Eagle was deeply drifted. Amber was greatly excited by the appearance of Schuk's horses and her response to their whinnies made us realize just how lonely our little Arabian mare had become since Trigger's death.

During this last short visit before heading south, Chuck discovered the frozen carcass of a cow moose in the ice of The Narrows. There was little we could do about it, at the moment. It would be up to Mildred and me to get rid of it when the ice was

finally gone. The moose had broken through ice thinned by the hot springs and had been concealed by frozen snow.

Becoming apprehensive of the softening condition of the thawing earth, the hunters took their final departure on April 7 riding the borrowed horses back to Schuk's ranch where they had left their truck.

Amber frequently lay dozing in her corral, or at other times in our cabin clearing, while Vevette raced in wide circles and leaped teasingly around the little mare's head, trying to coax her into a romp. Amber's udder was swollen and we were sure her foaling time was near. With the prospect of the foal—another pet—to offset the sadness we felt over the death of the aged Trigger, we were both cheered. Amber's response to our frequent petting and other attention was always a manifestation of the Arabian's affection and she often followed us on walks in the cabin woods. Obviously she was lonely. Her presence and the swarm of birds we were feeding, the squirrels, the chipmunks, the flocks of newly arriving geese, the drumming grouse and a happy little poodle enlivened our days. We could not suspect, under these circumstances, in this first week of a spring warming April, that starvation and death were already riding down from the Arctic Barrens to engulf the Chilcotin Plateau in a storm old-timers still recall as "the big Easter blizzard."

Within the week midday temperatures were in the high sixties. One evening at sundown we were puzzled by the appearance of a strange brightness in the western sky. The unusual light stood as a wide, almost vertical column extending from below the jagged horizon of the Coast Range to gradually widen and fade into the apex of the heavens above us. It closely suggested the shaft of a giant searchlight—a pale milky streak, mysterious in its vast proportions, cleaving the early evening blue of the sky. At this hour a light but chilling breeze was coming out of the northwest.

Near midnight, the mercury dropped to twenty-seven degrees and the wind, shifted into the north, was moaning under the cabin eaves. In the morning we moved Amber back to her stable when we found her restlessly pacing the square of the old corral. We bedded her box stall with dry hay, gave her a drink of water from which Mildred removed the icy chill with a kettle from the cabin heater and filled her manger with a thick flake from a bale of alfalfa.

On the morning of the ninth, we dispensed with our usual coffee-before-breakfast, feeling an urgency to get out to Amber. Vevette seemed to sense our excitement and ran ahead of us as we neared the little log stable. As Mildred and I approached, Vevette was standing in rigid transfixion before the closed door. Then we saw in horror a bloody little hoof protruding beneath the bottom edge of the door. Blood dripped from the hoof in a scarlet streak down the face of the sill to a darkening pool on the ground.

"Oh! Oh!" Mildred wailed. "It's dead!" But I saw a slight movement.

Releasing the barrel bolt on Amber's door we discovered her first born prostrate, the small body awkwardly twisted from an exhaustive struggle to free the trapped hoof. We lifted a little sorrel filly from a sodden bed and carried it into the sunlight, Amber following on our heels. The foal was unable to stand. In the early morning light we discovered the filly's left hind leg had been skinned from fetlock to cannon, bared to the bone in the struggle to free the hoof from the slot beneath the door. We were heartsick...and we had thought we had prepared carefully for the birth!

Vevette became almost unmanageable in her happy excitement over the foal. When Mildred hurried back to the cabin for first aid supplies, she took the poodle and left her to get her out of our way. Returning, Mildred brought a kettle of hot water, wash basin, some bandaging and a bottle of disinfectant. We tried to draw the torn hide back over the raw wound but the skin had shrunk away from the bone. As we worked to bathe and cleanse the injury, Amber stood at our backs, her soft muzzle roving over our shoulders and gently nudging, the while mother-talking to her helpless baby. I am sure the mare understood our efforts.

To restrict further bleeding, we applied carbolated vaseline and a dusting of scorched flour, over which Mildred wrapped a complete bandage. Carefully, then, we raised the filly onto its wobbly legs and guided its muzzle to Amber's milk. After some experimental probing, the little one found the source of needed nourishment and fed eagerly, but we had to support the filly's weight to prevent collapse. We were surprised and more hopeful of success when the foal stood unaided an hour later in a miraculous recovery of strength. She moved about now, shakily following Amber's movements. After nursing a second time the filly lay down in the sun and slept.

Our very old and outdated farm horse book served as our only guide. The nearest veterinarian was in Williams Lake. Roads were impassable; and though veterinarians fly into the Interior, a plane could not land on Eagle Lake's rotting ice, even if we could reach a telephone...which we could not. We would simply have to make-do without the aid of a vet.

As we made a final check on the condition of the new foal and saw our stock comfortably bedded near midnight, Mildred remarked on the sudden fall in temperature.

When we awakened on the morning of Sunday, April 10, a foot of new snow lay over the land. It was sixteen degrees above zero, a paralyzing north wind was whining over Eagle Lake and a flock of hungry birds fluttered excitedly on our window ledge. I'm afraid my greeting of "Happy Easter, Honey," to Mildred lacked some enthusiasm.

Within hours we were blizzard bound, the mercury stood at zero minus two degrees, our little filly was dead, and the gentle throaty rumbles of Amber's mother-talk had turned to a heartbroken whinny for a baby that no longer responded.

The storm saw the mercury swiftly tumble below zero while snow fell to lay as a shroud over the Plateau. The welcome signs of returning spring which had been manifest a few days before were buried under deep drifts. As the snow deepened the north-easter added to the new misery of the wilderness.

Our anxiety for the birds became an immediate and absorbing concern as we sought to relieve their hungry suffering and served to push from our minds the deep sorrow we felt over the loss of Amber's new foal.

137

We were at this time feeding an estimated twenty or thirty newly arrived birds. Our small patch of open feeding ground under the protection of spruces near the cabin became alive with a great many more birds. Scratching and fluttering hungrily where we scattered quantities of seeds, their numbers soon swelled to more than 200.

With a push broom and shovel I managed to work some of the snow from an area about twenty feet square just beyond the south windows of the cabin. Here there would be at least some protection from the chilling wind. I swept and scraped down to the frozen ground and over the duff scattered a gallon of wild bird seeds and corn meal. Mildred added some of Amber's rolled oats to a pan of corn meal and spread it along the feeding board in the south window. The birds moved in greedily even as we worked among them. Because we had been feeding the birds in our cabin woods since the first snows of winter, our supply of feed—originally a small barrel of it—was already low when the unseasonal storm struck the high Plateau. Now, suddenly, our bird population was increasing, the demand for sustenance was greater and the available supply diminishing daily.

That night, I dipped a coffee can into the seed barrel and prepared to scatter more seeds so the birds would find them at daylight; the can scraped bottom. I knew then the old truth that only the strongest survive under nature's rules would soon be manifest.

We were not aware of the great number of redbreast robins already in the country until the April blizzard struck and these birds moved in with the many others already with us. The feeding area by the cabin, out on the old moraine at the edge of the lake, around our canoe dock and among the spruces now swarmed with birds. We walked among them and they fed fearlessly within inches of our feet. Many thumped loudly in wild flight against the cabin windows. This amazing number of birds, which we estimated at well over 300 at the peak of the storm, was the greatest and most varied we had ever seen anywhere at one time.

By April 10, it was impossible to count the fluttering birds. There were great numbers of juncos, robins, varied thrushes, red-wing and Brewer's blackbirds, chickadees, flickers, woodpeckers and a few starlings. We saw but one Hepburn's gray capped rosy finch, one fox sparrow and a pair of beautiful mountain bluebirds. Within days the count increased until the feeding spaces in our cabin clearing literally bounced with a continuous flutter of birds. We saw a few mergansers and goldeneyes in open puddles in the lake ice and an occasional bald eagle flew over. The geese had left Little Eagle for better shelter elsewhere. The Canada jays were strangely absent. The grouse, which had been drumming night and day before the storm, were completely silent; probably, we thought, content to remain in warm cover under the snow.

On the morning of the eleventh, the mercury stood at two degrees above zero when we went out to scatter more seeds from our scant supply. An inch of new snow had fallen during the night. It lay like dry, powdery crystals over the old crust and glinted coldly in the feeble light of daybreak. Through a curtain of haze that hung low over the surface of Little Eagle, sunrise cast a pale glow through the mist and against this background of deathly cold the erratic flight of hundreds of birds could be seen. Their wild flocking through the low haze above the lake had become an aimless, winged search for sustenance now buried beneath new snow and, for hundreds, the search ended in a dance of death on the small spot of feeding ground we had struggled to keep bare in our cabin woods. Within an hour of our watching, this morning, a new and larger flock of robins arrived. When I had counted sixty, the new arrivals were flopping about on their frozen feet and feeding so wildly that further accurate counting became impossible. By now it was a constantly fluttering mass feeding at our feet and around us with a disregard for fear or danger born of extreme hunger.

How these birds knew something to eat could be found in our little clearing was a mystery to us but Mildred and I concluded, with a conviction sharpened by this experience, that the birds must have communicated the information that the Jenkins' cabin had food to offer.

We swept the new snow from our thirty-five-foot-long dock

and over the crusted ice on the boards scattered additional feed and sand. Quickly the dock became alive with birds and relieved some of the crowding on the cleared space beneath the spruces and the stump and window feeders. On the dock the birds ate greedily, then hopped to the very edge of the ice on the lake shore, where they drank from a thin seepage of water. Here the morning sun burned against the low overhang of the shoreline to produce a feeble trickle of water, but the moment the sun was gone it was ice again. The water proved a vicious trap for thirsting birds, as many of them were observed awkwardly hopping about with balls of ice on their feet. Most of these we would find dead by another morning.

Many different kinds of birds were feeding together on the dock and beneath the trees now with little thought for the quarreling so common under less adverse conditions. Each was intent upon only one objective and that was food.

Mildred mixed some of our seeds with bacon grease and we smeared blobs of this mixture on the tops of stumps in the clearing. She made another mixture of grease with some of Amber's rolled oats.

By three o'clock in the afternoon, on the third day of the blizzard, it was the third time we had scattered a sparing quantity of seeds from our nearly empty barrel. Within minutes hardly an overlooked seed could be seen. I reswept and raked over the ground duff hoping to turn up seeds that had been covered by scratching and, as I worked, hungry birds fluttered and hopped—and quite a few were already staggering—around my feet. We noticed, now, that others, particularly robins, were sitting slumped among the spruces where the misery of their hunger and cold would soon end in death.

Once we were surprised at the remaining strength, especially of the juncos, when a marsh hawk flew low through the foreshore trees. The feeding birds rose in a swirling swarm to disappear among the dense foliage of the spruces. Within seconds of the hawk's passing the birds were fluttering back to the frozen earth like leaves in an autumn wind.

Finally our seeds were gone. Now Mildred dug into our

storeroom supply of breakfast cereals. To these, which were not plentiful, she added some dry raisins, some chopped old apples, a jar of peanut butter, a two-pound brick of cheese and a scrap of suet she had saved until the last.

At five-thirty on the morning of April 12, the temperature had climbed to twelve degrees above zero. There was no wind and no haze. In the faint early light of a morning that would dawn crystal clear, we could see the birds feeding on what we knew to be the last meal for many, as among them some were now barely able to stand on feet already frozen. They hopped drunkenly, feathers fluffed against the cold, or sat in the stupor of approaching death. Others hunched on the limbs of the spruces from which they would tumble to die on the hard crust below. Fifteen robins hobbled about on the feeding board in our cabin window at one count, as we sat down to breakfast, and among them were the braver of the juncos and chickadees, seemingly aware of the fact the robins no longer possessed the strength to drive the small birds from the board.

The stumps where Mildred had spread the wads of her mixture were so crowded with birds the stump tops seemed alive. A young spruce near our windows, which we had often thought of as a beautiful Christmas tree, by reason of its symmetry, was this morning ornamented with clusters of redbreast robins who sat in a droopy daze, a sad decoration for the young tree. Beneath the spruce the frozen snow was already dotted with the red of robins that had toppled from their perches during the night.

Daytime temperatures slowly raised into the warming high thirties during hours of sunlight, causing the crusted snow to soften and become watery. It had settled down now to about three inches in depth but the softened condition froze with the low nighttime temperatures, making a solid sheet of glaze. This condition prevailed even in the dense stands of spruce and jack pines. The more fortunate squirrels, with underground food stores, seldom appeared now. The problem was even less for the chipmunks, not yet out of hibernation enough to be bothered.

Fresh thin ice had formed again in The Narrows and the

smooth surface was strewn with frost diamonds sparkling in the midday sunlight.

The unseasonal storm was still taking its toll. Daily we gathered dead birds around our cabin and under the trees. Some had frozen hunkered beneath the eaves. We also found their stiffened bodies in our woodpile where they had crawled seeking shelter.

The crows continued to call loudly among the pines to our north and west, but did not come to feed, possibly fearing attack from such a great number of smaller birds. The crows occasionally flew over our camp, eyeing the scrambling birds on the feeding area, but they did not stop. They would scream and caw loudly, probably aggravated by this sight and their own hunger. They seemed fully aware that their natural enemies were too numerous to risk open warfare and remained away, preferring to feed on the dead scattered among the trees.

Strangely, to us at least, there were more deaths among the varied thrushes, the so-called winter robins, than there were among the robin redbreasts. One day we found nine dead thrushes under the spruces where they had fallen during the night. These larger birds, like the robins, needed bugs and worms, which they would be getting at this season under normal weather conditions. But there was nothing normal about this April in the Chilcotin. In time we lost count of the dead. We picked them up, almost everywhere about camp, and burned them daily.

Vevette, whose bird hunting instinct is a natural inheritance from her ancestors, came to the cabin a dozen times a day with a dead bird in her mouth. She sniffed the bodies out and found them where we could not see them, and was a great help in getting them quickly gathered and disposed of.

Months after this blizzard passed, we were still finding the skeletal remains of robins, thrushes and other birds about the cabin area and on our walks. Perhaps not so surprising, because they are native to this wild plateau, the little blackcap and mountain chickadees appeared to withstand the severe cold better than many of the larger birds. This was also true of the juncos and jays.

On April 15, we fed the last of anything we had that would pass as bird food. For two days the daytime sun bared wider patches of earth around the trunks of the trees. We observed many of the birds going to these newly exposed areas, making an effort to find their natural food. But a sudden snow shower recovered the earth with an inch of new snow on this day marking mid-April. The birds came swarming back. We noticed the varied thrushes, in particular, were in a condition of advanced torpor, staggering weakly. The big die-off continued during the next several days.

Afternoon temperatures gradually climbed again to the high thirties and low forties; the snow was gone by the sixteenth and old ice on Little Eagle became a glaring wet sheet in the midday sun. There was a widened open stretch in The Narrows and some open water around the east and west sides of the islands. The thinning influence of the hot springs was plainly evident in the rotting condition of ice in The Narrows.

A few mallards, some scaups and several American mergansers moved in. Until now the geese had been seldom heard but one morning eight of the big honkers settled down in a broad pan of slush which they seemed to enjoy although the water spreading over the ice was too shallow for swimming.

The geese talked a lot among themselves and then we noticed there was a definite pairing off as they moved about, two by two, and gradually separated in pairs a little distance apart.

It was at this time my wife and I observed a pantomime revealing the crafty hunting nature of our coyotes. Returning to the cabin from a hike to The Ponds, we were having lunch and a pot of hot tea while watching eight geese from our cabin windows, when two lean coyotes emerged onto the ice from the south shore. Trotting swiftly side by side, they headed straight for the geese, which by now were hunkered down in pairs and appeared to be sleeping.

The coyotes were within about 200 yards of the big birds when one of them, probably sleeping with one eye open, raised

143

its head, noted the approaching hunters and alerted its sleeping mates.

As the long necks stretched upward, the coyotes came to a quick halt. Motionless as a pair of gray statues, they stood gazing at the geese. Then, one of the wild dogs began a slow trot obliquely away from its partner and headed toward the south shore of Bird Island in an attitude of complete indifference to the presence of the geese.

Alone now, as if it had been abandoned by its mate, the remaining coyote sat on its haunches, gazing at the geese, tongue dangling. There was no movement among the birds but all eight of them were alertly watching the predator. The staring stand-off lasted perhaps two or three minutes; then the coyote began a slow, leisurely approach. The geese raised onto their feet. The coyote halted. Another minute or two of staring followed. The distance separating coyote and geese had narrowed to perhaps 100 feet.

We looked for the coyote that had moved off toward Bird Island but were unable to detect it, though we knew it to be somewhere in the line of willow along the island shore. If it was now endeavoring to attract the attention of the geese from the lone coyote on the open ice, the ruse was not succeeding. Two of the honkers were obviously watching the island shoreline, but their mates were also watching the coyote on the open pan, and this one was moving slowly forward again.

Now the coyote slackened its pace, began a slow walk somewhat obliquely away from the geese, turned, reversed the angle and walked back again, in an almost leisurely attitude that might be interpreted as a gesture of only casual interest in the presence of the geese. The honkers remained standing in the slush, with only a turning of heads as they followed the deviative movements of the wild dog.

At a distance which we estimated to be not more than thirty feet from the geese, the coyote again halted, sat for a moment, haunches on the ice, and then much like any old lazy dog we had ever seen, stretched out full length, rolled onto its back with feet in the air, squirmed and relaxed on one side, head turned toward the geese, red tongue still dangling.

Such an attitude of indifference, such casual unconcern! The coyote lay thus for perhaps two or three minutes as we continued to watch. The birds were now evincing more concern for the nearness of their natural enemy who, it would appear, had only the most friendly of intentions. Now the coyote was up again, walking diagonally back and forth with seeming disinterest. In these movements the closing distance was again narrowed, now to perhaps no more than twenty feet. And as the geese began to stir nervously, the coyote again lay on its side, rolled away from the birds but with head twisted back over its shoulder, eyes watching, tongue a-dangle from its open mouth.

We watched with nervous fascination.

The geese, previously separated in pairs, now converged into a tight cluster on the pan. Then, as if emerging from a conference of elders, one of the larger geese walked away from the flock, began a slowly paced but deliberate approach to the coyote, which slowly rose onto its feet. It was at this moment, as the closing distance was no more than a few feet, that I heard Mildred gasp: "That crazy goose is committing suicide!"

With a sudden pounding slapping of wings we could plainly hear, the goose rushed toward the coyote as the coyote charged the goose. In an upward burst of power, the challenger soared clear as the coyote leaped, its open mouth missing the belly of the goose by inches, but receiving blows from the powerful wings. The air was filled with loud piercing cries of the flock as it swept above the ice, wheeled and bore away, to land again in a wide area of slush near the center of the rotting lake ice.

The coyote sniffed briefly where the geese had vacated the pan, then trotted off toward Bird Island.

When the coyote finally disappeared from our view on Bird Island, Mildred hurried out to our canoe dock to watch for the reappearance of the hunting pair.

Beyond the easterly point of the island there was still a great expanse of old ice, which bordered the open water of The Narrows. On the ice several mergansers were sleeping, a few others preening themselves, while several goldeneyes were idling in the open water.

When she returned to the cabin my wife told me I had missed a second performance. She had witnessed the reappearance of both coyotes from Bird Island, one of them resorting to the distracting bag of tricks which included lying prone and rolling on the ice and casually sauntering back and forth, while its mate, far out beyond the island, slowly approached the sitting ducks. But, as in the attempt involving the geese, the ducks had become alerted and the ruse had failed for a second time within the hour. The ducks flew away and, when last seen, both coyotes were trotting off toward the far south shore of the lake in their continuing search for food.

An old Chicano in the Sonoran Desert once told me, years ago, that El Coyote is the smartest animal of all; that, as a hunter, he is never without a plan and that, in pairs, their success is often realized as the result of a clever system by which one attracts the attention of an intended prey while its companion makes the unobserved stalk and kill.

"Then you see," he said, eyes twinkling, "they both eat."

I am inclined to the belief the desert coyote's cousin of the northern bush is no less an expert, but on this day he had met his match.

# Amber Joins the Wild Band

On June 3, we realized the musical tinkle of Amber's halter bell had not been heard since the previous morning and began a search for her. We drove the truck over the Old Tatlayoko Road looking for horse tracks but found none that were fresh. Then we left the truck road for the bush and continued our search, always listening for the bell.

Ten days after she had wandered out of our hearing we again heard the music of her brass bell about midmorning. The bell's soft tinkle came drifting over the lake from the wild meadow west of the cabin. Hurriedly picking up a carrot and a short halter rope, we headed for the meadow. We were surprised to find the tracks of several horses in the dust of our road close to the old Indian corral. The tracks had been made during the night. Evidently the band had been attracted by some old salt blocks under the spruces in the corral. We thought it strange, then, that we had not heard Amber's bell, if she was, in fact, running with the feral band.

The fresh prints led us into a dense thicket of sapling lodgepole pine bordering the meadow. We approached the thicket cautiously, avoiding noisy dry twigs, hoping to get close to Amber without startling the mare or the wild ones.

In the thickest of the pines we were suddenly startled by the pounding hoofs of a horse crashing away through the lodgepoles and within seconds the hammering of running feet exploded throughout the dense woods. By the sounds we knew they were heading for the north ridge and dense stands of pine beyond. We saw none of them, but then we heard Amber's bell. By its wild jangling we knew she was running, in fast pursuit of her new friends.

Taking the rope and carrot, Mildred headed for the meadow

while I made a swing out over the North Ridge Road in the pickup, hoping I might head them off.

At the junction of the North Ridge Road and Old Tatlayoko Road I met my wife returning from the meadows. We had found no tracks of the band. We knew it would be useless to attempt further search here, as the dry hard scrabble of earth in those woods revealed no visible hoof prints.

We drove a mile or two north and at one stretch of soft earth found tracks of one horse which had crossed the road during the past day or two but the tracks were not Amber's.

Finally that day, as we sat in the pickup, listening, we caught the far faint jangle of Amber's bell, deep in the forest far east of the road. And then a plane flew over, the heavy drone of its propellers drowning out the bell. When the plane was beyond hearing we could no longer detect the sound of the bell and headed back to camp.

As we turned onto the north ridge at our junction we paused to listen once more. Suddenly my wife said, "I smell the horses! They've just gone through here!" Then we saw hoof prints of the running band. Apparently the entire band had been concealed in the pines and had passed north over the ridge while we were listening to the airplane. The air was heavy with the scent of sweating horses but they were already long gone from the ridge. Unable to read further sign in the dry floor of the ridge or in the dense woods to the north, we gave it up and returned to the cabin.

On our return, in the softer dirt of the truck road, we found the tracks of several horses, those of Amber and a young colt among them.

During the next several weeks we alternately searched for the horses and worked on an addition to the cabin. In our searching we covered many miles of the wilderness lying north of the lake; a rolling, undulating region of lodgepole pine, swamps, small lakes, rocky outcrops and wild meadows. We enjoyed the long walks despite the disappointment of losing the mare. Our return to camp was almost invariably by some new route and often we were bone weary. To rest from these day-long treks through the virgin wilderness we alternately worked on the roof of our new ice house and storage shed, setting up pine rafters and nailing down the rough sheathing. We also managed a few turns around the lake in the canoe, in particular to check on the progress of a nesting loon we knew to be sitting on two beautiful light olive brown eggs on Loon Island.

One very calm and sunny morning as we had breakfast and, as usual, were watching the lake, Mildred spotted the pair of loons in the water just off the nest area and with them one baby. We watched with the binoculars but could not see another baby. We gulped our breakfast, gathered cameras, and put out in the canoe to check the nest. By now the adult loons with their lone baby were cruising some distance from the nest site.

Mildred said if they had left one egg she was going to collect it for a specimen of its strange beauty. As we neared the nesting spot, paddling quietly, Mildred stopped her paddle, saying, "Listen...I hear a peeping." I was sure she was mistaken, but I listened anyway. No doubt about it. A very distressed peeping sound was coming across the still water. It had to be from the loon nest. We hurried on and came alongside the nest, which lay at the water's edge, and there on the wet trampled reeds sat a lone loonlet, crying its heart out. It was about the size of a tennis ball, a soft pastel-sooty little infant with stuffy out-flung wings. On webbed feet it staggered awkwardly toward us as we moved in close. It plopped into the water, its paddles outstretched like outriggers, and working vigorously as it came right up to Mildred in the bow of the canoe, its clear small cries plaintive in the silence of the early morning.

We were puzzled because the parent loons were so far up-lake with one chick while this one had remained at the nest, unattended and unprotected from eagles and hawks. We concluded either this infant had been abandoned by the old birds, or it had hatched after the threesome had gone up the lake this morning. We had heard it said that swallows and other tree birds are known to eject weaklings from the nest to assure the survival of only the fittest and pondered the notion this may have happened here. But this baby loon seemed anything but a weakling; in fact it was active as well as lustily noisy.

Mildred took pictures of it with two cameras, then used up the remainder of a roll of movie film. That meant going back to camp for more film. Carefully, we returned the chick to its nest. By the time we had swung the canoe around the little one was back in the water, swimming in desperate effort to follow us. We managed our escape, however, and soon returned with cameras re-loaded. This time the baby was some distance away from its nest and again came swimming happily to meet us.

As we drew close, its stubby little wings stuck out horizontally, trembling and fluttering in expectant greeting. Mildred said maybe it was cold, cupped it in her hands and held it to her cheek. The plaintive peeping stopped as she held it and it made little contented sounds, until she tried to put it back in the water. Immediately, the little guy began crying again.

"What are we going to do?" Mildred began worrying. "What if the parents have deserted it? What would we feed it?" Then she laughed as she remarked, "Maybe we'll have to regurgitate fish!"

From far up the lake, where the parent loons and the solitary chick could be seen cruising in a small bay, came the clear sharp cries of the older birds, which we knew had been watching us.

"Do you suppose we could take the baby up near the parents and let it loose?" Mildred suggested. "I wonder if they would take it then?"

That didn't seem too likely a means of restoring it to its parents. Finally, we decided to leave the chick and attempt to "shoo" the adult birds back to the nest by herding them with the canoe.

Mildred set the baby back in the water and we headed up the lake, paddling fast to gain speed enough to escape the weeping chick. Its cries of distress followed us. The parent birds were more than a mile away by now. We swung well outside their bay to head them off and prevent their going farther up the lake, finally bringing the canoe about well beyond them, then slowly paddling back.

On the smooth water we watched their movements and their rippling wakes and, as they turned one way or another at our approach, we swung the canoe about like a cutting horse to keep them properly headed toward the island and their nest. The male swam well ahead, followed by the mother with her baby alternately behind or beside her. Now and again the adults broke the silence with worried calls.

After an hour of this very slowly paced and watchful herding, we had covered perhaps half the distance in return to the island when the mother, seemingly aware that her off-spring was tiring, got behind it, urging it forward. The parental calls now became more insistent and in more varied tones. The male began to grumble in a deep throaty voice and the mother tried to hurry the baby by again swimming ahead, though she kept looking back to her chick.

We were still a considerable distance from the nesting island when we again heard the peeping of the deserted baby, saw it emerge on the water beyond the end of the island, swimming toward our returning entourage. The male bird apparently saw it also and swam directly to meet it. Our earlier concern that the baby had been abandoned was quickly dispelled when the adult loon and the infant became reunited, their affection manifest by excited conversation. There was a recognizable contentment in their tones and actions. The male circled the chick several times, closely scrutinizing the sooty black miniature; then both swam to meet mamma and her remaining off-spring. Muted loon talk drifted across the lake to us as we idled in the canoe. We felt relieved by the obvious concern the older birds had shown for one we had mistakenly believed abandoned.

It was not until later years of experience with loons on Little Eagle that we learned it is the habit of these big birds to train and discipline their young by taking out a single chick at a time for parental instruction in the ways of survival.

On this day of our initial encounter with a loon baby training session, Mildred was anxious to get some movie footage of the birds. We applied our paddles to shorten the distance and as the film in Mildred's camera wound to its end, the big male raised to a standing position on the surface of the lake, flapped his powerful wings with a loud slapping and ran off on pounding feet, uttering fearsome cries.

When we did not follow the male away from his family, he repeated the standing act, flopped on his back as if mortally injured, then ran off again, cries of anguish echoing against the hills. We paddled a bit closer to the hen and two babies and one of them—we think it was the one Mildred had held in her hand earlier—swam right up to the canoe, peeping loudly. Then, however, some natural instinct must have sparked in the infant brain, as it suddenly turned away from us to swim back to its mother, even attempting, awkwardly, to dive beneath the surface.

Our two hours of loon herding with the canoe had paid off and we felt grateful for the success of our rescue as we headed back to the cabin.

Later that evening we observed the two adults again near the island. We watched with binoculars as one of them waddled from water to nest. It appeared to be inspecting the premises, then returned to the lake and swam off with its mate. When the big birds began splashing, standing up, racing and diving, my wife surmised their actions were in joyful release from parental anxieties of the past few hours.

"I think mamma just tucked the babies in for the night, and now she's joined papa for a little relaxation," was Mildred's conclusion. "I know just how she feels."

The next morning, as we were watching the nest area with binoculars, we noticed that one of the adult birds was far up the lake; the other, obviously the hen, sat just off the east point of the island. She remained so stationary she appeared to be anchored, but her black head turned constantly from side to side and she was emitting a series of strange-sounding low cries such as we had never heard until now.

"There is something wrong over there," Mildred said. "That loon is really worried. I can't see either of her babies."

"Papa's gone fishing and mamma's just mad because she's home alone and the kids haven't had their breakfast," I said. But I realized suddenly that I had made light of a serious situation that was, in fact, on the border of stark drama when the big male loon came sweeping homeward in response to the urgent calls of its mate. At that moment a huge but immature bald eagle, which

152

until this instant we had not seen, leaped upward from its perch in the top of a spruce above the loons' nest, swept low over the loons, hesitated momentarily to hover above them, then flapped away to disappear in the distant timber of the north ridge. It was then we discovered the two baby loons as they popped out from under the hen's protective wings. When the eagle had finally disappeared, the adult loons swam off toward a distant bay, each with a baby riding piggy-back. Unseen by us, the baby loons had been concealed under their mother's wings during the time she had been calling for help from her mate.

In the days that followed we saw our loon family many times. The infants developed fast and were soon diving as expertly as their parents. We lost our contact with Little Sooty for he never again offered to come to the canoe. Apparently he was receiving his training and adhering to it.

* * * * *

No journal on life in the Chilcotin would be complete without at least an honest, if short, reference to mosquitos, as they are admittedly here in quantity from breakup to freezeup. I am not informed as to which of the various dipterous insects of the family Culicidae the British Columbia mosquito is identified, but the females are equipped with a proboscis that will puncture a moosehide shirt and draw blood all in one lightning thrust and they are not to be underestimated. Fortunately, our cabin is located on the north side of Eagle Lake and summer's prevailing winds are from the southwest to northeast quadrant. Brisk and cooling breezes come to us across a mile of open water and here, to the leeward shore, few mosquitos make the trip across from the muskegs and swamps to our southwest. The incoming breezes fresh off the lake also tend to sweep the insects back from any northern approach out of the pines. We have mosquitos, of course, but in such limited numbers we are grateful. Only on a dull hot and listless day do they become an aggravation and then copious applications of spray repellent are in order.

We have spent many pleasant weeks without being aware of mosquitos. Ordinarily, here, there seems to be about three to four distinct mosquito seasons during spring and summer, as the hatches occur. But even at their worst, a few hot summer days seem to burn them off. There have been times when we have heard the high hum of mosquitos among the pine and spruce tops and have mistaken the sound for that of a swarm of bees. We have seen clouds of them passing overhead in a crazy zig-zag flying pattern, the whole swarm moving up, down or drifting off sidewise in a sort of heaving, rolling unison.

Horses on open range in the Chilcotin are often seen wildly head tossing, tail switching and closely bunched in any available shade in mosquito season; at other times lunging madly through pine thickets or willow bottoms in an effort to brush off the biting insects. Few of the horses in this region have ever experienced the luxury of a repellent spray. The feral bands lead a hard life, between seasons of swarming mosquitos in summer and near starvation in winter, when snow overlays a range long since overgrazed by cattle.

Just at dusk on June 24 we heard Amber's bell at the west end of the lake. We were tempted to go immediately to try and coax her to us, then realized it was so near darkness that the attempt would be wasted. We decided to wait until daylight, hoping the band would remain in the meadow.

By daylight we were up. Amber's bell could still be heard. From the rhythm of the sound we knew she was grazing and had not moved out of the meadow. Following a hurried breakfast we shoved off in the canoe, taking a can of oats and some carrots. Now the sound of the bell had ceased and we were afraid the band had wandered farther away. Mildred suggested, hopefully, that they were sleeping.

Swinging well to the south of the meadow in order to keep out of sight of the roving horses, we approached stealthily. Finally, from behind a thick screen of willows, Mildred stood up in the bow of the canoe for a cautious look and whispered that the wild band was scattered among the grassy knolls and lodgepole pines and, most of them, including Amber, appeared to be dozing in the warm morning sun.

There were seven in this bunch, among them two young colts

and a big black stallion. Amber was standing motionless, well off by herself. Apparently she had not been fully accepted as yet.

Squatting in the canoe, we whispered our strategy. I would ease the canoe along behind the screen of willows until our position would place us approximately between Amber and the rest of the herd. Mildred was to be ready to land. Then, hopefully, while I held the canoe against the low bank of the meadow, Mildred would cautiously but speedily approach our little mare, the can of oats and carrot in one hand, a halter rope in the other.

The horses would most certainly bolt from the meadow the moment they saw Mildred. It was our hope that Amber would remain behind if she realized Mildred had grain for her.

We had Vevette with us, of course! Lately she had been well-behaved in the canoe, when we gave her commands. But now, the poodle seemed to sense our excitement and I am sure she could smell the horses. Mildred was shushing her, ordering her to stay in the bottom of the canoe.

"Don't pay any attention to the puppy," I told Mildred, as the canoe eased into the bank of the meadow. "If the horses begin to run, just try to keep Amber from going with them."

The horses had seen us as we crossed a narrow channel of open water to reach the meadow bank. Heads up, ears thrust forward, they began to swish their tails nervously. Watching us as I pushed the canoe for a landing, they began to mill about. Amber still dozed. At this instant Vevette, recognizing Amber, made a wild leap from the canoe, missed the bank, and hit the water with a loud splash! Mildred stepped out hurriedly as the canoe touched the shore, dismayed at Vevette's unruly action, but started to run toward Amber as the screaming whinny of the big stallion pierced the morning calm.

The wild band bolted, then, raced into the bordering pines. I saw my wife running toward her pet mare, hissing loudly at Vevette to "Go back! Go back!" Then Mildred, wildly waving a threatening arm at Vevette, threw herself off balance in a muddy spot and down she went in the mud. Amber, suddenly wakened by the thundering hoofs of her companions, bolted after them, never seeing Mildred, the halter bell clattering loudly as she entered the woods and disappeared with the other animals.

My wife scrambled out of the mud and ran, slipping and stumbling after the mare, a joyful poodle leaping wildly about in the tall grass and joining merrily in the chase.

Mildred was calling, "Amber! Amber! Come back, Amber!"

I could only sit in the canoe and be a spectator to the exciting tableau in the meadow. Mildred followed her mare into the pines, still calling. Vevette finally returned to me as I sat and waited.

When my wife came back she said she had gone as far as The Ponds, had heard Amber's familiar whinny as she raced after the departing herd. Mildred gave up the pursuit when the clatter of Amber's bell finally faded in the distance and it was obviously useless to attempt to overtake the mare.

Following a brief rest, my wife was all for going after the little Arabian again. I returned to camp in the canoe while Mildred walked north on the Old Tatlayoko Road to look for sign. I drove our pickup out to the junction of our own road and met Mildred there a little later. We walked over the north ridge, found some scattered tracks and some steaming droppings that proved the horses had eluded us.

We drove on out to Tatla then and spent the balance of the day at the annual Tatla community gymkhana. We passed the afternoon witnessing some expert horsemanship, content to rest from the exertions of our own earlier "show" in the wild meadow.

# Amber's Birthday

Usually by July 1 there are several nests of ruffed grouse among the aspens around our cabin and during this time we have had to watch Vevette closely. The nesting season seems to sharpen her natural hunting instincts. She came to Mildred once, carrying an unbroken egg in her mouth, her short tail buzzing with excitement, for which she got a severe scolding.

We let her go out again and followed her as she headed back into the aspen grove. She ran directly to the foot of a willow clump and there on the ground was a nest with four eggs. We could hear the nearby grouse mewing softly. Mildred held Vevette's nose to the nest and proceeded to give her a harsh-voiced shaming and marched her back to the cabin.

Late in the afternoon we again checked the nest and the four eggs had hatched. The hen and chicks were gone. Near Amber's stable a drummer was noisily beating its wings.

The male ruffed grouse in fan-tailed strut, in the presence of the hen, is the essence of arrogance and vitality. We have watched them from our cabin windows, taking their slow, deliberate steps, black-barred tails at full spread. Head erect, the male's slow even-paced approach to the hen is broken by occasional pauses and sudden short runs of a few feet. Often he rushes at an angle away from the hen, whose own actions seemed to be in complete indifference to the antics of her lover. This pantomime is frequently terminated by the hen's sudden flight or running departure, the male in fast pursuit.

Once, when some fishermen were camped in the little meadow at the west end of Eagle Lake, the grouse were drumming incessantly during the night and particularly among the aspens around our old corral. The next day when the campers drove down the Old Tatlayoko Road to the ranch home of Ed

Schuk, one of them asked Ed if he knew the people living in a cabin on the lake. Ed said it was the Jenkins who lived there and the fellow said, "Somebody ought to go in there and fix his damned light plant. We heard him trying to start the motor all night long!"

What the campers had mistaken as noise from an exhaust pipe—closely similar to the throbbing of an old Model T—was the sporadic drumming of grouse.

In the years we have lived in their habitat, the ruffed grouse have been on the increase, probably in conformity with nature's cyclic system, in which the bird population builds gradually over a period of about ten years and then declines quickly. The cause of these population cycles which occur not only among the grouse, but among lynx, snowshoe rabbit and other animals, is one of nature's secrets, the answer to which scientists have sought and argued for more than half a century. Not knowing the answer, we simply refer to these cycles as the balance of nature. It is most obvious and clearly apparent in the cycles of the lynx and snowshoe rabbit, or varying hare. The hare is the natural and most easily obtained food of the lynx. There is an old-time acknowledgment among the natives here that when rabbits are scarce, there are few lynx; that as the rabbit population returns to full saturation of its habitat, so also return the families of the big cats in ever increasing numbers and the cycle is renewed.

Less known to us are the sharp-tailed grouse, the "chickens" of the Chilcotin, a pale-colored bird of light brown and ocher bodies with whitish bellies and tails; less familiar mainly because despite the fact we have often heard their throaty cooing on the grassy knolls at the west end of the lake, we have seldom succeeded in a stealthy approach across the exposed grasslands. They favor the parklike area with fringes of hardwoods and conifers, as compared to the ruffed grouse's choice of dense hardwood bottoms and deciduous thickets.

Of all the birds who share our summer life in the bush, I think perhaps we have had more real pleasure from the hummingbirds, attracted to the sweet red fluid of the glass feeders Mildred has hung from spruce limbs and stumps within good watching range of our cabin windows. During warm days of summer they become numerous and Mildred often refills the nectar tubes twice a day. The brick-tone metallic red of the rufous hummers and their green females have been our best feeder customers. The bulletlike speed by which they disappear among the trees has made it difficult to locate nesting places but Mildred found one, quite by accident, while walking near the cabin one day. It was on the topside of the low bough of a spruce sapling, not over three feet above the ground. It was about the diameter of a fifty-cent piece, having a very shallow, open cup of a gauze so fine it was translucent in the sunlight. After seeing this tiny marvel of the hummer's nest-building skill, it was not hard to accept the statement that these fairy nests are actually constructed of the infinitely small particles of lichens, held together by strands of cobweb.

We have often sat within two or three feet of the feeders to catch a better identifying view of the hummingbirds. Seemingly, the red coloring in the feeder liquid serves only as an attraction for the birds which are quickly drawn to anything crimson. We had noticed this strange fascination for the red tail lights on our pickup truck and also found that wearing a red bandanna pinned to our straw hats, or a blaze-red hunting jacket, also brought them right up to us; often so suddenly close to our faces it caused us to squint.

The feeding mixture we have had the best success with has been a combination of sugar and water, boiled together slightly and reddened with vegetable coloring. Red ants are a problem where the feeders are fastened to a tree trunk and the hummers will refuse to patronize the feeders once the ants have swarmed onto the nipples. Hanging the feeders from a swaying branch has its drawbacks because wind action causes them to drip and lose their fluid. Mildred finally came onto a pretty good solution for the ant problem. She punched a very small hole in the center of the lid removed from a two-pound coffee tin and forced one end of the feeder hanging wire through the hole, converting the metal lid to an effective ant guard.

We soon had another feeder robber on our hands, however,

when a pine squirrel discovered the sweet red drip from the tube. Hanging by its hind feet from the tree trunk and gripping the tube in both forepaws like a baby holds a nursing bottle, the squirrel gulped and sent the tiny air bubbles flying up the tube. Since that day we have had both squirrels and hummers at our feeders and, eventually even the chipmunks would come to enjoy the red nectar. There have been frequent squabbles between hummingbirds, squirrels and chipmunks for possession of the glass tubes. The hummers usually win such contests, however. The squirrels and chipmunks are not inclined to do battle with the little winged lightning bolts.

On August 28, we were returning from a trip Outside for needed supplies. At Chilanko Forks we saw Doug Schuk who told us his father had seen Amber with a band of wild horses a few days earlier in Tachatolier Cabin Meadow. The meadow was on our way home and as we approached we caught a glimpse of a wild horse band grazing at the far end. Passing the long-abandoned sod-roofed Indian shelter known as Tachatolier's Cabin and coming nearer the open meadow, we saw eleven animals in this herd. There were the seven we had seen with Amber in June at Eagle Lake, plus an additional young stallion and two mares.

As we studied the distant band with binoculars we saw one light sorrel mare among them, a rather small animal with white blaze. This had to be Amber, though it was impossible to observe her leg coloration since the herd had been grazing in swampy country impregnated with alkali. The legs of all the horses were caked with chalky clay.

We had no grain with which to attempt coaxing our mare away from the herd. The band was becoming nervous, the stallions suspicious of us. We decided to go on to camp to avoid spooking them. We would unload the truck, pick up a saddle, bridle, lead rope and grain, and return to Tachatolier's meadow the next day.

We did just that, but the next day we found only an empty meadow. We spent the day walking to some high ridges near the old cabin but found no trace of the missing horse herd. The band had evidently gone south into the thick timber between the meadow and Little Eagle.

We stalked the grasslands around Tachatolier's old ranch again on September 1 and as we drove within sight of the big meadow discovered the herd had returned. We eased the truck forward cautiously for we had been warned we could never get anywhere near these wild animals. Stopping momentarily to glass the grazing horses, we then moved slowly forward again. They looked up, all heads raised as we approached, but did not bolt. The day was muggy hot and their stomachs bulging with the lush grass of the wild meadow probably stifled the urge to run.

We were finally within fair binocular range and scanned them closely, looking for Amber in particular, but as yet unable to read a brand. The little sorrel we had seen previously was there but she was partially hidden. Off to our right stood a beautiful dark chestnut mare, obviously a young and spirited animal, with a larger older dark bay mare of typical mountain breeding. Mildred and I both remarked on the beauty of the little chestnut, which we considered far above average in this mixed company of feral, half wild horses, and said something should be done about her.

The band momentarily split into two groups as the two stallions pranced and showed an inclination to fight. The action put the sorrel somewhat off by herself and Mildred began a low, gentle calling: "Come Amber, come Amber," but got no positive response. Then Mildred said the sorrel's legs looked too white and her blaze, a little left of forehead center, too large. I said I thought that was because they were all clay caked from feeding in swampy ground. This just had to be Amber.

Taking advantage of the confusion of the sparring stallions, I got Amber's pan with some feed oats from the truck. I shook the grain in the pan, lightly, hoping this old mare-fetching trick would create attention and bring Amber to me now as it had in the past. I slowly moved a short way from the pickup while Mildred continued to call Amber, but the little sorrel paid no heed whatever. Then the dark chestnut we had been admiring, and her older companion, began easing toward me. They would hesitate now and then, and again move up, until it finally occurred to me the grain must be an attraction for the chestnut, probably a well-bred animal far from her rightful owner. Mildred still sat in the truck, calling Amber, and glassing the main herd, and at the same time noticing the two coming closer.

"Try to encourage those two to come up and maybe Amber will notice and come too," Mildred said.

Now the wild bunch started milling nervously. The two stallions squared off. There was a start of rearing and vicious biting and then as suddenly the action ceased and the animals resumed grazing. Mildred continued to call Amber, far off to the side. By now the beautiful chestnut was coming right up to me, neck stretching toward the oats. I held the pan in outstretched hands and she came on, to bury her muzzle into the grain. The older mare hung back a little.

I let her eat a little, then held the pan away from her, pushed her head aside.

"Let her eat," Mildred whispered from the truck, afraid of spooking them. Then louder she called, coaxing, "Amber, come Amber!" watching the distant sorrel for some response. But there was none. "Don't scare these," Mildred whispered again.

"But I want to save some of these oats for Amber," I said. I let the chestnut have some more, anyway. She was now persistent. And I also thought maybe by feeding this mare Amber could be coaxed out of the herd. We were feeling desperately disappointed that Amber paid no attention and would not respond to our calls.

It was now I noticed the chestnut wore an old neck strap, so high and snug it lay almost concealed under a fold of fat close behind her jawbones. As she ate I slipped my fingers under the strap to feel its tightness. She allowed my touch, then I turned her head slightly to one side to look at her, and was amazed to read the J/J brand on her right shoulder! There was only one J/J brand in British Columbia and it was ours!

"This is Amber!" I yelled to Mildred, hardly believing it, and walked around to check her scarred foot.

"What?" Mildred all but screamed, disbelieving. And I repeated, "This is Amber!"

Forgetting all about not spooking the wild band, my wife jumped out of the truck and came running to bury her face in Amber's neck. "I can't believe it, I can't believe it!" she kept crying over and over. "Our own beautiful Amber and we didn't recognize her! But look how she's changed! Are you sure?" We were both crying and laughing at the same time.

"Here's our brand!" I said, proving that point. "And I've checked her foot. This is Amber all right."

I was holding Amber by her old neck strap, though her brass bell had disappeared in the time she had followed the wild band among the jack pines. Her former sorrel coloring had darkened to an almost mahogany chestnut and her legs were clay coated to the knees, adding greater deceit in her natural coloring.

Mildred and I were both dumbfounded. We had owned and raised horses for nearly thirty years but this beat us! She had changed from a light sorrel to a dark and solid chestnut in less than three months. The little sorrel we had been trying to coax out of the wild herd looked much like Amber had looked in June when we had last seen her and thereby lay the answer to our confusion.

Vevette had set up an excited barking in the cab of the truck and was up on her hind feet clawing wildly at the window. We now realized the poodle had recognized the approaching chestnut mare long before we did and was clamoring for a reunion, squealing in the cab and trying to get out.

While we stood talking to Amber and petting her, she finished her oats and was nudging us for more. Then we noticed the whole band had been moving up closer, especially Amber's companion. We had been told by experienced ranchers on the Plateau that we'd never get near that bunch of wild horses, that they would spook the minute we stopped the truck...that we might as well give up trying to catch our mare. Right now we wished these experts could see the "wild" horses. In fact, the band had come so close, Mildred became a little apprehensive that we might be going to have trouble. But these horses all had their ears pointed forward in curiosity and anticipation; no indication of fear or belligerence.

Mildred said, "You know, I believe we could call up the rest of them with a little time and patience. Wish I could try." But there wasn't time now, we had to get Amber home. Mildred brought the lead rope and we snapped it onto Amber's strap. I led the mare a short way to a low hollow, out of view of the feral herd, while Mildred brought up the truck. It was while we were brushing mud from the mare's legs that Mildred remembered that this was September first, and she exclaimed, "Why this is Amber's birthday and I'd forgotten all about it in our excitement."

She went to the back of the truck and rummaged in her groceries, coming out with some carrots. "Happy Birthday, Amber!" And Amber was in for some more loving. "She's six years old today. What a day!"

After a good brushing, I saddled her, loosely cinched, and led her off toward home. Mildred followed some distance back with the truck. In a few minutes I mounted and started the ten-mile ride back to camp. The mare whinnied a few times as we left the meadow but there was no fuss. After a mile or so, when she began to lather up, I drew up the overhand knot in the latigo just enough to snug the saddle to her round fat back and we pushed on with no arguments except for an occasional head tossing whinny or two. I knew she was reluctant to leave the band, probably the big dark mare in particular.

When we were sure of no difficulties, Mildred went on ahead with the truck and had coffee ready when I rode in. My wife said when she drove in and let Vevette out of the truck, the poodle ran as fast as she could to the horse corral, looking for Amber.

The solution of our horse problem was realized not long after that day, when we turned Amber over to the care of Ross Wilson, whose young daughters took the mare to their hearts as one of the family and Amber was again among the Wilson's horses—all seventeen of them.

We often went to call on Amber and take her oats and carrots and she seemed pleased to see us. The following summer she had a new foal to show us, lovely, but definitely of the wild stamp.

# Beavers Move In

In the erratic surprising nature of weather on the Chilcotin Plateau, temperatures which had dropped to fifty-two degrees below zero in the dying days of January, suddenly shot upward as February appeared on our wall calendar. We sensed the promise of breakup. But winter did not die willingly. There was a wild convulsion of high and low temperatures in this first week of the new month. The mercury danced in the tube of the registering thermometer, from below to above zero.

Our transistor gave us the news that winds up to 100 miles an hour were lashing the Queen Charlottes and the West Coast. And on this day the Coast peaks were again blanketed in deep new drifts. A gusting southwesterly wind became a steady blow, ripping billows of snow from the sides of Splinter Mountain and sending them in long smoky curtains across the slopes of the foothills.

The wind completely obliterated the moose tracks at the water holes. The snow caps on tree stumps around the cabin tilted crazily. At times the air was charged with a fine mist of frost particles that sparkled brilliantly in the sunlight. We restocked our bird feeders with more suet and seeds.

The blow was of short duration.

Fresh tracks punched in the old winter crust revealed a moose had come to the area of the hot springs, found one of the old holes covered by drift and pawed it open to drink. From there its tracks came off the lake ice to pass within a few feet of the cabin and disappeared among the naked aspens beyond our clearing.

As we viewed the roughened condition of the lake crust torn up by the moose, a flock of about twenty white-winged crossbills settled in the tops of the lake shore spruces and fed noisily among the ripened cones. They remained for about thirty minutes and took their departure en masse.

It was twenty-four degrees by eleven-thirty that morning, the air tempered by a light southeasterly. The softening breeze prevailed for the balance of the day and by 3:00 P.M. the temperature had climbed to twenty-seven degrees. Some dark shining areas appeared on the flat face of Little Eagle's winter crust. Mildred, examining the changing scene with her binoculars, surprised me with the announcement she could see vast pools of water rippling over the surface of the ice off Goose Island. Checking our old diaries for the breakup dates of former years, she discovered this February 9 was the earliest we had seen "open" water.

To celebrate the promise of early liberation, we popped a big bowl of corn and wrote letters until midnight.

There would still be some nights below zero but we knew that breakup was hovering over the wilderness.

Through January and February the snowshoe rabbit is almost pure white and at times, in the glare of bright sunlight, almost invisible, particularly if it "freezes" in its tracks, squatting motionless in its awareness of danger. We have seen them running over the snow in midwinter when the only discernible movement was a brief apparition of slightly dusky ears as the hare flashed into action, seeking safety under a cover of blow-down. In summer their coat is a dusty brown and, in that season, still an excellent camouflage among the duff of the forest floor, where they shelter under such meager cover as withered branches and sunburned needles of fallen lodgepole pine.

Where the grouse survives largely on the winter buds of aspens and soapolallie bushes, the hare seems to fare equally well on the tender bark of young aspens, sapling pines, such buds as it can reach and grasses found beneath the snow.

Not being previously prepared for the event of Valentine's Day, we resorted to "make-do" for an observance for which Mildred has had a lifetime of sentimentality. She made up a large red jello heart and this with a wild blackberry pie became the featured treats of our Valentine dinner. My contribution was also a heart—a large red one drawn with crayons on which was superimposed the portrait of a bull moose, his wide eyes burning with love in the presence of a blushing cow. This seemed appropriate to the occasion, as moose had been seen about our camp almost daily.

Vevette would leap into the wide window ledges, watching for the big animals. Her growling and barking told us they were around our cabin, or among the near trees even though not within view from the windows. The poodle had become nervously concerned by the presence of so many moose during recent days and we kept her under close surveillance for her own safety. It had become necessary to restrain her, on opening a door, so strong was her impulse to go dashing out, the pompom of her little tail a stiff vibrating flag. In her mind's eye, moose were obviously unwelcome invaders of her realm.

It was not unusual to step outside the cabin to discover a moose or two feeding among our aspens or standing in the truck road, eyeing our movements.

Where we had spread a layer of sawdust over the path under the gallery roof, morning sunshine reflected its pleasant warmth from the log walls of the storeroom. Snow had not reached this narrow, protected strip of earth and here our winter birds found the new warmth of February sun to their liking. In a matter of days, since the ever-lengthening hours of sunlight were increasing, the path under the gallery became a favored place for birds and for the pine squirrels that competed with them for the sunflower seeds we scattered there. Though ruffed grouse are bud eaters and disdained our grain, they too were attracted to the path, and here they fluffed their feathers and dusted in the luxury of sun-warmed sawdust.

Enjoying their presence and not wanting to frighten them, we avoided the path as much as possible, though detouring around the storeroom in a circuitous route through old drifts to reach the toilet or woodpile was not easy. I finally dug out a new path on the opposite side of the storeroom, turning the gallery path over to the birds and squirrels.

Of all the birds that wintered with us the chickadees were our favorites. There is an easily encouraged friendliness in their nature. A few offerings of seeds, bread crumbs, peanut butter or suet and these little birds are readily adopted. They seem more willing to accept the presence of humans in their wilderness habitat than some of the larger birds, with the possible exception of the sly, quiet Canada jays that glide on silent wings the moment food of any kind is offered. We spent many hours throughout the winter watching the chickadees on our window feeding board and among the suet stations in the spruces around the cabin. The light, high-pitched melody of their song filled the air about us, often as the only sound in the deep cold of the woods. They came to expect our routine appearance with bowls of feed, and often fluttered about our heads in noisy greeting.

February 20, one of our most beautiful days, dawned at eight degrees below zero.

We bundled into warm parkas, took our breakfast coffee pot and cups out to the canoe dock to enjoy the unfolding beauty. As the warming sun burned off the haze, the skies over Little Eagle became clear and flawless; deeply blue in the far north and northwest horizons; still blue but faintly tinged with a pale saffron to the east and south. Not so much as a solitary puff of cumulus hung above the sharp summits of the Coast Mountains and the Niuts glistened in the brilliance of their deep glacial ice from which the late February snow had disappeared.

Recognizing the high brilliance of sun, sky and frosted snow as a day for picture-taking, we were out with Mildred's cameras as soon as her light meter promised good results. One of our favorite subjects is trees in winter dress. We found, among the aspens and pines, the cold white fire of hoarfrost where the overnight fog from the lake had frozen into a thick and snowlike flocking.

As the sun climbed, the frost coated limbs of the aspens became a network of jewels against the blue of the clear Chilcotin sky. As we walked up the trench of our road, selecting the best of nature's beauty for our films, the tight bunches of green needles on the lodgepoles flashed in the fire of ice diamonds fine as dust.

By midafternoon the thermometer read forty-two degrees,

the frost was gone and the "show" was over. The wheel ruts in our truck road were rivulets of melt water.

We were conscious of the near approach of breakup—that one begrudged, spongy season of soft aggravating mud usually lasting several weeks that marks the death of winter and the birth of spring.

Bringing in supplies from Williams Lake on May 24, the Chilcotin road was torn and deeply rutted. Where breakup damage had been repaired, a mixture of pit-run dirt and boulders up to and including the size of grapefruit had been dumped into the chuckholes and soft frost boils. The spreading and leveling of this "Chilcotin gravel" as it is called in familiar contempt by the Interior ranchers, had not been completed on our return and we were bone tired from seven hours of jolting. We turned in early, our sleeping bags spread on the gaucho bunk.

We awakened to the drumming of grouse, the early morning gossip of the geese and the loons, the scratchy mutterings of mergansers in The Narrows and the thumping of a squirrel running the length of the bird feeding board in the window. We had slept the sleep of the weary, to be roused by familiar sounds as the sun, already high, flooded the cabin with its cheerful warmth. I opened my eyes to find Vevette standing on my chest, punching me with both front feet in a demand for attention and, when Mildred stirred, the poodle immediately divided her attack to include both of us. Then she ran to the door, jumping against it, demanding to be let out of the cabin.

Our breakfast was hurried. Anxious to again feel the smooth glide of the canoe, I went to get it ready while Mildred gathered her equipment. Vevette raced ahead, anticipating the canoe ride. We would make a reconnaissance tour of the nesting islands to check on this year's activities.

We headed for Goose Island first. We have visited and made a count of goose and loon nestings over recent years and have found as many as five goose nests and one loon nest in a single season. This year there was but one, the nest of a honker. The loons were elsewhere.

We came around the north side of the island, moving slowly

and quietly. A watchful gander moved from his guard station in the west end shallows, angled off a short distance the while talking quietly to his nesting mate.

Maneuvering the canoe into the overhanging willows until they could be grasped, I held our light craft against the low rocky slope of the island while Mildred stood in the bow endeavoring to penetrate the wall of brush with her eyes. The nest could not be seen. We circled the island, then, chose another landing spot and again my wife stood in the bow. She could not catch a glimpse of the sitting goose. Finally she climbed ashore and while she was stepping as quietly as possible through the undergrowth, the goose we sought rose almost vertically from her well concealed nest at the edge of a thick clump of low-bush juniper. Startled to discover she was standing so close to the nest without being aware of its location, Mildred stepped backwards, almost losing her balance. The goose was off and away on loud flapping wings, crying her protests and was immediately joined by the gander in a repeated noisy circling about us.

Mildred observed and made notes of the six eggs closely bunched in the nest of breast down and we took our departure. As we moved over the lake for our next inspection on Loon Island, near the south shore, the geese swung in to a smooth landing near their nest and we soon saw the hen's return to her eggs while the gander resumed his look-out on the point.

In a matter of days these geese learned, as others had in previous years, that we meant them no harm and they came to accept the offerings of cracked corn we left on the island. On the days we called to make the egg check, they gradually became less suspicious and simply swam off a short distance, returning to the nest almost immediately on our departure.

This year we found no evidence of a nest on Loon Island, though both loons and geese had hatched their young here in former years.

We moved on to Coyote Island, the last of our nesting prospects. Coyote lies a short distance off the south shore of Little Eagle, enclosing a bay whose bottom is creamy white sand. Here we found a scattering of water plants, their long slender stems topped with delicate pointed leaves that lay floating on the surface. The island protects this little bay from summer's westerly winds. It is a calm place of clear, crystal water and plant life that presents a picture of near tropical beauty. The island is also favored by other small birds, as well as by geese and loons, and we have never wearied of its restful influence...lilting songbirds and the droning of honey and bumblebees.

As we idled along its south shore, letting the canoe drift silently, off to our east, in the shallows of a reed bed we observed a goose moving among the tall stems. Then he set up a burst of gaggling, obviously to call our attention away from the island. We felt sure we would find a nester there. We circled close to shore, Mildred trying to locate the sitting goose before going ashore. Finally, just as my wife spotted the long-necked bird, she bolted into the air with loud cackling and wing beats and settled on the water, the gander joining her. The nest was well concealed under the boughs of a spruce. With only five eggs, we assumed the hen was still laying. We left immediately.

That was the only goose nest on Coyote Island this year.

When a westerly wind began to whip the lake into a choppy turbulence, we swung away from Coyote Island, heading for the protection of the north lake shore. We took the waves at a quartering to the wind, in order to lessen the pitch and roll of the canoe and still hold our course to the shelter we could expect in the lee of Bird Island.

Vevette did not like wind in her face. Our poodle curled herself under Mildred's forward seat for the lake crossing, keeping her head below the level of the gunwales. The crossing was bumpy but made with the added speed of the wind. We circled Bird Island, came around into the wind in The Narrows, cut across the channel and beached the canoe, returning to the cabin with appetites eager to augment our late sketchy breakfast.

When the wind had quieted, we returned to the canoe and drove it east, close under the sheltering north shoreline, to check on the extent of some new beaver cuttings we had noticed during the past fall.

In our early years at Eagle Lake we had come across old

cuttings where beavers had left evidence of their activities, but the mammals themselves had been long gone, the result of a century of unrestricted trapping. Then one day while Chuck and Wilma were passing along the north shoreline in our canoe, a couple of years following our arrival as settlers, they discovered a lone beaver sunning on a point of land projecting from the slot of a small narrow lagoon. It moved to the water, dived with a resounding tail slap and disappeared. There were a few fresh cuttings around the lagoon. That was the first beaver seen on the lake since their near annihilation and the new cuttings were a bright fresh evidence of their return. Since then, the cuttings have become general wherever there is water and aspens in our region of the Plateau. The beavers have made a remarkable recovery since Eric Collier, the late and talented naturalist-rancher of Meldrum Creek, brought a pair of beavers to inhabit a man-made pond at his wilderness home and established the forerunning parentage of a great new rehabilitation.

Less than two miles east of The Narrows we came upon such a jumble of freshly felled aspens we were convinced the beavers must have a lodge somewhere near. We began to search in earnest now, taking note of the direction in which many of the saplings had been dragged into the water from the sloping banks of the shoreline. We checked into a couple of small bays, expectantly, only to be disappointed. Then Mildred saw a wet, mud-padded streak through a clump of pine grass and wild rose bushes which bore the telltale drag-marks of working beavers. We roped the canoe to a sapling and climbed out for a better look around. Just beyond a narrow dike, not more than ten feet wide, and separating it from the main lake, we saw a pond thickly grown with watery grasses. The pond was about forty feet wide, the dense mound of a lodge in its center. The impounded water here served as a perfect moat for the lodge which was almost completely concealed by a jungle-like tangle of blow-down and brush. We found it was actually linked to the lake by a slender canal and the slot itself was densely overlaid with dead cuttings all around.

Unable to approach the concealed pond and lodge without

173

being heard, as we worked our way through the tangle of brush, we saw no beavers, nor did we expect to. The evidence of their presence was convincing, however, and we turned the canoe toward camp, well pleased with our discovery. In recent years the beavers have built several new lodges on the lake and elsewhere.

# Sasquatch and the Keekwillee Holes

Through June and early July our transistor radio picked up the news of final preparations of our space scientists to put Americans on the moon. As Mildred and I stood on the canoe dock one evening enjoying the beauty of a huge full moon rising above the skyline of the Cayuse Range, we decided to go Outside for the event; that is to say, in order to witness the historic blastoff and the progress of Apollo XI on television.

On July 20, we sat spellbound as Neil Armstrong set foot on the dead planet, heard his prophetic—"One great leap for mankind!" But when a million dollars worth of scientific equipment was jettisoned at Tranquility Base to become the first exportation of American garbage beyond the already fouled surface of earth, I told Mildred my enthusiasm was waning and I wanted to get back to the tranquility of the Chilcotin Plateau.

We returned to find that even here, in the deep of wilderness, more changes had taken place. A row of freshly blazed aspen posts set into the rocky soil of the lake shore east of our cabin bore the printed notices of new land applicants. And a half mile of new road had been slashed through the pines along the north ridge where the applicants had cut out an access to their locations.

We would be sharing our idyllic seclusion in the future. Our decade of blissful isolation had come to an end.

The natural parklands that lie as small open glades of sweet pine grass and clustered groups of lodgepoles along our north ridge have always held an enchantment for us. Leisurely walks here became one of our early pleasant habits. The north ridge is forever a place of wild beauty, in sparkling frost of a winter day when the pines are flocked in new snow, in midsummer when Indian paintbrush and wild roses flame in tall grass beneath the conifers and in the soft glow of a full autumn moon when long shadows lend mystery to the silence of wilderness.

Over the years, Mildred and I have come to walk in the beauty of the ridge as a routine of unending pleasure. I sometimes think my own affinity for this restful place lies in the fact it was through an opening among the pines one September day when we first glimpsed the turquoise depths of Little Eagle Lake shining as a jewel at the foot of the mountains and fell in love with it.

Our roadway climbs from the cabin woods to extend along the summit of the ridge on the route out to Tatla. In winter snow, the road through the pines is criss-crossed by the deep tracks of foraging moose, the pad marks of cougars, lynxes, coyotes, snowshoe rabbits, ermine and squirrels. We often go up there in the sharp cold days of deep snow just to learn the movements of the animals that winter here; to read sign, as the old-timers would say, and to maintain a sort of fraternal relationship with the denizens of our woods. In summer, when the last moisture from breakup has been drawn off the Plateau by days of hot sunshine, the forest floor becomes dry and brittle duff. In the gritty soil of the ridge, then thick with pine grass and wild flowers, few of the trails of the habitants are visible; yet we know they are still here except for the moose, which by now favor the high cool summits of the hills where there is some escape from the flies.

We see an occasional mule deer here in summer months. The feral horses of the wild bands roaming the Plateau come through occasionally. Cougar, lynx and coyote remain here too, because snowshoe rabbits are plentiful. An occasional grizzly follows the ridge as a natural route of easy woodland grades approaching the high summits of the Cayuse Range, southeast of Eagle Lake.

Ever since Vevette came to live with us she has hiked, canoed, eaten and slept with us; so it seems needless to say that on our hikes to the ridge we are never without our happy little poodle. She quickly adapted herself to our habits and developed an early acceptance of our woods walks as a "must." They have been made in all kinds of weather, good and bad, known to the Plateau.

For Vevette, the ridge is an excellent place to satisfy the inborn hunting instincts of her breed. She is a natural hunter, sharp eye, ear and nose; and on her feet, lightning quick. In September there are grouse to flush, squirrels and hares to chase and, though she seems never to quite catch up with them, her pleasure is great if the rapid wagging of her stubby pompom is a measure of joy.

The thought that we might someday encounter the threat of tragedy in our walks to the ridge had never entered our heads—up to one bright and frosty September morning.

We were moving at a casual pace up the gentle rise of the roadway sloping to the ridge when Vevette disappeared on one of her exuberant bursts of squirrel chasing. Ordinarily she would be racing back to us in a moment or two. We were not greatly concerned until, of a sudden, the poodle's excited yelps, deep in the pines, quickly became a high-pitched series of terrified cries.

"She's hurt!" Mildred exclaimed, and began calling frantically to Vevette. We both started running toward the sound of her anguished cries when she came bursting out of a thicket of young lodgepole saplings, ears flapping back, eyes wide with terror, her little tail clamped down tightly. Still screaming in a voice unlike anything we had ever heard from her, the poodle leaped into the sanctuary of my wife's arms, whimpering, trembling in the reaction of intense fright.

"Cougar!" was our first thought. We had often seen the big cat tracks here in winter snow. Or, possibly, I thought, it could even have been a Canada lynx, for they are fearless felines with a reputation for great ferocity in times of hunger. We could find no marks of violence on Vevette. Whatever it was, she had escaped it unmarked.

Mildred soothed and tried to quiet the poodle. We waited a few moments, our eyes searching among the pines, but could see nothing beyond the wall of saplings skirting our road. Then we started on toward the ridge again, keeping watch for the cause of the disturbance. Mildred put Vevette back on her feet. She immediately chose to walk on the opposite side from the source of her fright, crowding against Mildred's leg.

We had gone only a short distance when Mildred whispered, "I see it!" We stopped, keeping very still. Mildred whispered that she had caught a glimpse of movement among the pines. The early sun was bright in our faces, then we saw the glint of sun on the fur of a large animal, partially concealed by the pines, moving stealthily toward us. We froze, not particularly from fear, but hoping it would come out into the open. The animal, obviously seeing us better than we could see it, stopped as an obscure dark form behind a screen of low limbs and hooshum bushes. Mildred again took Vevette into her arms. We strained our eyes against the morning sunlight to identify the animal. Vevette was again whimpering and quivering.

The moment of confrontation lasted perhaps ten or fifteen seconds, then the animal moved off, fading back into the density of the trees where its dark outline merged with the shadows of the forest.

"I think it's a wolf," I said, conscious of how tall it stood. We walked slowly up the road again. Within 100 feet we came to a narrow opening where Mildred and I had slashed out a survey line by limbing the saplings with a machete. Here I could see down the straight line of the slash for several hundred feet. As I looked along the length of the narrow opening, I got one final glimpse of the animal. Its huge dark skull, thickly pointed black ears, shaggy shoulders and the high arc of thick tail, convinced me this was my first sight of a live timber wolf since we had settled at Little Eagle.

Mildred and I have since wondered about this incident many times. Around Lac La Hache, 100 Mile House in the Central Cariboo and in the Alexis Creek and Redstone country on the Plateau, the big northern wolves had been seen in numbers during recent months, after a seeming absence of several years as the result of concentrated poisoning. They were thought to have been largely exterminated by the deadly baits dropped from Game Commission airplanes. But a recent predominance of coyotes, a more familiar animal, seemed to indicate the baits had long since disappeared from the cattle ranges. The return of wolves in Jameson Basin, around Tatlayoko Lake and the Homathko River was an established fact. With Eagle Lake thus lying between two known wolf ranges, their presence in our woods would no longer be considered improbable.

While we discussed our excitement later in the day, Mildred reminded me that Vevette was familiar with coyotes and had never shown a fear of them. We had fed as many as eight coyotes at one time around our trailer while camped in the Sonoran Desert. It had been necessary then to restrain our poodle's desire to romp with them.

There is an old contention among the Shuswaps, the Thompson River Indians and the tribes of the Lower Fraser around Yale and the Harrison Lake country, that hairy giants known as Sasquatch roam the wild Interior of the Coast Range. The Indians describe Sasquatch as an anthropoid—admittedly humankind in most physical characteristics—but of massive and fearful proportions. To Indian children, Sasquatch has goblin connotations and threats of dire consequences at the hands of the hairy giants have been used to maintain good juvenile behavior in tribal wickiups for many years.

"You know," Mildred remarked, "that thing Vevette saw must have looked as big as a Sasquatch to her." I agreed with the comparison. Thus I was not surprised to hear my wife telling Vevette that it was Sasquatch—that she was never, not ever, to run off into the woods again or Sasquatch would surely get her!

Passing the place of her terrifying encounter on our road, on future walks, Mildred would remind Vevette of Sasquatch. The poodle would again crowd Mildred's legs, walking on the far side, begging to be picked up and carried past "the place." Or in our pickup, going to Tatla on mail day, she would stand in the cab window, watching intently as we drove by the scene of her great adventure, turning her black eyes knowingly to Mildred when my wife whispered, "Sasquatch is out there!" Even now, at the mention of the word, Vevette has a far-away look, remembering.

Lou Haynes said Vevette's being female may have had a lot to do with the fact she escaped harm. For my part, I like to think she came face to face with a big northern wolf with a chivalrous respect for a maiden silver poodle, but it is difficult to be convinced such may have been the case, for in the wilderness, the laws of survival are steeped in the blood of bird and beast. Predation is the unwritten code by which the strong survive on the flesh of the weak. Yet it has been my own observation that even in the enforcement of her unrelenting code—by which a finely balanced level of wildlife is maintained—nature has somehow imparted a lack of fear in some of our fauna that encourages coexistence even where the threat of sudden death is ever present.

We have seen this apparent tolerance of danger or what might be construed as willingness to accept calculated risk, where the bald eagles and nesting geese were involved. Geese we frequently observed sitting on eggs nested without regard to protective overhead cover or camouflage, on Goose Island, while eagles occupied good spying positions on spruce limbs above the nests. It was obvious the nearby gander guarding the goose and her eggs was fully aware of the eagles and the constant menace of their presence. And yet, the nest had been fashioned with down plucked from the breast of the hen, the full clutch of eggs laid and finally hatched, under the watchful eyes of two bald eagles.

One calm September morning Mildred and I observed two adult eagles, both balds, in repeated downward swoops on a grebe swimming in open water near the middle of the lake. At every downward plunge the big birds forced the grebe to dive. Working as a team, the eagles circled above and alternately dived on the grebe with such rapid frequency the water bird soon weakened from lack of oxygen, finally fell as an exhausted prey to one of the hunters and was carried off swiftly to Loon Island and devoured.

But on this same day, within another hour, we saw other grebes in the same waters, swimming and diving for sucker fish with apparent indifference to the presence of eagles soaring above them.

Seemingly, in some respects at least, nature in her maintenance of harsh rules of survival has been charitable enough to spare, or omit, an acute sense of fear among those decreed to die that others may live. I do not presume to insist this is a fact; but it has been a repeated observation through years of wilderness association, that the near presence of a roving predator is frequently tolerated with little more than a casual alertness.

Among the fauna of our wilderness we have seen the tracks of lynx, made during early morning, crossed by the tracks of a snowshoe rabbit, where the hare had passed later the same day. There was no indication the hare had been alarmed by the fact a lynx had been abroad that day, as the hare's imprints in the snow were even-paced, unhurried, mute evidence of lack of concern. It was simply going about the business of searching out its own food.

Around Tatlayoko Lake we have found the winter yards of bands of mule deers criss-crossed by a maze of cougar tracks and often two of three kills in close proximity to the yards, where the cats had fed. Yet there had been no sudden departure of the deer; rather, they had remained, attracted by the available browse, and I became convinced that only in the moment of attack the deers were sufficiently alerted to their peril to attempt escape.

In the sheep range of the Thompson River, Mildred and I one time surprised a young stone ram on a narrow ledge, by coming in above it within a distance of perhaps twenty-five feet. It could easily have escaped. Instead, on seeing us, the ram simply "froze." After about five minutes, during which we watched and the ram remained unmoving without so much as a blink of its glassy eyes, it resumed feeding on the leaves of hardwoods growing from a cleft in the ledge. When we finally moved off, the ram observed our departure with a sort of idle indifference.

* * * * *

A little distance south of Cougar Marsh the loggers, in early September, cut out an access road to Tatla Hill. The new route goes deeply into the heart of the last stand of old-growth Douglas firs on the hill, which is west of Eagle Lake. Judging from the size of the stumps and a count of annular growth rings, these magnificent old conifers condemned to the sawmills had mantled the south slopes of Tatla Hill for the past 400 years. Soon only stumps will remain where the giants once stood. And it is doubtful such trees will ever again be seen on the Chilcotin Plateau, for man's quest for material gain under the banners of "progress" here, as elsewhere in our land, has had little in sympathetic common with the ecology of the realm in which he lives.

Where the heavy blade of the loggers' "cat" turned west from the Old Tatlayoko Road to gouge and grade a truck route to the hill, the machine tore away one corner of an ancient man-made revetment of earth and stones. This was a portion of earth wall, or footing, where the primitive people of a near forgotten time built their keekwillee; a pit house covered with a sloping, dome-like roof of poles and sod.

How long ago?

Who knows? Along the banks of the Fraser River in Southern Cariboo and elsewhere, including the Plateau, the keekwillee builders dug their pits and roofed them with frameworks of carefully fitted logs, overlain with layers of reeds, grasses and sod, long before the first white man's wanderings brought him probing into the western wilderness.

Kee-kwill-ee, or kee-kwul-lie, or, if you prefer, kik-hwili. The word is Salish and in the Chinook jargon used as a preposition, meaning low, down, below, under, or as a depression or pit. How you might spell it is of little importance because the Indians didn't "spell" the words they spoke. White man couldn't pronounce them as the Red man did and attempts to assert the true pronunciations or spellings of the jargon have never produced anything but a corruption of the spoken word of the First Americans.

We know of a rancher who converted the pit of an old keekwillee to a root cellar on his spread and called it "an old kwiglee," so that's another version.

On the Plateau, keekwillee is more or less accepted with accent on the second syllable.

There are several of the ancient pits along the slopes of the north moraine of Little Eagle Lake. Two relatively small ones we found in our cabin woods. These are circular and from the angle of the present slope of the weathered excavations, we judged their original diameter to have been about ten feet and depth about four feet below surface level. We showed one of these to our friend Lou and it was his notion, quite logical, we thought, that this small keekwillee may have been the original shelter of a newly united couple whose early family needs were few and small. Chiefly they required shelter from the rigorous cold of the Chilcotin winters.

The big pit south of Cougar Marsh is of a size to suggest it may have been occupied by more than one family during winter months. It is approximately twenty feet square. The only evidence of the original walls is the parapet of sod and heavy boulders around the rim of the hole. We suppose the boulders were used to add weight and strength to the footings of the log walls. The lodgepole pines that make up the present surrounding forest are of about eighty to 100 years standing and some are growing from the floor of the pit.

Knowing of their old-time customs, it is probable the women dug the pits for these houses, using their digging sticks and hand trowels of wood or bone to fill carrying baskets with the loosened earth. The dirt was conserved in nearby piles, to be used as the final roof covering.

Anthropologists believe the log framing of the sloping roofs of such houses was begun by first setting four upright posts in a rectangle near the pit center; that the logs or heavy poles of the main rafters were set with their upper ends fitted into notches in the tops of the uprights, their bottom ends dug solidly into the earth at the rim of the hole. Over the heavy main supporting braces other logs were laid closely parallel and when completed the roof work presented a semidome shape with a squared hole in the center. Here a deeply notched pole stood approximately upright, projected through the hole from the floor of the pit. It

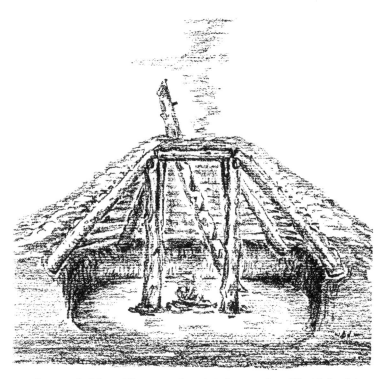

served as a ladder. The opening in the roof sufficed both as a smoke hole and a means of access.

Where available, reeds and sedge grasses were used to make a thick mat over the roof logs—it could have been pine needles and willow brush—and over the mat a layer of sod completed the job and provided a solid and warm shelter for the occupants of the new keekwillee.

Mildred and I often walk the route of the old original Tatlayoko Road south of Little Eagle, beyond Cougar Marsh, past the wild meadow we named Horse Heaven because our saddlers loved its sweet grass and the cool water of its small lake. As a general rule, we go at least as far south as the big keekwillee hole and look at it again, before heading back to camp.

How many times we have done this! But the hole always seems to draw us. Though it still appears as we first saw it—except for the corner rooted out by the bulldozer—my mind still contemplates the people who once lived here. It is as if I expect to see this ancient dwelling as it once was and I imagine how it would be to walk up the slope of the sod roof, step up to the hole at its center. I can almost feel my feet on the notches of the single pole ladder, sense the smoothness of its vertical trunk in my hands. The smell of wood smoke from a cooking fire drifts idly up to meet me; the pungence of pitch pine, of fat venison roasting above aspen coals; the smells of an ancient home and hearth deep in the wilderness of Chilcotin 100, 200 or more years ago.

In a trance of the imagination I see the pit house buried in the white robes of winter, serving its main usefulness as a warm shelter and the sounds I hear are the voices of women at their never-ending work in the dim room below. Their low spoken conversations, in their quiet, almost whispered way of speaking, comes up to me thinly, lightly, in the gray smoke rising from the squared opening. I hear the fretful wail of a newborn babe seeking the breast of its young mother and the laughter of children. These are the sounds I hear standing above the opening of a keekwillee whose roof and walls, and whose people, have long since disappeared through the alchemy of time. Only the pit they dug in the enduring earth remains. One sound I do hear that I am sure of is the voice of a light breeze through the lodgepoles standing in a mute ring of gray and green at the rim of the vanished pit house. The windsong in the pines is a melancholy moaning and I am a little sad too, realizing that what I came here seeking has been long gone from the face of the moraine.

Now the loggers are here. Soon the old-growth firs the people of the keekwillee knew so well, when they were all young together, will also have vanished from the slopes of old Tatla Hill and only the stumps, like the empty holes, will remain to mark the passing of a race of big trees and a race of forest people who knew and cherished the gifts of wilderness.

* * * * *

Though fog lay like a woolly gray blanket over the calm face of Little Eagle when I awakened in autumnal daylight, early sun quickly burned it away, revealing the sharp crests of the Coast Range against the intense blue of the sky. Our registering thermometer had settled on an overnight low of thirty-six degrees, but by the time I was finally up and around the cabin was already warming from hot sun through the lakeside windows.

Beyond the windows the shining red leaves of willows and wild roses dripped brightly with the sparkle of heavy dew, the harbinger of another warm day. And this one, I knew, would be what Mildred calls another bonus day in our satisfied lives. We were soon well up on our road to the north ridge, drawn by the charm it has always held for us. This time, however, I carried my old Springfield with a full magazine, sure in my own mind I would never use it, but nevertheless feeling more security for Vevette in the event of an encounter with another wolf.

In the early sunlight shafting through the crowns of the tall shoreline spruces and filtering back among the aspens along the road to the ridge, we were amazed by the vast profusion of spider webs, their silken traps shining in the sun. They lay and hung among the limbs of the hardwoods in wavering veils of finest gossamer, glinting with the wet diamonds of morning dew.

Underfoot, the yellowing pine grass was overlaid with the network of webs spread as snares for ground insects and overall was the wetness of the heavy dew.

From the ridge this morning, the sky was revealed to us as a wide blue dome above a landscape of greens, copper and gold. Not so much as a single cloud lay in the still air of the void. Thin veils of mist, slow rising in the early warmth of the sun, were lifting from the deep canyons of the range and from the low valley of Tatlayoko as we stood in reverence of the beauty around us.

For three days now we had been enjoying the full richness of Indian summer: cloudless, calm days dawning cool with dew, becoming warm, even a little sultry by midafternoon; calm, cool and star-flaming at night. On some recent mornings there had been light frost. Along the ridge this morning a big band of crows moved noisily among the pines. They appeared restless and I wondered if perhaps they were making plans for the warmer south country. There were now few small birds around other than jays and chickadees.

I had almost forgotten how beautiful the bronze winter leaf

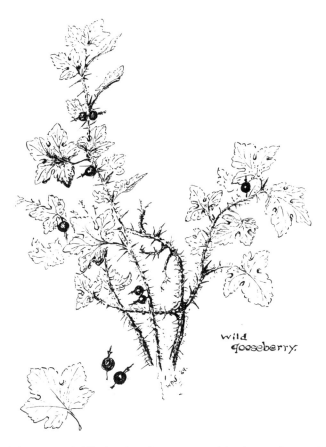

wild
qooseberry.

buds of the soapolallie bushes become at this time of year. Now
their fruit—the hooshum berries so appreciated by the tribal
Chilcotins—was entirely gone. The crop had been unusually
light. But here were the new, thickly clustered buds as a promise
of renewal, tight bunches of small beads shining like new copper in the notches of the twigs and dark stems. I broke off some
branches for Mildred to arrange in a hand-crafted green pot-
tery bowl, with sprigs of red wild rose hips, scarlet willow and
wild gooseberry, to make a bright centerpiece for our table.

As we stood on the ridge today our ears picked up the distant
gaggle of geese. A quick search of the sky revealed two long
wavering wedges of the big honkers high above the lake. We
judged their numbers at several hundred. They were over Splin-

ter Mountain when we first saw them, heading southeast toward Chilko. In the clear silence of the morning their cries still drifted back to us when the geese had finally become mere strings of beads above the distant horizon.

Winter migration had begun.

In some areas of our cabin woods, aspens had almost entirely shed the golden abundance of their foliage while others were still green, or just beginning to "turn." Near the stable, the aspens are quite tall and slender where they are partially shaded by the shoreline border of spruces. Here the aspen leaves had become a rich harmony of copper, gold and ripe apricot in a blending of pastel shades. The leaves of a few cottonwoods around the edges of the little wild meadow beyond the stable were the color of ripe pumpkin. We have often said we are glad the hardwoods do not all come into the full glory of their fall coloring at the same time and thus shorten the season of our enjoyment.

By late afternoon a southwesterly breeze developed. It became blustery, shaking the aspens and sending down showers of golden leaves thickening the ground cover. The low slant of sun angled through the frothy ruffle of waves rolling over the face of the lake, backlighting the whitecaps until the jade green depths appeared to be shot full of snow. It was nature's annual "Fall Showing" of her finest treasures.

As it seems generally to do at this season of the year, the wind fell away and a dead calm returned to Eagle Lake as the day neared its ending. From our canoe dock we watched the sunset. As the fireball lowered into a notch in the Coast Range that we have always pictured in our minds' eye as the probable low pass to Bella Coola, long rolls of new cumulus drifted in from the Pacific. The clouds became anchored among the crags of the Niuts above Tatlayoko, like fat pillows of pink cotton.

A sudden clouding over following sundown brought a mixture of rain and hail. The icy pellets bounced noisily on the cabin, tumbled into the valleys of the roof, and rolled from the eaves to bounce again as they whitened the ground.

I stood in the cabin doorway, enjoying the quick hammering of hail on the roof. As I listened, the haunting cries of another high passing flight of geese came down through the overcast and though I could not see them I could tell by the direction of their fading voices that these, like the flights we saw earlier, were heading south. The sky became a convulsive turbulence of dark and ragged clouds and spasmodic bursts of low sunlight. I watched as the sunset spread narrowly between the horizon and an overlay of solemn nimbus boiled in from the Pacific, its low angle throwing flattened shafts of flame-light burning red among the snowfields. At that moment, as Mildred came to watch with me, holding Vevette in her arms, a huge double rainbow stood high and brilliant in the mist, one end of its multicolored arch sunk in the depths of the lake. The clouds above Splinter Mountain fell apart for the brief moments left of daylight and as we looked into the fading afterglow we saw the thin bent line of the southbound geese.

But they will be returning in another spring and, surely, we will be here to welcome them.

# The Changing Wilderness
## 1967

By the third year of our retirement, Mildred and I had developed such acceptance of our lone habitation of the big valley of Little Eagle Lake, we had grown possessive. The mere distant echo of a rifle shot would rouse my wife's immediate resentment.

"Some darned hunters!" she would say in disgust.

"Probably some Indians getting their winter meat, "I would offer, trying to sound practical about it.

"They don't have to come in here!" she would insist; and there would be an all-inclusive sweep of her arm in a gesture that took in the eight-mile length of the lake and the surrounding mountain ranges to the far horizons!

I sometimes wondered if the idyllic charm of the big wilderness of Chilcotin would ever really change. This seemed improbable to me, for here, so remote from the pressures of expanding populations, we had felt no threat of invasion.

In the fall of this year we went again to the American Southwest to visit our U.S. Air Force son Will Jr. and his family, for some rock-hounding, and to soak up some warm sunshine. We returned to Little Eagle in late spring, to discover surprising changes.

The loggers had arrived!

We had neighbors.

The Old Tatlayoko Road, the rough and rocky winding wagon trail we had followed with so much pleasure where it twisted among the pines, had been bulldozed to a width of twenty feet and straightened by loggers who were even then hauling out mammoth loads of old-growth timber to a new sawmill near Chilanko Forks.

At the outlet of the lake, where the natural overflow drained westerly to feed the series of big ponds, the beautiful rocky creek bed we used to ford on our trips to the Cougar Marsh had been "improved" by two huge corrugated iron culverts. Over the culverts an earth fill had raised the road bed about four feet. To secure material for the fill, the bulldozer crew had gouged off the entire dome of a grassy little meadow that had been, probably for centuries, the dancing and mating ritual ground of generations of sharp-tail grouse. Now only the imprint of the scouring 'dozer treads remained. In the little meadow where Mildred and I first stood to gaze on the unspoiled magnificence of the natural parklands, two tar-paper shacks and a litter of tin cans and old clothes, the wreckage of an old truck, a discarded bed spring and scattered empty beer cartons proclaimed the arrival of industrial progress and "civilization."

I wondered, then, if this was the trend and policy to be expected in British Columbia's industry-oriented government. Destruction and pollution was already rampant here, even in the area officially mapped and dedicated as "public ground," the beautiful little natural park set aside as a campground administered by the Forest Service.

At Cougar Marsh the wanton destruction of the natural park had been repeated, the grassy, flower-studded knoll bladed away for "fill" dirt to cover a culvert. The young pines and aspens that had graced the knoll were now a ragged heap of trees and roots pushed aside by the blade of the loggers' dozers. There had been plenty of fill dirt available elsewhere with less destruction. The little parkland had been sacrificed simply because it was "handy."

On the slopes of the hills to the south the fresh scars of logging slash were already visible. On calm days the distant whine of chain saws and the clatter of "cat logging" on the steep hillsides could be heard. Above the pines bordering the new logging roads, great clouds of yellow dust rose in the wake of trucks rolling to the new mill with their loads of old-growth fir.

While we were sorry to see the big trees coming off the hills to our south we were at least heartened since the timber along our north ridge had not been invaded. Here there is little timber of merchantable quality in stands sufficiently dense to warrant logging—at least for the present!

We came to the realization rather suddenly that we were no longer alone. We were sharing the backlands of the ancient plateau with a clan to which the sanctity of nature and the unpolluted ecology had little, if any, aesthetic significance. We could take some satisfaction from the fact that so far the logging operations were beyond the confines of Eagle Lake. But the far faint whine of chain saws and the rattle of the loggers' "cats," like the echo of those rifle shots, we heard as the anguish of a dying wilderness.

A short distance west of our cabin we now had neighbors. Lou and Doris Haynes were camped in the midst of piles of lumber hauled in from the sawmill at Tatlayoko and other supplies intended for home construction.

Summing up the changes that had taken place, Mildred and I talked of the significance of our diminishing isolation. Little Eagle would never be quite the same. We tried to admit, however, that from a practical standpoint we were undoubtedly fortunate by having good neighbors. The prospect of being snowbound, inherent hazards of sickness or injury, were lessened by the presence of other humans. The potential security would likely outweigh the loss of our blessed isolation...or would it?

Our sons and their wives, who often expressed concern because their mother and dad were "off on some wild trip again, the Lord knows where!" seemed relieved that we were no longer completely alone in our wilderness paradise. They were quick to remind us we were "much better off." We simply accepted the facts of change, but with a nostalgic memory of Little Eagle the way we originally found the blue jewel of the Chilcotin.

We were happily surprised to discover a healthy growth of leaf lettuce, chives and onions in our planters. Deep snow had lain as a protective blanket over the planters while we were away. Our green garden was ready for use. Mildred shared some of it with Doris and Lou Haynes, who had material on hand to build a greenhouse but hadn't gotten around to it yet. Of course there was the constant danger of frost, even in July. We contrived an overnight cover with a roll of black building paper which we removed during the daytime. On July 31, the mercury stood at an even thirty-two degrees at sunrise and the planter cover sparkled with frost, but our garden was safe. We were enjoying leaf lettuce daily.

Mildred's diary for August 2 relates: "My planters coming along. Tomato plants thriving...cuke, chives and seed onions up. Also a few onion sets from last year. The marigold, petunia, lobelia and alyssum plants I brought in are doing nicely. Have some calendula and bachelor button plants coming from seed...the parsley did not come up...only a few chard and some kale. Very few of the wild plants we dug and brought in are growing...we need more top soil."

Among the shore birds that seasonally come to the interior bush and frequent the lakes and ponds of the Plateau are the Bonaparte gulls. At times we have been fortunate in seeing sizeable flocks of these beautiful birds, conspicuous by their jet black heads and snowy bright bodies, circling the lake near our cabin and perching in the trees of Bird Island. The Bonaparte is the smallest of our western gulls and, in our estimation, the most beautiful. *Larus philadelphia* is quite readily identified in summer breeding season by the coal blackness of its head (which is white in winter) and the white outer primaries of its wings. Its nesting place was for many years an unsolved mystery. In recent times it had become a generally accepted belief that the Bonaparte, a Pacific Coastal migrant passing inland in breeding season, is a tree nester. We have confirmed that fact, observing nesting pairs in the spruces near our cabin.

One August morning, as we were having our sunrise coffee out on the dock and savoring the piney fragrance of the sun-warmed air, the plaintive cries of the Bonapartes came to our ears. Though, at this time, out of sight from where we stood, we knew they were on Bird Island. We slid our canoe into the lake and eased out quietly, moving slowly around the east side of the island. We soon spotted a solitary Bonaparte perched in a small spruce at the water's edge. It was asleep, head under wing. A few cautious strokes of our paddles brought the main flock into view.

About thirty of the birds had settled in a dead spruce on the west shore of the island. There was one immature bird in this flock. Appearing larger than its attendant mother, the baby sat stuffily on the tip of a limb off to one side of the main flock, its mottled tannish gray coloring betraying its immaturity in contrast to the brilliant whiteness of its parent. She sat closely attentive, her black head glinting in the sun.

We paddled quietly around to the west side of the island in such a way as to obtain a more favorable light. Still they sat, unperturbed by our appearance and the hum of the movie camera. We were now almost directly beneath the youngster and mother. Finally, to get some action in our pictures, I waved my Chinook paddle overhead. In a chorus of loud cries the Bonapartes rose swiftly up and away, as our tape recorder and movie camera captured the beauty of their voices, the wild flash of snowy wings against the flawless blue of the sky above Bird Island.

A day later, a flotilla of nine big northern loons—the most we had seen at one time—came cruising in their slow, majestic poise into The Narrows. They came silently, at times dipping their bills into the water up to their eyes in a movement we interpreted as a searching action, scanning the shallows for fish.

We obtained no film footage of the loons but succeeded in getting an excellent tape recording of their trilling cries. Seeing us, the loons reversed their course back toward the deeper water of the lake. There began, to our delight, a rising chorus of wailing, sharp, clear and prolonged that echoed and re-echoed among the hills, to become a captive recording on our tape as the loons moved ever farther away. Our album of bird and waterfowl "music" was richly enlarged this day. By now Mildred had accumulated a collection sufficient to provide us with more than an hour of bird and animal calls, including, in addition to the loons and Bonapartes, the big northern owls and Canada geese, an excellent coyote chorus from the Chilcotin bush to augment those from the Sonoran desert. To these we added the zoom of rufous hummingbirds and the drone of our lazy bumblebees and songbird melodies. There was also the wild lashing sounds of Eagle Lake's ice-bound contractions. The record also included some excited barking by Vevette as she joined in our wildlife adventures.

By mid-August, Little Eagle had absorbed a sufficient amount of sunshine to lose some of its iciness, at least in the shallow bays and we swam in its crystal depths. We favored the spots where the warm springs that kept the lake ice open in winter served to temper the lake in summer as well. Vevette swam with us, to her great joy.

One morning, as we were having our coffee on the canoe landing, a young Pacific seagull came swimming through The Narrows, eyed us momentarily as we stood quietly watching it, then to our surprise, it swam slowly but directly toward us. We were amazed when the little gull came within about thirty feet of the dock and then proceeded to sit, idly observing us in a curious way. Occasionally the gull would execute a small circle, swim off a little distance, then return. Finally it came within perhaps twenty feet of us, swam back and forth in short turns, never taking its eyes from us.

It probably sounds ridiculous to say so, but this little gull actually acted as though it wanted friendship or at least some attention. It got it. Mildred eased herself slowly back off the dock, hurried to the cabin and returned with some pieces of bread which she tossed onto the surface of the water. The gull moved off when Mildred began throwing out the chunks of bread but when we both stood still it returned and quickly feasted on our offerings. We saw the friendly little gull on this day only. We had hoped it would favor our company and remain around The Narrows, but we did not see it again.

Hot weather annually brings the curse of forest fires to the Chilcotin Plateau and this year the pall of smoke again hung along the northeast and west horizons as more than 100 separate blazes crackled through the tinder dry lodgepole, fir and spruce and turned the sun to a dull red blob. Then one day heavy smoke billowed up over the far summits of Splinter Mountain, to our southeast, as a new fire roared through the timber near Chilko Lake. We went to Tatla for mail and groceries and learned the Forest Service had made such a demand for food supplies to take care of a big crew of fire fighters, Graham's store was practically emptied of available groceries.

It was several days before the Chilko fire was contained and finally defeated but in the meantime some massive fires burned out of control on the Coast and Vancouver Island—the heart country of the last great stands of virgin old growth on the North American continent. These fires sent the overspreading billows of their heavy smoke to spread inland through the river canyons of the Coast Range. It hung as a somber blanket over the Plateau. It was depressing, as our beautiful snow-capped mountains were shrouded in the death robes of forest destruction. We were thankful when the worst of the fires had been conquered or burned themselves out and our skies cleared again, in September.

We added a propane gas refrigerator to our camp equipment, taking advantage of rockgas which had become available through a tanker service at Tatla. The quality of our meals was radically improved. The six-cubic-foot 'fridge proved a real blessing. We bought it secondhand in Williams Lake and with a minimum of extra copper tubing and a few fixtures soon had our cold box working. Now we could keep milk, eggs, fresh meat and other foods on hand in quantity. The threat of summertime spoilage was reduced to a minimum. Then Mildred, acting on a suggestion from the man who sold it to us, closed off the lower half of the box with a cardboard panel blocking the extreme cold from the lower compartment and, by turning up the flame of the refrigerating unit, created a larger freezer in the upper half. Our thermometer soon registered twenty-two degrees in the frigid upper section, keeping our stocks of meat solidly frozen. A casual check of our propane freezer would usually reveal ample supplies of frozen roasts, steaks, ground beef, milk and bread, while the bottom half contained, unfrozen, our eggs and fresh vegetables. The quality of our food supply was changing.

We shut off the flame during the cold months. After freezeup there was little need for mechanical refrigeration. Old Man Winter solved the problem of food preservation and seldom released his frigid preserving grip until late February or early March. In winter it was more a problem of thawing frozen foods, as needed, or keeping them in frost-proof storage.

The walls of our ice room, like the rest of our cabin, were built of spruce logs standing vertical. Double-walled with the inner walls of heavy planks, the space between averaged two feet of sawdust fill. A near three-foot depth of sawdust lay over the top of the chamber. We fitted a heavy door which originally served in a similar capacity as the door of a coastal cold storage plant. This door we bought secondhand at quite a reasonable price. Being of metal construction and weighing about 500 pounds, it was hauled in from the Coast in our pickup truck. We slid it out of the truck on jack pine rollers and positioned it squarely before a previously constructed wall frame of heavy timbers on a stone and cement base. We levered it up and into the opening with the aid of our truck jack. Some careful checking and re-checking of frame measurements had assured both of us this big door would fit the opening, once we got it up-ended with the jack, and it did, to a "T." The insertion of eight machine bolts capped with hex nuts and iron washers secured the big door, once we had it properly placed. The interior of our ice room is six-by-six feet deep and wide with a six-foot ceiling and readily holds close to four tons of lake ice if we choose to fill it up.

* * * * *

We decided to enlarge the outer end of our dock with an L-shaped platform. Then we would have room for our folding camp chairs and a card table, as well as for occasional guests who might want to join us in our early morning coffee hour. To get the project moving, we first cut out some green aspen poles about eight inches in diameter and built a rectangular log crib three feet wide, three feet deep and eight feet long. The crib we put to-gether resting on the outer end of the existing wharf. The crib's corners were notched and fitted snugly "cabin style" and rein-forced with galvanized eight-inch spikes. The bottom of the box was planked.

When finished, we used a peavey and an iron bar to slide the green log frame sideways, off the dock. Being heavy with sap and of low natural buoyancy, the crib floated low and sluggishly in the water. Wearing a pair of swim trunks, I went over the side and held it in approximately its proper position while lifting some loose boulders off the lake bottom and dropping them into the bin. We soon had it settling to the bottom. Just before the final weight of rock fill was added, we inched the heavy box into its final and previously measured position. Then we dumped in the last of the rocks and our crib was solidly settled on the lake bottom, as the first of two piers we would need to support the stringers for the L extension of our dock.

The next day we built and sank the remaining crib. We soon had the stringers bolted and the new deck of one-by-eight-inch rough sawn boards nailed down. The L added a deck eight by twelve feet in area and it has since proved its usefulness many times over.

Some old fire hose nailed along the outer edges of the deck made a good bumper strip.

We were definitely aware now of a change in the temperature of the lake. August had given us some good swimming days. But September already had the feel of fall in the air. There was new snow on the Coast Range and the two days in which I sank and filled the log cribs, up to my waist in the water, were chilly reminders that summer had passed.

While I worked on the new dock extension, Mildred used a pair of long-handled brush cutters to prune down the willows along the lake shore. These had grown so tall in one season we were no longer able to see the shoreline from our cabin windows, or the deck of our dock. The wharf was a favorite roosting place for a family of mergansers—a hen and eleven youngsters that came almost every sunny afternoon to climb up on the boards for an hour or two of siesta. They repeatedly messed up the deck before taking their departure. In fact, despite my daily scrubbing with a heavy bristle broom, the dock soon took on the appearance of having been whitewashed. But we liked our fish-eating friends too much to risk offending them by driving them away, although Vevette frequently charged the sleeping flock and sent them running on splattering feet across The Narrows, the hen protesting loudly.

* * * * *

Two huge granite boulders, each probably weighing well over two tons, had plagued our efforts to eliminate them. One lay where our new truck road came into a turning area back of the cabin, the other in the line of our walkway along the north cabin wall where we were continually forced to go around it.

We had once attempted to loosen and roll off the grade the big rock in the driveway using a log chain and grab hook attached to Ross Wilson's big diesel truck but the result was only a broken chain. We had failed to move the big rock out of its resting place, but had managed to tip it up sideways in the hole. We were looking at this boulder more closely one day and discovered that it was finely laminated, like much of the flag stone we had gathered from the lake.

We obtained a set of gads (slender, tapered steel wedges) and found that by driving them into the seams of the rock with a sledgehammer, it could be split into big slabs. This rock was a beautiful dark green stone. The seams of its lamination were from five to seven inches apart and approximately parallel. In two days of hammering on the gads, we reduced the huge boulder to a mass of heavy slabs, all of which were quite uniformly flat and smooth and very beautiful.

The largest of the slabs, two of which were approximately four feet long by two feet wide and seven inches thick, we moved on pine log rollers. The real job was to get the heavy stone slabs onto the rollers. This we accomplished by jacking up one end of a slab until a roller could be shoved back under the stone to near the center of its weight. Then, using the log roller as a fulcrum and a peavey as a lever, the slab could be teetered onto a parallel roller with a forward push and we were on our way.

To make a smoother surface under the log rollers we laid a loose track of planks from the pit where we split the boulder to the front entrance of the cabin where our first steps would be built. The distance was about 150 feet and, fortunately, the route was practically level, though a crooked one.

To get around the corner of our ice house and between the toilet and a big wood pile, then to avoid a clump of spruce trees, some old stumps and other obstacles, we had to change the angle of our log rollers frequently, using the sledgehammer to knock them around to the proper alignment on the track of planks. I worked in front, shifting the rollers ahead of the slab as Mildred levered the big rock along with the peavey. I was somewhat amazed as well as quite proud to see my wife, who weighs a shade over 100 pounds, boosting the tremendous weight of stone along the crooked route to the cabin with the skill of a hand-logger.

Old Cheops and his slaves at El Giza had nothing on the slaves of Eagle Lake. We had gone back into methods as old as the pyramids to move mammoth blocks of stone that had lain where the great ice cap dropped them perhaps 25,000 years ago. There was this difference, however, Cheops' stones had been moved to the tune of whips cracking over bloody human backs. The stones at Little Eagle were being moved to the tune of "rock and roll" pouring from Mildred's tape recorder. And this was a labor of love and fun.

The big rock that lay deeply set in the earth at the north side of the cabin could not be split. It was an igneous boulder with no seams into which we could insert a wedge. We tried for most of a day to find a weak spot in which to start a wedge, then finally gave up the idea as hopeless. I was about to abandon hope of ever getting rid of this big boulder when Mildred suggested that maybe we could just dig a hole alongside of it, roll it in and bury it. So we began to dig.

In two hours I was hip deep in a hole four feet in diameter and still had not dug below the bottom of the rock. During the late hours of afternoon the pile of earth and small stones that I picked and shoveled out, going forever deeper alongside the big boulder, grew until I had to give the shovel an extra heave to clear the heap.

Finally, at a depth of just over four feet, we came to the

bottom. We propped the great stone with jack pine timbers to hold it safely in place while I undermined it with my pick. Eventually, satisfied by measurements taken with a steel tape that sufficient width and depth had been reached, we dug a shallow adjoining pit into which we inserted a heavy pine pry pole about eight feet long. We got out on the end of the pole, using our combined weight for greater leverage, and with one big heave tilted the rock off balance and into the deep hole we had dug. Joyfully we found our measurements had been correct. When we finally shoveled back a covering of earth above the spot where we sunk the enemy, it lay well below the surface, no longer an obstacle in our path.

With the benefit of a rich cement and sand mortar, the slabs of greenstone became front and rear entrance steps to our cabin, colorfully complimenting the rough gray stone foundations below the log walls.

It was mid-September when we finished mortaring in the last of three entrance steps.

In late September, we turned to cutting a fresh supply of lodgepole for our winter heater wood.

Rustling up a big pile of sweet scented pine is always a happy task. I love woodpiles, especially the good smelling kind, like pine and old-growth Douglas fir. I not only like to smell the wood piled up for winter; I want it to look proper. A woodpile to be viewed with pride should be made up of equal lengths, neatly stacked, ends squared and top layers level. I learned that from my grandfather, who was an expert wood cutter.

As our woodpile grew, this year, snow deepened on the summits of the Coast Range.

Then came other harbingers of winter.

The big owls returned to the spruce belts bordering the lake. Their hooting would start near dusk. Frequently, by late dark, we would be hearing three or four of them at one time, calling back and forth across the lake. On nights of quiet air, their calls echoed and re-echoed among the hills until their numbers seemed to have multiplied.

Mildred's diary for September 29 recounts: "A big thrill

before daylight this morning. (Will) wakened me, asked if I wanted to tape the owls. Of course I did! They were really singing. I carefully and as quietly moving as possible, set the recorder near an open window in the as yet full darkness. We taped a very good reproduction in a few minutes as there were at least three different owl voices just outside the window."

On this date her diary also noted the changing color of foliage around our cabin. The aspens were blushing in soft shades of copper and gold; willows were beginning to redden. Everywhere the wild rose leaves were turning to crimson and purple. Out along our new road toward the north ridge, the aspens in one area were a deep red, intermingled with shades of rich ripe apricot and from pale to golden yellows. A few were already curled and browned by frost and we would be surprised, in the deep cold of winter, to discover that these seemingly dry and lifeless leaves and twigs of the aspens would be sought out by moose, deep in snow, for the nourishment nature had stored in the cured foliage.

# Tom Hance: The Pilgrim of Chilcotin River Valley

Looking back over the approximately forty years of my life on the Chilcotin Plateau, many events of historical significance came to my attention; in the following chapters I have attempted to account for them in their natural sequence. Chief among them, in my personal contacts, was the story of Tom Hance who crossed the great western plains from Pennsylvania to California in the 1860s and who's credited with being the first white settler in the big valley of the Chilcotin River. Other stories in the following pages include the remarkable events surrounding the early life of Charlie Skinner who brought purebred horses to the valley and precipitated a feud among cattlemen that led to one of the greatest slaughters of wild horses in the history of British Columbia. Skinner drifted into historical oblivion leaving a matis daughter named Chee-Wit who became a legend in her own right as a phantom of the wilderness near my home.

I believe the readers of Chilcotin history will be interested in some varying viewpoints on the real cause of the Chilcotin war. It is the story of Klatassine, the tribal leader of the fierce band of Natives that precipitated a clearly unjustified conflict between the Indians and whites in Waddington's attempt to build the gold road from Butte Inlet to the gold fields of Cariboo in the 1860s. Among Klatassine's followers were Old Dog, whose warriors armed with only bows and arrows easily out-shot the Imperial government's military with a rain of arrows which out-flanked the speed by which the militia could fire and resload their long barreled single-shot rifles. The chapter is devoted to what Old Dog called the difference between the stick guns (bows and arrows) and his reference to the iron rifles which he called the white man's chickamin gun because it was made of metal.

I lived to know the personality of an American named George Turner who drifted into our area from Bella Coola and who lived and died under the cloud of an unproved suspicion that painted him as a fugitive from justice. The series includes a chapter on Memaloos, the Indian's word for death and my personal experience with a little girl named Gloria who was a near victim of what many whites consider a vicious practice among the nomadic Indians of the Chilcotin Plateau. Then there's the story of Jimmy Brown, the hermit of the Klinni-Klinni River. Included is a story of a young couple and their infant baby, lost for nearly a week, and who survived by living on pine tree sap.

I have attempted to interlace tragedy with humor and I rounded out the series of my personal experiences with chapters that reflect a more joyful side of the wilderness of Canada's last frontier.

In the big valley of the Chilcotin River, Chinook terms and the tribal jargon are inter-mixed and often in conflict which confuse a reader. In our area, the Homathko River flowing from the plateau to Butte Inlet drains a valley as to a lake designated by map makers as Tatlayoko. I never heard an Indian call it Tatlayoko. Their word for this lake was Tatla-ko. You can take your choice.

\* \* \* \* \*

Midsummer. 1868. A tall young man not yet thirty years old, stood on the high eminence of land gazing northward into a wide expanse of rolling grasslands once known as New Caledonia but by now more generally known as Chilcotin Country. He said to himself, "It's free and empty, there'll be no southern sympathizers and I believe it's the place I want to be." He had come west from his native Illinois in a covered wagon—four months in crossing the plains to California. Tom Hance was a veteran of the Northern Army in the Civil War, who had abhorred the bloody slaughter between north and south. He regarded the war as a suicidal conflict of father against son and brother against brother.

In his mind it had been triggered by wealthy southern planters in their white pillared mansions when the southern confederacy fired on Fort Sumter and left President Lincoln with no alternative but to declare war to save the union.

*Oh my darling Nellie Gray,*
*They have sold you far away;*
*And I'll never see my darling anymore...*
(Old Negro lament from the days when slaves were sold in the Deep South.)

On the long plodding haul ever westward, Tom Hance "the loner" made his night fire of buffalo chips and made his bed on the prairie sod beneath his wagon while his weary horses grazed at the ends of staked out tethers. He would think of home and play his violin.

One morning as he lay in his blankets waiting for the sun to dry the dew, his horses began to whinny, sensing the approach of riders. Tom aroused himself to see a small group of Indians approaching on their ponies. Hance immediately took up his violin and began to play, keeping his bow hand lowered close to the butt of his pistol, which was stuck in the waistband of his homespun pants.

The Indians halted their horses some little distance from the wagon, then slowly approached, their leader holding up one hand in the peace sign of the Prairie Indians. A few minutes later from a "possible bag," Hance withdrew several small pocket mirrors to present one to each of the Indians, who evinced a pleasurable surprise at seeing their images in the glass. A few minutes later, the Indians went on their way. Months later, when he reached San Francisco, that same violin would be heard again, played by Hance, who had become a member of John Philip Sousa's Marine Band.

The route Hance followed when he left California to come north is conjectural, even among his descendants. If he was still traveling by horse and wagon, possibly by some of the roundabout primitive roads through Oregon, he logically could have come into the Puget Sound area in the vicinity of Nisqually Flats (near present Olympia).

In that time, the Hudson Bay Fur Company dominated the flats with a large outpost where they had extensively developed agriculture, growing potatoes and wheat among other things. Also in this period, the Hudson Bay Fur Company steamboat *Beaver* was operating in coastal waters and it would be logical to assume that aboard the *Beaver* he probably made his way to Victoria, it being his purpose to determine the facts about so-called "free-land" in Canada.

It was there, at Government House, he obtained the help of a young girl, Eleanor Verdier, who assisted him with all available information of the times.

Weeks later, Tom Hance's eyes swept the green waters of the Chilcotin River again. He turned his saddle horse around, swung back south to Canoe Creek, skirting what was known as the Gang Ranch. It is interesting to note that in this area of benchlands, Hance had encountered remnants of a group of southern sympathizers who, during the Civil War, Lord Lytton, the territorial secretary, had warned to cease their efforts to stir up trouble between Americans and Canadians or be expelled from Canada. That's how Gang Ranch got its name—by which it is still generally known—though, it has long since come into more peaceable hands.

At Canoe Creek, Hance swam his horse to the east bank of the Fraser River and again took up the northern route of the new Cariboo Wagon Road and proceeded on north to Soda Creek. Here he again swam his horse back to the Chilcotin Plateau, turned south on the grassland he had recently viewed, onto an Indian Trail that would eventually become known as the Medrum Creek Road. Riding on the north bank of the Chilcotin River, Tom Hance picked a spot about twenty miles west of Riske Creek and built his cabin.

The place would eventually be known as Hanceville. It would become the sight of the first post office of the big valley of the Chilcotin River, a trading post where Tom Hance did business with the Indians. Once a month he would ride back to Soda Creek where there was a grist mill and post office and return with mail to Hanceville, which soon began to attract settlers.

Tom Hance was an energetic man, well-liked by the Natives. He became well-known for his honesty. One night as he lay in his lonely cabin, the vision of the smiling face and the eager enthusiasm of the young girl at Government House repeatedly crossed his mind. They had corresponded briefly over a period of months and her letters warmed his heart. He realized he had been in love with this girl since the day they met. The age-old appeal for companionship had been strengthened by the passage of time. On sudden impulse, Tom Hance was again in the saddle heading for Victoria.

When he asked Eleanor Verdier if she would marry him, her eager response was the only answer he needed.

Their wedding trip followed a few days later and, together, they returned to Yale from Victoria. At Yale, Tom and his young bride bought saddle and pack horses.

As Tom and Eleanor Hance wended their way north of Yale, the newlyweds discovered Chinese miners at the China Bar, for whom the bar was named, still recovering gold from the sands of Fraser, which had been overlooked by white miners. The Chinese were secretly hoarding nuggets of pure jade which they were exporting to the Orient. At Kanaka Bar, they discovered a group of Negro miners who the Natives believed were Hawaiian, hence the name Kanaka Bar. It was assumed at the time these blacks had originally been smuggled into Canada by northern sympathizers during the Civil War and had fled westward out of fear of being recaptured or reprisal from southern sympathizers.

The famous Cariboo Wagon trail was built by the royal engineers. The bulk of the big stampede of prospectors had passed, but the new road was still being traveled by throngs of gold hunters from all over the world. The heavy freight wagons of drovers like Sam Bass and trains of camels imported from Arizona by Hi Jolly and the mule trains of the Catalonian Jean Caux, who everybody knew as "Cataline," were moving supplies into the far northern regions for the miners and the new Northwest Mounted Police. Few of the stampeders on the Fraser were interested in the vast expanse of the Chilcotin Plateau, west of the Fraser River. The main interest being chiefly gold.

The newlyweds threaded their way through the placer mining camps for more than 400 miles to Soda Creek. There they swam the Fraser to the Meldrum Creek Trail and returned to Hanceville. Eleanor Hance had become the first white woman to settle as a homemaker in the vast valley of the Chilcotin River.

In the course of time, Eleanor gave birth to five children, Grover Orlando, the first white child born in the Chilcotin River Valley, Percy Royal, Hattie Eleanor, Thomas Ray and Edwin Rennie. Hattie Eleanor became the wife of the late Tom Witte, the father of Irene Bliss of Willow Springs.

Among the early arrivals in the valley of the Chilcotin River were the Bailiff family, from England, in the early 1880s. Their family for many years was so completely isolated that to this day descendants of the original settlers still speak with the delightful British accent.

\* \* \* \* \*

Today, the once-thriving village of Hanceville is but a matter of memory. In October of 1993, a visit to Tom Hance's old homestead revealed no trace of the buildings that once housed a population of more than a hundred settlers, in addition to Tom Hance's trading post and a saw mill. The site is occupied now by a cluster of small modern tourist cabins and the headquarters of a dude ranch. The only physical trace of Hanceville is on a gently sloping hillside where a weathered picket fence encloses a primitive cemetery, completely overgrown by juniper and other native vegetation. There are no headboards or other grave markers. There are probably other graves there without markers so long since taken over by nature they bear no visible trace.

There is, however, a plaque, erected some years ago—I don't know how long—by the Williams Lake Historical Society, bearing the names of Tom Hance and his wife. (Mrs. Irene Bliss informs me the date of deaths are as follows: Tom Hance, August 11,1910; Eleanor Hance, May 31,1935; and Judd Thomas, Mrs. Bliss' uncle, 1927.) I left this place with a feeling of sadness for the fact that so little is known about the Chilcotin Valley's famous original settlers.

Coming down the hill from the summit below Hance's woods at Lee's Corner, there is a sign erected by the highway department that says, "This is Hanceville." It stands near the old Lee Ranch, which now occupies much of the area.

# The Chilcotin "War"

Choelquoit Lake lies among the rolling parklands of the Chilcotin high country under the shadow of the Potato Mountains. Like so many others of its kind that enhance the wild grandeur of this land, it is regarded by many as one of the region's most beautiful; a turquoise jewel so clear that on calm summer days the mirrored reflection of surrounding hills and the cotton clouds above picture a landscape upside-down. Mildred and I go here often. There is a tranquillity about this place, imbued with the beauty of wild flowers, that makes one wish to linger in the quiet peacefulness of a garden.

With friends of long standing, Floyd and Ruthella Cyr, we camped one night in early fall on a grassy slope bordering the starkly white beach of Choelquoit's eastern limits, where an ancient Indian trail extends a short distance to the old sod-roofed cabin of Eagle Lake Henry and the fish smoking racks of the Indians on Chilko River. As we settled in warm sleeping bags that night and visited quietly among ourselves awaiting sleep, flocks of ducks—we thought that they were probably golden eyes—sailed in so close over our heads, the whistling of their wings was sharp to our ears. They splashed into Choelquoit's safe resting depths and were muttering peacefully as we fell asleep by the dying coals of our fire.

This had not always been a place of peace for the human race. It was here that Klatassine, the fiery war chief of the Chilcotins, came in to William Cox's vigilantes under an invited flag of truce to end the Chilcotin War in 1864. The truce was arranged by Chief Alexis who "sold out" to Cox, it is said, for British coin and a few trinkets.

The white rag of surrender on a stick that Klatassine held in his hand not only rang down the final curtain of the Chilcotin

War after two years of bloody struggle, it also signaled the death of the Homathko war chief at the end of the hangman's noose and the demise of the ill-advised Waddington wagon trail from Butte Inlet on the Strait of Georgia to the gold fields of Barkerville. Klatassine was said to be a blue-eyed Indian, whose deep-set orbs were a bewildering mixture of the ancient brown of his tribe and a strange shade of gentian that flared with puzzling fierceness when his anger was aroused. He was possibly the result of some early Coastal white man from a trader's windship or some very early Frenchman prowling the Interior and bedding down with some dusky maid long before the British took over in New Caledonia. There are no records.

Alfred Waddington was a London born Englishman turned "forty-niner" in the California gold rush. He joined the stampede to New Caledonia in 1858, as word of new gold strikes excited the civilized world. Waddington's business in San Francisco was a grocery firm known as Dulip & Waddington. It was in that year he went to Victoria, where he set up a branch which thrived on the mad gold rush to the Fraser River.

When Alfred "Old Waddy" Waddington planned to build a wagon road to the rich gold fields of the Cariboo, he was guilty of an Englishman's arrogance concerning the "lowly" Indians and the Indians' willingness to kill when abuse inflamed the primitive instinct to violence and revenge. In temper so fierce, the superstitious Native would rip a white man's heart from his chest and chew the bloody gristle to capture his enemy's strength.

This will be a brief summary of the so-called Chilcotin War, which was actually a manhunt. The Homathko Indians had become virtual slave labor of Waddington's white road crew. Firstly, Old Waddy displaced the Homathko's from their ancestral home at the mouth of the Homathko River to build headquarters for his enterprise. He was financed by a generous appropriator from the Colonial Coffers and Victoria's businessmen. The Indians were hired to do the hard work of road building, their labor to be paid in measured "powder and ball" for their old muzzle loaders. No money or food included. The white men reasoned the Indians had always lived "off the land" and fish and game and with black powder and shot furnished by Waddington, could continue in their present method of obtaining enough food to sustain their strength. Thus, the road builders would not be subjected to the indignities of hard labor.

The plan worked for a while and the Indians foraged the wilderness for food. But before long the woods ran out of a source of deer and bear. A salmon run failed one fall in Homathko River and the Indians began to hunger. They begged for food, snatching for scraps discarded by the white man. The Indians squatted on the ground with empty bellies while the white crew (most were political hacks sent up to Waddington by patronizing politicians in Victoria) dined on the best foods available and smoked their long-stemmed clay pipes.

In two years only a dent had been made in the road work. Waddington had little foresight. He soon found his Indian hand labor was inadequate for the scientific engineering the job required. As they faced the perpendicular stone walls of the canyon, every facet would require heavy blasting to make even a narrow trail up the horrendous gorge of the river before the high-level grasslands of the Chilcotin could be realized beyond the ramparts of the Niut Range at Tatlayoko Lake. Beyond Tatla Lake the road would be in MacKenzie Country and the Blackwater River Road. The last mileage to Quesnel Forks being, comparatively, much easier.

Suddenly realizing the formidable obstacles that faced him, Waddington dispatched a small crew from his camp at the mouth of the river to explore the feasibility of his substitute route. This small band of searchers climbed the high walls of the canyon, crossed the Homathko to the opposite bank and proceeded northward seeking a more tenable route, reaching a point on the Homathko where a stream known as the west branch joins the river. They mistook the branch for the main stream and followed it deeply west of the Niuts before they realized they were lost. They climbed a spur of the Niuts skirted by the west branch and from this elevation could see in the far distance the open rolling grasslands of the Chilcotin Plateau. Near starvation, the searchers returned to Waddington's camp to report their discovery.

While Waddington was in Victoria, the Homathko's finally threatened to refuse to work and the white road builder foreman made the final mistake. Small pox had all but wiped out the Coastal Indians long before Waddington's time, the dread disease killing thousands. "You work or we will bring back the small pox," the foreman said.

That was when Klatassine decided the Indians had had a bellyful of the white men's treatment, if not of food. Klatassine and his crew decided to declare war in the early dawn of April 30, 1864. They crept among the tents of the white men, slashed the tent ropes to drop heavy canvas over the sleepers and then proceeded to fire their muskets into squirming bodies, hacking with axes and stabbing with their hunting knives.

The "Chilcotin War" was on! Soon there was a manhunt for Klatassine and his followers by both federal militia and a mob of about 400 vigilantes from Barkerville's placer mines. Meanwhile, *The Colonist* in Victoria, headlined the massacre urging a policy of shoot first, to kill, and ask questions later.

In flight, Klatassine and a small group of followers climbed the shear slopes of Homathko Canyon. Pursued by the "militia" and civilians, they eventually reached Tatlayoko Lake. They waded the shallows at the south end of the lake. They climbed onto the high natural "flat" to an old trail south of Potato Mountain, emerging at Chilko Lake where they hoped to find fish. But scouting ahead, they discovered the Chilcotin ancestral fish camp occupied by the "military." They were exhausted and starving near Choelquoit Lake. There, Klatassine finally chose to surrender. Lord Lytton had sent word promising a "fair trial."

Shackled, they were taken to an old log jail at Quesnel Forks and chained to the wall. In the stench of their own filth, they squatted for weeks against the wall awaiting trial. A priest came daily to convert them, but when Lord Lytton decided they should hang, Klatassine was surely puzzled about "fair trial." "We are here as warriors, not as murderers," he insisted. When the priest told him God loved the five condemned to hang, Klatassine asked, "If God loves us, why are you killing us?"

"Hanging Judge" Matthew Baillie Begbie supervised the execution of the five condemned. An elaborate gallows was erected at Quesnel Forks and drew a large crowd of spectators, including women.

On October 26, 1864, the traps sprung and the necks of five "warriors" were snapped as the ropes vibrated. Thus ended the Chilcotin War. British justice had prevailed.

Old Waddy's hands never wore any of the blood of the conflict. It was during this time that Waddington, in his self-anointed importance, named the highest peak in the west coast of British Columbia as Mt. Waddington. Old Waddy eventually went to Ottawa, where he died from (of all things) small pox, the white man's threat of using the dread disease to enforce slave labor that had caused his downfall at the mouth of the Homathko River.

At Choelquoit Lake, the mirror of its placid surface still reflects the beauty of the mountains and the soft clouds of summer sky and, if you camp there some night as Mildred and I have in years gone by, you will still hear the whistling wings of the golden eyes splashing into the lake as dusk settles over the quiet beauty of this restful place.

# Old Dog

I want to tell you the story that I got from Old Scotty Shields about a year before he died, down in Tatlayoko Valley. This is a story of an Indian they called Old Dog. He had an Indian name, of course, but I could never pronounce it and Scotty couldn't either, because he couldn't speak like an Indian who talks from the bottom of his throat. So I'll just call him Old Dog, because it sounds pretty much like that and that'll save you from scrambling around like I do, trying to pronounce words like an Indian.

Old Dog lived over in Nemiah. Old Dog was talking about the Chilcotin War and the manhunt for Klatassine, the blue-eyed Indian who led the uprising at the mouth of the Homathko River, when Waddington was building his road up the canyon.

He told about the soldiers coming after Klatassine, who fled into the mountains in the Chilcotin and described how the Indians resisted their advance, coming up the precipice from the Bella Coola River. They met the soldiers with their only weapon, which Old Dog called the stick gun, meaning a hardwood bow with arrows.

He said, "Inj'n only have stick gun. Soj'er have chickamin gun (those old long-barrel muzzle-loaders that fired black powder and shot)." Old Dog said, "Inj'n know soj'er coming. His drum go 'pum pum pum, pum pum pum, pum pum pum' you know. So Inj'n hide in olallie bushes (berry bushes), and soj'er climb up hill where Inj'n hide. Inj'n make olallie bush move and then hide, close to ground or behind tree. Soj'er boy fire chickamin gun where he see bush move, but Inj'n not there. When soj'er shoot, Inj'n jump up, put arrow in stick gun, shoot at soj'er. Some fall down. Some not get back up again. When some soj'ers stand up, have to load gun again, have to put gun on ground beside soj'er, put more powder and shot in barrel. That when Inj'n jump up, shoot stick gun and more soj'er fall down again."

Scotty said Old Dog didn't talk much more that day about Klatassine, the war chief, but he did say descendants of some of those Indians still live in the Chilcotin hills.

# So—They Shot Ol' Charlie's Horses!
## (The Legend of Skinner Meadow)

On old, "early" maps of Chilcotin country, the mountains lying north to northeast of Choelquoit Lake are designated the Cayuse Range. Some of it is densely timbered with lodgepole pine and staggered stands of Douglas fir, but there are also areas where pine grass grows lush and wildflowers in their season give the region riotous beauty so unique as to defy description.

The name—Cayuse Range—was not chosen by the map makers with reference to the tough broncos that still roam much of the open country of the North American west. It was actually a misnomer, because the horses that inspired the name were, originally, some of the most beautiful purebred animals the Chilcotin has ever known: Clydesdales, Percherons and purebreds imported from the United States by a man with a dream.

The man was Charlie Skinner, of Seattle, in the state of Washington, who came into the high plateau region west of Fraser's River along about 1910. Charlie was a horseman by nature; he came looking for a "spread" where he could promote his longing for a horse ranch. He found what he wanted in the deep pine grass of the rolling parklands around Choelquoit—the lake that lies like a jewel in the shadows of the Potato Mountains and the Niuts—and in the sprawling flat of the wild grass and muskeg that would become known as Skinner Meadow.

The meadow itself was what interested Charlie, in particular; lying broadly at the foot of the mountain which today also bears his name, the flat is estimated to exceed 600 acres, more or less. There are areas of muskeg and peat that make much of it a bog,

217

but there is still enough usable wild hay land to winter a sizable herd of Herefords, which it does to this day.

Skinner Meadow became the heart of Charlie's dream of horse heaven and it was into this realm of wild grass he brought his basic stock of registered Clydesdales, Percherons and quarter horses, which my old friend Lou Haynes will tell you were some of the most beautiful animals the Chilcotin had ever seen. Being pedigreed, forty-odd head of breeding stock entered Canada duty free and, for a long time, Charlie Skinner was the envy of the pioneer ranchers west of the river, whose saddle stock in those days was mostly Indian-bred and "rough stuff."

Thus was born the Skinner horse ranch and Charlie's three-star brand, which would, in a few years, become the nemesis of surrounding cattle ranchers of the west Chilcotin. It was here that Charlie Skinner's dream of horse heaven became obscured by the vision of a railroad! The "old CPR Survey" was still alive, a sequel to the memory of Waddington's ill-fated wagon road and the Chilcotin War of the 1860s. The Canadian Pacific survey proposed a railroad over much of Waddington's old route from Butte Inlet to the Chilcotin Interior and Charlie Skinner became suddenly inflamed with the notion Skinner Meadow would be an ideal site for a railroad "Y," or "turn-around," for trains seeking such an accommodation in the otherwise mountainous Interior. Obsessed with visions of financial reward, Skinner's attention to his horse empire seems to have developed a lot of foot dragging. The horse herd, already expanding in the next few years, got completely out of control. By the 1920s, Charlie was paying range fees of fourteen cents per head to the Forest Service on 400 head of stock, which he admitted wore his three-star brand. But, he refused to admit his herd already exceeded that number and were then spreading far and wide beyond the Choelquoit hills and heavily depleting the available natural grasslands of the open range from Riske Creek to Chilanko Forks, to the thinning fringes west of the Klinniklinni River. James ("Scotty") Shields, one of the Chilcotin's best known old-timers who came from his native West Calder to Canada in 1920, probably knew Charlie Skinner as well as anyone in the Tatla-ko Valley. Scotty told me he really felt sorry for Skinner, but he was more sorry for Skinner's horses.

"They were beautiful animals," he said. "Those first forty or so stallions and mares he brought into the country; magnificent Clydes and Percheron and purebreds, sleek and proud, a thrill just to see them racing over the open range.

"Trouble was, Charlie got so fired up with his notions about the railroad, he lost all control of his horse herd and in a few years the result of in-breeding began to show up in the runty, scruffy-looking animals you saw everywhere. The range was soon crowded with Roman-nosed jugheads that eventually numbered an estimated 2,000 animals by about 1929 or 1930, and the once lush grasslands around Choelquoit Lake had become rolling hills of yellow dust.

"That's when the Forest Service finally stepped in and put a bounty on all unbranded horses: three dollars on every stallion and one dollar on every mare. A pair of ears would be accepted as proof of a mare destroyed; the testes of stallions drew the three dollar bounty.

"There were the usual complaints from some horse lovers when the destruction of the wild bunch was finally authorized by the Forest Service," Scotty recounted. "Naturally some people are very sensitive about such things and it's understandable. But here was a herd completely out of control and becoming an economic problem in cattle country where range was already limited. Only scantily fed in summer, by winter they were starving on a diet of tree bark and dead brush. Pawing through frozen snow in search of grass that no longer existed, they walked and staggered on bloody feet, gaunt and weak."

Scotty told me that of all the feral horses he had seen shot by bounty hunters during the three or four years "horse hunting" was at a peak in the west Chilcotin, he, himself, had never seen Charlie Skinner's three-star brand on more than four. He thought Skinner had never branded more than a few.

Horse hunters during the campaign launched by the Forest Service included young and newly married Bill Bliss of Willow Springs Ranch west of Alexis Creek, Ken Moore of Tatla-ko,

Dan Weir of Riske Creek, Eddy Ross of Redstone and Eagle Lake Henry of Mountain-House, who hunted around Quitsene (Cochin) Lake. By 1930, Scotty said, there were more "wild" horses than cattle on the open range, as far north as Chezacut and west to the Klinniklinni River.

At one time, in a sporadic attempt to confine his best stallions, Skinner had built a crude pole corral linking the east end of Choelquoit Lake with the west end of Goose Knob Lake, but it soon fell apart under the pressure of too many animals for the holding capacity it possessed. They simply knocked it down and ran away.

You talk to old-timers and you get a lot of estimates on "the kill"—and a lot of arguments. Scotty seemed to have a more impartial and somewhat sympathetic view of the massacre. He told me he thought the total was probably between two and three thousand.

Charlie Skinner became a drifter, punched cows here and there—for Duke Martin on the C-1 Ranch, and others. He lived for a time in a cabin on the shore of Quitsene Lake. In the early years of his fantastic enterprise on Skinner Meadow, he started construction of a beautiful log house, on a gentle slope overlooking the broad expanse of his once grassy empire. Frank Render, an old-time expert with the broad ax, hewed and artfully dovetailed the logs of what promised to be a mansion. Work got as far as putting up rafters when the big dream died and Charlie Skinner left the region. Hunters, indifferent to its beauty, have despoiled much of the ruin, using it for camp fires.

Scotty Shields, who had collected his eighty-fourth birthday when we visited in his snug cabin on Homathko River in August of 1986, predicted a repeat performance in the "horse problem."

"Right now," he said, "nearly all the ranchers have horse herds of twenty to forty or more. The Indians have more horses than ever. The range is again being depleted by horses that will never be saddled because everybody rides in pickups or ATVs. You're going to see history repeat itself in the grasslands of West Chilcotin."

In the way of the times in Skinner's years on the big meadow, he took a Chilcotin woman as his mate and to this union was born a daughter, who, like Charlie, became a legend in her own time. The Indians called this metis child Chee-Wit, which, in the Chilcotin tongue, means Chickadee. Mildred and I knew her briefly. I'll tell you more about Chee-Wit.

# Chee-Wit: The Phantom of the Woods

Her given name was Lilly, matis daughter of a white man and a Chilcotin mother. Her girlhood was besieged by the animosity of tribal members, whose generations of hatred for the white man was reflected in their rejection of Lilly because she was a "breed." Often deprived of the nourishment and companionship she deserved, she grew to a frail young womanhood, a virtual outcast. Her lot was not improved when she became the wife of an alcoholic, who frequently beat her unmercifully. Finally, in desperation, Lilly ran away. As she fled to the woods one day, following a severe beating, Lilly snatched a coil of her husbands snare wire from a nail in the filthy sod hut of her home and a scrap of canvas.

In outward appearance, Chee-Wit (Chilcotin word for chickadee) would be taken for a full-blooded Chilcotin. She was well named, I thought, because the calves of her legs below the hem of her ragged dress were emaciated from childhood rickets. Her only means of survival during the first winter of her escape being the length of snare wire with which she trapped rabbits. I first saw Chee-Wit in Betty Linder's kitchen in The Big House of the Graham Ranch at Tatla Lake during a severe midwinter blizzard.

It was the middle of January and the mercury in Fred Linder's porch thermometer said it was forty-six degrees below zero. It was "mail day" in Tatla. Mildred and I had managed to coax our old pickup truck through about eight inches of new powder snow the ten miles from our cabin on Little Eagle Lake to the Graham Ranch. We had come stomping out of the drift against the wide front porch of The Big House, on Betty's invitation to some good hot tea before starting homeward.

"This is my friend Chee-Wit," said Betty. We said "it's nice to meet you," or something like that, and Chee-Wit's response was no more than a slow turn of her gaze in our direction, which she immediately reversed.

A small, thin wisp of woman, she sat silent and uncommunicative, without expression that I could interpret as either pleasure or displeasure when Betty introduced us. Her thin face showed no trace of whatever emotion she felt, if any. She could have been in her early thirties, I thought, or she could have been in her fifties. Her face wore the strange stamp of unpredictable age. She sat in stony silence so close to Betty's big cookstove I wondered if she was conscious of the high heat radiating from its firebox.

We directed our conversation with Betty and Fred, hopefully to include the "little bird" sitting in near-scorching proximity to the stove. Linder, starting as usual with comments about the deep cold of mid-January, the talk and the chores of feeding the big Graham herd of Herefords from snowbound stacks of winter hay near Tatla Lake. The usual always started with weather talk.

I noted, as I could now and then without seeming to stare, that over ankle-length moosehide moccasins, encased in a pair of white man's "rubbers," Chee-Wit was wearing what appeared to be several pairs of very worn old stockings, some black, some brown, all with ragged holes as evidence of much travel through the windfall of dead "jack pine," which is notorious in our woods for its ability to ravish any legwear. Obviously there were also two or three old dresses, their cloth below knee level also ragged, and two faded woolen sweaters tightly buttoned over whatever else she wore. A dark scarf covered the black hair of her head.

I had already begun to shed my stag shirt, due to the heat of the kitchen, before I had observed these things about Chee-Wit, wondering how she could stand the kitchen heat.

Fred made tea in his usual way of being overgenerous with its strength. We had visited for perhaps half an hour when Chee-Wit, who had not spoken once, rose quietly from her chair. She walked out the door and headed into a new swirl of wind-blown snow that quickly became a curtain behind which she faded dimly for a moment and then disappeared completely.

When I asked where she was going, Betty said, "I'm not sure. Probably to a little wickiup she's made somewhere out in the bush. She comes in only once in a while, sits by the stove for a couple of hours and then leaves. It's as if she just comes in to soak up some heat and take it with her."

In time that year I learned a little more about Chee-Wit—but very little. She was a loner, living in solitary existence away from her kinfolk. Over a period of years, her small brush-covered pole shelters, usually set up tee-pee fashion, frequently had been found by hunters or ranchers rounding up cattle from the lodge-pole thickets. Quite often such shelters had shown evidence of only short occupancy and it was apparent Chee-Wit was often on the move in the vast Chilcotin wilderness. Betty thought that was probably because Chee-Wit existed primarily on the meat of rabbits—the big snowshoe hares that are excellent "eating." She was a known expert at setting snares.

It was also known, however, that Betty Linder provided her with flour, salt, bacon and other staples on occasion from the Tatla Lake General Store, which in those days was a business segment operation of Graham Ranch. In fact, meeting Betty and Fred in their pickup one winter day, I noticed a large box of staples, including bread and a slab of bacon, in the rear of their vehicle and when I asked the usual "Where you folks headin'?" Betty said, "Oh, just down the road a little to an old friend we haven't seen in quite a while. Just going for a little visit."

Just down the road a short distance near old Burnt Corral, I had noticed a slim wisp of smoke rising above the pine tops a few days back and I was pretty sure Chee-Wit was at the source of the smoke. Snow lay deep over the Chilcotin.

Betty had made a valiant effort to make Chee-Wit's life a little easier, furnishing one of the old original Graham Ranch cabins with a good bed, blankets and food, telling Chee-Wit it was all exclusively for her comfort. The cabin had a good stove and was well stocked with wood. It's old sod roof above the long ceiling of the pine log cabin was assurance of warmth in the coldest of weather. Then Betty managed to get Chee-Wit placed on welfare, which would guarantee her future sustenance, but when checks for Chee-Wit arrived in the Tatla post office, Chee-Wit was not around to put a thumb print above the signature line and the checks simply piled up in a pigeon hole of the post office. She would come to Betty's kitchen, but never to the post office. I never learned the outcome of this problem. Only Betty knew and, when she died in 1982, Chee-Wit had been long gone from the Tatla Lake area, her whereabouts as unknown locally as they had been in the years the hermit woman had roamed the endless miles of the Chilcotin hinterland. She was strictly a loner.

I recall driving west of Chilanko Forks one day when I got a fleeting glimpse of her, heading west as I was. She was in the edge of the lodgepoles bordering the heavily rutted road. I slowed down, about to offer her a lift, but on seeing Mildred and me in the pickup, she turned abruptly into the woods and disappeared.

Ross Wilson, storekeeper and cattle trucker who lived at Chilanko Forks in those days, told me one time, "You know, she thinks she's a grizzly bear."

"Where'd you get that?" I asked Ross.

"Oh, that's what an old Indian over at Redstone told me. It's something about being reborn."

Well, I was aware of the fact most Indians regard the subject of reincarnation with the dignity of their own, sincere convictions. Like the Alaska Eskimos, the soul at death is believed to be reborn in the life of an animal, and vice-versa. So maybe she was a grizzly. Old "Tsiam," the grizzly. She was little and thin, but wiry and tough. She had to have some of the qualities of a grizzly to survive as she had, against all the hardships the wild Chilcotin bestowed upon her.

I heard, in 1992, that Chee-Wit had finally left the Chilcotin. She died at the home of a sister on the Alkali Lake Reserve, where she is buried. I have always wished I had known Chee-Wit a little better.

# Jimmy Brown

One of our better known neighbors, by a distance of some forty-five miles by road and trail, who departed this life a few years ago, was an old trapper-prospector by the name of Jimmy Brown. Jimmy lived alone, "down in the hole" of the Klinniklinni River southwest of Kleenakleene. His home was a one-room log cabin among a grove of huge old-growth Douglas firs on the banks of the river.

Jimmy Brown's cabin and out-building had been built to suit his own needs. The log walls of the cabin had been put up with the butt ends of the logs on two opposite sides, all to the north, and the tops all to the south. As a result, when the walls were finished, log rafters were laid up with all the butt ends on the north wall and the cabin had a sloping shed roof. Then a doorway was cut through the north wall just to accommodate Jimmy's short stature. Somewhere, he acquired a full-sized "citified" door and hung this on the outside wall. Anyone over about 5'8" had to duck their heads to enter the cabin. The little outhouse was to one side and was a solid structure of carefully notched logs. It stood perfectly plumb. No door got in your way as you sat and relaxed, looking out to a beautiful view of the valley with high mountains on both sides. A hawk's wing hung on a string to fan yourself with on a hot day or when the flies were bad.

Jimmy cleared about an acre of ground each year to pay his taxes.

Jimmy Brown was a self-educated woodsman who had never gone to school outside of the one known as Hard Knocks. Our son, Chuck, and his friend, Dick Pearson, while hunting cougars in the big hole country where the Klinniklinni drains deep into the Coast Range, had been a guest of Jimmy's in the winter of 1954.

Chuck recounted that on their first meeting with Jimmy "down in the hole," the old-timer was met on the trail riding an aged horse that Bruce Kellogg had given him. He was sitting in a tattered saddle. At this meeting, Jimmy apologized for not getting off his horse to visit a little, saying, "I'd get off, but the saddle would fall off" (the saddle had no cinch). The next thing Jimmy said was, "Do you have anything to chew?" They found out later that Jimmy had a tobacco habit that only surfaced when he was around people. Quick as he was back home alone, he would throw his tobacco away and could go without it for weeks or months. But as soon as he encountered another human, his tobacco habit returned in just a few moments.

In the short space of a few days holed up in Jimmy's cabin while a blizzard exhausted itself among the crags that rim the valley, a lifetime of one man's struggle to read and write was revealed. An old and battered Bible, and heavily thumbed copies of Mark Twain's accounts of *The Adventure of Huckleberry Finn* and *Tom Sawyer*, were Jimmy's "school books." These, and an assortment of labels on canned goods such as Pacific Milk and Fort Gary Coffee, which are as standard equipment as a woodsman's ax in this country, were his reading materials.

In some disparate manner over a period of years "down in the hole," Jimmy Brown had acquired a sketchy ability to read by learning the phonetics of the alphabet and applying them, laboriously, by light of candle or kerosene lamp on long winter nights.

The Bible's word he trusted and respected, although he said he found it much more difficult to decipher and understand than Tom Sawyer and Huckleberry Finn, because these characters did things just like ordinary folks. In a little more than two years he had "word sounded" his way through Tom Sawyer and you knew he had read it, to hear him recount the adventures of Twain's famous characters.

"He sure was quite a boy," Jimmy would say, relating the results of his reading efforts. Jimmy could tell you everything the printed labels had to state on cans of Pacific Milk or Fort Gary Coffee. Also some other standard items, especially those where brand names were clearly obvious by the contents. When it came to writing, his letters were characteristic of the printed form, generally square-cornered and stiffly vertical.

About this same time, Jimmy told Chuck and Dick he had originally come from Montreal and he had recently decided to make a trip back home to look for any of his family that might be alive. He said that when he left home he had left behind nine brothers and sisters. His last correspondence with them had been about 1925.

Chuck and Dick had to make a trip out to Williams Lake for supplies. So, as it turned out, they were able to give Jimmy a 200 mile lift to Williams Lake to catch the train for Montreal. Chuck recalled as they passed the Indian cemetery at Redstone, Jimmy removed his hat and crossed himself.

When they left him in Williams Lake, Jimmy asked the boys to write him a letter sometime, but be sure and put it on "one of those machines," probably referring to a typewriter. "I can read readin' but I can't read writin'." To one whose schooling had been as difficult as Jimmy Brown's, this made understandable sense.

I later learned that Jimmy returned to the Chilcotin River Valley within a year. Chuck encountered him near his old home in 1959 and Jimmy expressed disappointment in his search for relatives. He related that one day in Montreal, he was inquiring about possible relatives from a hotel clerk, mentioning the names of his brothers. A man standing nearby, overhearing the conversation, stepped up and said, "I think I know of one you are looking for." The stranger arranged a meeting and Jimmy came face to face with a long-lost brother, who Jimmy said turned out to be the last living member of nine brothers and sisters. Jimmy said that beyond the handshake and introduction, "we could come up with nothing in common to talk about. And that's when I decided to come home where I could be happy again."

# The Legend of Turner

Along the south shore of One-Eye Lake in the west Chilcotin, there is a little mound—a sort of an islandlike place—that rises slightly above the level of the surrounding water and on it is an old Indian graveyard. The top of this little mound is festooned with lodgepole pine and spruce and below these trees lies a carpet of long strings of elkhorn moss and the bright red berries of kinnikinnick. It is a place of beautiful solitude. At the foot of these pines lies the grave of old Chief One-Eye, of a tribe that has long since departed from this area. And beside it, almost shoulder to shoulder, is the burial place of an American from Kansas. A fella named George Turner.

In the early years following World War I, George Turner came up from the valley of the Bella Coola River and topped out on the rim of the Chilcotin Plateau at the crest of a place called the precipice. That was at the head of an old Indian trail up from the valley. The sun was shining that day. The snow was nearly all gone and he marveled at the grass growing fresh on the vast prairie country, grasslands so extensive they seemed to fade into a blur in the far distance of the Fawnies and the Rainbows, which are foothills of the coastal sierra.

At Ike Sings' store, he dropped his big heavy backpack and made arrangements for some additional supplies. He told Ike Sing, a Canadian Oriental who ran the old log and mud roof store for many years, that he'd been trapping on the coast for the past three or four years, but tired of wet weather and wind. And he said, "If I continue to like what I see up here, I may just stay awhile."

Turner was a man probably 6'2", weighing more than 200 pounds, large shouldered, slim hipped and heavily muscled. He moved eastward on the old 300 miles of wagon trail that stretches between Williams Lake and Bella Coola, until he came to a place called Towdystan and the ranch home of the Engebritzen family (though by common use many of the old-timers called them "Englebritsen," as if the name had been spelled with an "L," which was improper). He said he was looking for work, and the Engebritzen's put him on as a ranch hand.

Fred Engebritzen, who ranched beef cattle on native grass in a stretch of wild meadow interlaced with muskeg, told me the following story of George Turner who had gone to work for Fred's folks when Fred was about six years old. Turner and an Indian were sawing and splitting wood for the ranch kitchen one day when a couple of riders came into view from the west. Fred was playing in the yard, saw Turner look and remark to the Indian, "Here they come now, and she's with him!" Turner was surprised. The riders' city clothes marked them as "Outsiders." Turner was not happy by what he saw. They rode up to Turner's chopping block and the man and Turner got into a quick argument, which obviously involved money. The woman sat silent.

Engebritzen told me that argument got so heated his father ordered his family into the cabin and, fearful there would be a shoot-out, told them to all lie on the floor, heads to the bottom log of the cabin wall as they sprawled down. Fred's father peeked cautiously from the corner of a small window.

He saw Turner yank his ax from the chopping block and step up to the man on the horse. But Turner stopped when the horseman pulled a big pistol from a holster under his jacket and told Turner, "Drop that damn ax or I'll blow your head off!"

Turner dropped the ax. The woman, who up to now had remained silent, laid a hand on her companion's gun arm, pressed it down and said, "Put that thing away before you get us all in a lot of trouble." A few moments later the couple rode away. Fred said his father later told him he believed the man on the horse was Emmet Dalton, the youngest brother in the Dalton Gang, who had attempted to rob two banks at Coffeyville, Kansas, in the late 1890s. Emmet survived a shootout with severe wounds, only to be sent to prison in San Quentin, California, where he served twenty years of a life sentence and was finally pardoned by the governor of California. The argument at the chopping block gave birth to a suspicion that would hang over Turner to his dying day. Oddly enough, nothing was ever proven.

Fred Engebritzen told me that Turner was an excellent worker; amiable, well liked. Fred said Turner could swing a heavy scythe all day in the prairie grass and never seem to tire. Evidently, he saw more of what he liked, including a pretty young Indian girl at One-Eye Lake, who was the daughter of old Chief One-Eye. The Indians called her Sitkum Memaloos. Sitkum, in Chinook, means "half"—half of anything—and memaloos has connotations meaning anywhere from "being badly crippled," to a serious sickness or even death and primarily the word means "dead."

Sitkum had only one good arm. In a fall from a horse as a young girl, she had sustained a serious injury. Her right arm was badly broken and being improperly set, reset, or not set at all, she had a crooked arm and a withered hand. She was otherwise healthy, as well as beautiful. Turner fell in love with her on sight.

Mrs. Joy Graham, a member of the old pioneer ranch family at Tatla Lake, told me of an incident which she thought described quite well the warm affection that existed between Turner and his Indian wife. She said on a hunting trip one time without horses, they came to a mountain stream that was a torrent of white-water and they needed to ford it to get where they wanted to go. Sitkum was a little timid about wading in because she was a slight build and Turner, the big fellow, hoisted her up under one arm and waded into the stream. Out in the middle, with water boiling around his knees, he laughingly threatened to set her down and she screamed in fright. So, he held her up and kissed her and waded on across, setting her down on the other side, where he hugged and kissed her again and they went on into the woods. It seems to me that was a rather significant demonstration of affection.

Turner worked on at the Engebritzen ranch for several years and in time became rather famous among hunters as an expert guide and woodsman. I think a lot of his popularity was due to Sitkum. As a native-born Chilcotin, she had inherited a gift of knowledge in the ways of wild animals and their habitat and where their nourishment was seasonal, and she often led the packstrings of the hunting party.

The story goes that one day at Towdystan, as they were about to leave with a party of hunters and several pack-horses, a young colt belonging to the bell mare broke from its holding pen and rushed up to the mare's side, causing some commotion. One of the hunters said, "Get that little rascal out of here because it'll cause us nothing but trouble."

Mrs. Engebritzen obtained a halter and a lead rope and retrieved the colt and as she led it back to the holding pen, she asked, "What should I call this little fellow?" At that time, Turner stood up in the stirrups of his saddle, turned around and called to Mrs. Engebritzen, "Call it Doolin. That's a good name for a little outlaw."

As she led the colt back to its holding pen, she said something about "Doolin. What a strange name for such a pretty little animal. I never heard that name before." The party rode off.

Fred said his father knew something of western American history and he recognized the name of Doolin as that of a Kansas outlaw. At this point, it seems essential to drop down to Coffeyville, Kansas, for a minute or two, because it's important to the story.

Doolin was a notorious gunman who rode frequently with the Dalton Gang—Grat, Emmet and Bob—on some of their forays of robbery. Doolin was perhaps the most notorious of the western bandits of the time; it's said he had twenty notches on the butt of his pistol, one for every man he had killed in his lifetime and was said to have killed his first when he was only ten years old. It was claimed that he would often, when drunk, brag that he'd never killed a man who didn't deserve it. Doolin, riding with the Daltons, had planned to rob the two town banks in Coffeyville, which stood opposite each other on the one main street of the town.

The story goes that a day out of Coffeyville Doolin's horse went lame and he stopped to remove a rock from a foot of the animal. The stone had become stuck on the frog of the foot between the corks of the sharp shod shoe. The horse had been limping for some time. Doolin told the Dalton's they'd have to go on alone, saying he'd be a sitting duck if they got into trouble in Coffeyville and he tried to get away on a lame horse, to which they all agreed. Doolin turned back toward the hills of Oklahoma where he was born.

The story of Coffeyville and the attempted robbery of the two banks by the Dalton Gang is too well known to warrant much elaboration in this story, but it is essential to recall that as they entered the town at about 8:30 in the morning, they found both banks closed with signs on the doors saying they would open at 9:00.

So they stood around waiting for the banks to open, their horses in the middle of the street. For some reason, at about a quarter to nine both banks opened. So Bob, Grat and Emmet and another gangster headed to one of the banks and the rest of the gang, which had split up, went to the bank on the opposite side of the street.

In the bank the Dalton's had entered was a lone teller who was sweeping up. The Dalton's weren't interested in the petty cash in the boxes in the teller's cages and they ordered him to open the vault. The teller protested, saying he couldn't because it had a time-lock on it and the only one who could open it without waiting for the time-lock was the president of the bank and he hadn't arrived yet.

One of the gangsters riding with the Dalton's had been drinking heavily and, holding a pistol at the teller's head, in a state of nervousness, squeezed the trigger and the shot killed the teller. The roar of his gun was heard in the street. Someone yelled, "They're robbin' the bank." Someone else yelled there were robbers in both banks. The townsmen immediately went for their guns.

The Dalton Gang tried to escape through the rear doors of the bank and found them bolted. Their only chance was back into the street for their horses. When they ran from the bank, they met a fusillade of gunfire. Eight died that day, including four townsmen. The only survivor of the Daltons was their younger brother

Emmet who fell, severely wounded, trying to reach his horse. Little more could be said about Doolin, who had gone back before the robbery took place. Doolin eventually met his fate in a mining camp called "Colorado City."

The Pinkertons were hot after him for some of his many crimes, when he came face to face with a deputy marshall who confronted him. Doolin, who had been drinking, had aged somewhat and his reflexes had slowed. His gun had hardly left the holster when the marshall's weapon put a bullet through his heart. Doolin died with his boots on—fancy Mexican boots with silver spurs.

Back in the Chilcotin, George Turner continued to work for the Engebritzens. He and his wife were living in a little cabin on McClinchy Creek.

It was the winter of 1955, from what I was told—Grace Kellogg said it was near Christmas-time—and there was about a foot of snow on the ground and it was near fifty degrees below zero. Turner had been ailing; in time he passed away. At his bedside was his son-in-law, Baptiste Dester. Before he died, Turner obtained a promise from Dester that he'd be buried beside his old father-in-law, Chief One-Eye, on that little mound by One-Eye Lake.

With the help of Tex Hanson, a guide and trapper from Clear Water Lake, some pine boards were obtained and a box built for a coffin. While at the gravesite on the little mound at One-Eye Lake, Tom Chignell and some Indians and other friends kept a fire going for three days, Mrs. Kellogg remembered, in order to sufficiently thaw the ground to dig a grave. They would keep a hot fire going for several hours and then push it aside and scrape away an inch or two of thawed out sod, and then return the fire. She said it was a slow and hard job, but they finally got it dug. On a toboggan they put the pine board box containing Turner and hauled it about a mile and a half through the snow to One-Eye Lake.

When Turner was finally lowered into his last resting place, Baptiste read from a tattered Bible he carried in his shirt pocket. He said a prayer and it is recalled that as the still hot earth was shoveled back over the coffin, the heat met the frigid cold of the mid-winter air and caused the vapor to rise above it into the limbs of the pines.

I have purposely omitted from this story the names of several of the off-spring from the union of Turner and Sitkum, because some of them are still in the area of the Chilcotin, especially around Williams Lake, and they are respected and very fine people, well liked by everyone. They are naturally sensitive about the rumor that hung over Turner for so many years.

Most everyone around the old Tatla Lake area who remembered Turner would tell you he was well liked, good-natured, never quarrelsome (with the exception perhaps of that one incident at Towdystan the day he confronted the two people on horses).

I need to recall for you a little something about Towdystan, because in the early days in the territory before white settlers came to populate the grasslands of the high country, Towdystan had been a place of rendezvous between the Indians and the fur traders of Hudson's Bay and others. Towdystan, Fred Engebritzen told me, is a Chilcotin name by which the location still goes and it means "whiskey" or liquor of any kind. The traders came in early spring or sometime after breakup to pick up the winter catch of the Indians.

The traders are known to have covered a lot of their trading with the potency of hard liquor and they brought diluted whiskey and wines, which would get many of the Indians uproariously drunk. These orgies sometimes lasted for a couple of days before the trading began and, when the trading did start, valuable furs were bought for pennies. Big copper pennies of the empire, the size of an American two-bit piece and little cheap mirrors, which the squaws loved in particular.

When the traders left with their rich bounty, the Indians remained with hangovers and bloody heads from fighting and a few copper pennies which they prized as the chickimen money of the white man, because it was soft and easily worked and made beautiful nose and ear rings.

The old rendezvous site is a place of quiet now and those wild orgies are a thing of the past.

235

# Memaloos

Explorers and scientists believe that in an ancient time Asiatics from the north polar regions of Siberia probably walked across the fabled land bridge believed to have spanned the fifty-eight mile distance between Siberia's east cape and that portion of the North American continent we now know as Alaska. They brought with them cultures and beliefs as old as civilization. These cultures, including spiritual, are believed to have influenced other peoples of the American north polar regions, including the Eskimo, who may or may not have been occupants of the American north polar regions even before the arrival of the Asiatics. Little is known beyond the evidence discovered in fossil remains.

In the Eskimo language it is said there is no word for murder and in their religion there is a similarity of beliefs of the North American Indians in the spirit world. From the far north to the Southern Hemisphere, there are many features of tribal spiritual beliefs that appeared to be similar, probably through centuries of inter-relations.

In this documentary evidence, the Eskimo believes there is both moral and spiritual justification for assisting aged and disabled Eskimos in committing themselves to death. The very aged, sometimes having reached a state of complete failure in the normal functions of the body, are known to request what they believe to be the blessings of death. In this, they are assisted onto the polar ice where they say their good-byes and are left to die. In the extreme cold of the Arctic, the old person soon becomes the victim of what we call hypothermia and deep sleep, followed by death. Like the Indian, the Eskimo also believes that in death there is a happy future in the spirit world.

When Mildred and I first went into the Chilcotin region more that fifty years ago, we heard the legend of memaloos (mem'-o-loos). Memaloos is a Chinook word meaning "to kill" or "death." Like other words in the jargon, it has many connotations, including any crippling injury that threatens death or a severe physical injury that impairs complete physical perfection, such as crippling arms and legs. There is a common term or sort of nickname for such a person known as Sitkum Memaloos or "half dead." Sitkum is a Chinook word for half.

We learned of different people called Sitkum Memaloos in the far west Chilcotin during our years in the remote wilderness of Eagle Lake.

It was at about this time I learned of the alleged custom among Chilcotin Indians living in remote areas of the high plateau of putting to death weak or deformed newborn babies. This alleged practice, I was told, was more a result of starvation or undernourishment, and the lack of nutrition was for many years common. For more than 100 years, the Chilcotin had been virtually trapped out of its wildlife in the wake of the great harvest of the fur trade and in this land where winter is frequently more than seven months of snow and extreme cold, starvation haunted the winter camps of these nomadic people. It is said that even the younger women lacked breast milk to nourish newborn babies, probably because their main diet was seldom more than shreds of smoked jerky or dried fish and roots, if they had been lucky enough to lay in a supply before freezeup. For many years before the advent of welfare, medical clinics and other benefits now enjoyed, the Indians had no knowledge of so-called family practice, including birth control, and babies arrived year-round as a matter of accepted nature.

It is said many of these babies were immediately disposed of by their mothers or others in the tribe as a simple matter of tribal survival.

From a Native-born farm wife of a white rancher in Tatla-ko Valley, I was told of an incident during her childhood which she referred to as memaloos. She told me of a Chilcotin woman who had come to the ranch house to bargain for food. She was accompanied by a small boy about four years of age, a lone survivor of

237

twins. The child possessed an unbound curiosity about the strangest things he saw in the ranch kitchen and was repeatedly scolded by his mother for examining everything that he could get his fingers on. Finally, my friend told me the mother made a move to chastise her son, but as she rose from her chair the little fellow made a face, laughing at her, and ran out the door. Returning from a futile attempt to catch her mischievous son, the mother turned back to the kitchen declaring, "By Damn, you know Miz'—I think so maybe I kill wrong kid."

And now I will tell you the story of little Gloria, the victim of an alleged attempt at memaloos in which we had a personal experience.

"Mother" Evelyn Wilson and her son Ross' young family ran the trading post at Chilanko Forks. One night in early November when this story has its inception, the high country was already facing freezeup and the earth hardening for the long winter.

It was closing time at the trading post. She had put a chunk of pine in the big wood heater to hold the fire against the growing cold. She was turning down the lamps when the pounding of boot heels and the music of spurs said there was a late horseman at the door. She called, "Come in." A tall young Indian entered, his moosehide chaps already stiff and crackling as he walked.

He said, "Miz' Wilson, I'm just come by camp people, little way old trail this place. I see light and smoke from chimney. People inside I hear talk and laugh—I think this good place I stop for night, tie my horse to tree. But ol' Kuitan not like where tie him up, blow hard, snort, yank back on halter rope, hold head down, not like smell. So, I look down to see what make ol' Kuitan jerk on rope. It's some old rags, on ground at foot of tree. I see baby in old rags moving, that scare my horse. I tell baby not cry, I go quick for Miz' Wilson."

"Miz' Wilson, this Nazko In'jun no want trouble in Redstone. I think more better you go get baby quick. She be memaloos by morning."

Mother Wilson said, "Put your horse in the corral and feed it." Putting the coffee pot on the heater and a mug on the table as she gathered up a heavy shawl and woollen blanket, she said, "Stay here and I'll give you a good dinner."

She was out the door. In a matter of minutes she was back, the infant in her arms. In the morning, Mother Wilson took the waif to the nurses in the old log hospital at Alexis Creek. When she returned, she had with her a constable of the Royal Canadian Mounted Police and documents prepared by a Justice of the Peace, providing for custody of the baby as a foster mother. In the presence of a Mountie, who witnessed the documents, the infant became a foster child. The parents willingly signed their release. Mildred and I knew her as Little Gloria.

We went south that winter to spend Christmas with family and friends below the border, returning some weeks later, in time for the annual festival in the Tatla Lake Community Hall. We were sitting on benches enjoying the program when I felt tapping on my back. It was Little Gloria, happily snuggled up to Mother Wilson as we turned to hug her.

The nurses at Alexis Creek had found Little Gloria to be suffering rickets in an advanced state of malnutrition. She was already sitkum memaloos when rescued by Mother Wilson and from that you can draw your own conclusions.

The provincial and federal governments have been beneficial. Many Indians now live on reserves, such as at Redstone, Alkali Lake, Alexis Creek (Anaham) and others. Some still live in sod-roofed cabins in the "outback" and no longer in the old "pit houses" (keekwillees). Some have become expert log house builders. The starvation the Indians once faced is no longer a threat to their future. You seldom if ever hear the story of memaloos anymore.

But these facts are the product of government bureaucracy and the pressures of white civilization, particularly the priesthood, which has closer contact with the Indians living on crowded reserves. It is said, however, that in the vast outback of this big wilderness country, far from settlement, when old Manitou blows his cruel midwinter winds down from the Arctic regions, the practice still prevails. In the distant outback where old sod houses are still occupied, death during the subzero months of winter ignores the white man's ways. Here, it is said, the ancient customs (which are as old as the pit houses of Kispiox and the keekwillees of the high plateau) are observed.

From a bundle of digging sticks tied to a rafter pole, a short shaft is withdrawn and with this primitive tool a pit is dug in the sunken earth floor of the isolated home which yields readily to the thrusts of an old grandmother or the child's mother herself, if she is physically able. Many of these floors of the old homes were originally dug down well below the level of the frost line, the surplus earth from the excavations being used for insulation of the walls and roof. It is said that in the little pit, the body of the child is laid in the soft fold of smoke-tanned buckskin over which the earth is returned.

Following burial, the rhythmic flat-toned thumping of a raw-hide drum may be heard above the singing of the family, as a rejoicing prayer to Mama Tomanowis, the spiritual maternal God and protector of The People.

# Secret of the Pines

The first time I heard the faint wailing I thought it must be a coyote pup. They make a sort of pitiful little noise when they first come from their den. Next day I heard it again. The wailing seemed to be coming from a grassy knoll where we had seen sharptail grouse dancing in early spring. This knoll was close to three sizable ponds at the western outlet of Little Eagle, then a beautiful reedy habitat alive with mallards and shore birds. Now the ponds are gone, dried up as the result of low water in the lake, to become one big grassy meadow in a few short years.

Taking my binoculars and a Winchester, I walked in the direction of the ponds and eventually came into view of an old and very ragged yellow umbrella tent where there were two young people sitting by an open cook fire. The woman was holding a very small baby in her arms and the child's face was red from crying. An old homemade packboard was so laced and equipped with willow bows I recognized it had been used as a "carry" for the infant, papoose style. There was not much evidence of a grub supply, but on the fire a kettle was boiling.

To open a conversation to disguise my curiosity I smiled at them and said, "What's for dinner today?" The girl returned my smile and I felt better. "Cattail roots," she said. "They're real good, too." Well, I knew the Indians ate them, so it was easy to get acquainted with these people and I learned they were from Buffalo, New York State. They were Mark and Christine Gillman. College educated. Victims of the asphalt jungles of the big cities. They had come west, looking "for a better way of life." The baby was Otis, six weeks old and not looking very healthy.

They had come to Chilcotin in an aged, beat-up stationwagon, at the moment parked in the brush off the old Tatla-ko Road about a mile from their camp.

241

"We had an old boat we lived on, on the Coast," she said. "But the boat was no good and we let it go and just lived on the beach for a while." I envisioned them digging clams, living on the bounty of the sea. I know all about the clams and crabs of the Puget Sound country and when she said, finally, "It rained and the wind blew so much we gave it up and came to this country," I knew about that too. Both Mildred and I had grown up on the coast of Washington State, where it rains a lot.

At Big Creek in the Chilcotin, Christine had gotten a job as a fill-in school teacher. Most of the kids were Indians and the new teacher soon became acquainted with some of their kinfolk, which has a lot to do with this story. An aged squaw tutored both Mark and Christine in the use of the edible foods of the Plateau country, including cattail roots. The Gillmans thus became somewhat obsessed with the idea they could live off the land, or almost, anyway. And here they were boiling up a cattail dinner the day I got acquainted with them. They were the first newcomers we had seen on Little Eagle since 1954.

In time the Gillmans took up a small patch of Crown Land about two miles up-lake from our cabin. Mark was no woodsman but he sure was a willing pilgrim. We showed him how we had solved our own cabin building problem by cutting spruce logs in eight-foot lengths, ripping flat sides on them and standing them on end for house walls, stockade style. Easier for two people to handle that way. So Mark and Christine built their cabin of small poles cut from a dense stand of lodgepole pines. It had only a door, open when light was needed; a dirt floor. No window for the time being. It had a flat roof of poles overlaid with tar paper backpacked from the general store in Tatla, twelve miles away. Mark had a 7-mm Mauser and soon moose meat added much to their diet. In time, Christine acquired a good hand grinder and Mark backpacked in several seventy-pound sacks of wheat that became the basic source of their sustenance during their first winter on Little Eagle. From then on it was moose meat, grouse or rabbits, whole wheat bread, cattail roots, some herbs and other wild forage from the woods and fish, including squaw fish, which they smoked. They had learned from the Chilcotins how to live like Indians. We seldom saw them during the winter, did not visit much, but they were good people. Mark helped us put some windows in our own cabin and he was a good and willing worker. I think the thing Mildred and I appreciated most was the fact they were true conservationists with a deep appreciation of the wilderness. That, also, they had learned from the Indians. Some good books lay on a rough shelf in the little cabin, which they had been smart enough to build small and tightly chinked to withstand winter cold known to go beyond sixty below zero in this region.

One day in early April—Otis was now about seven months old—an early breakup came on the heels of a sudden warming sun that started the ice on Little Eagle to wail, groan and rumble the message that winter was passing. Snow that had lain among the pines since December disappeared. Geese arrived to quarrel over spots of open water around the islands. Bald eagles were overhead daily searching for squaw fish in the shallows where the ice had thawed, crows following them closely for a chance to snatch from the eagles as they fed. The woods were alive with the chatter of squirrels. When the sun warmed the earth you could smell the pungence of spring. It was on such a day the Gillmans decided to go for a bit of exploring. In their old station wagon, parked in the road a full two miles from their cabin, they drove to Tatla, got a tank of gas and a sack of apples. Planning to be gone only a few hours, they made no other provisions and headed for the Bidwell Lakes, exuberant in the start of a hastily planned one-day outing.

The Bidwells lie in a remote pocket of the Cayuse Range. They could be approached by a fair road branching from the old Tatla-ko road for a distance of about sixteen miles to the east, somewhat beyond Choelquoit Lake. The final stretch at that time was just a dim wagon trail worn into the wilderness by the Indians many, many years ago. No fit road for an automobile, by any stretch of imagination. But it was a beautiful sunny day and the Gillmans were confident they could drive to the Bidwells for a picnic. As a result, they got stuck in a mud hole that let their old station wagon settle until only the body remained above the suddenly thawed surface of the trail. They were about thirty miles from home.

Mark and Christine struggled for most of the remainder of the day to free their aged vehicle from the gumbo in which it had settled. They ate a couple of their apples and Christine nursed Otis, who cried a lot. That night the little family huddled around an open fire as the Chilcotin weather lived up to its reputation for quick change and the mercury dropped below freezing. At daylight, Mark resumed his efforts to free the vehicle from the mud, but the old shovel they carried was no match for the gumbo. Finally, the Gillmans realized their only option was to start walking and that was also when they made the mistake that has so often been made in a spirit of desperation by people inexperienced in mountain travel: they decided to take what they thought was a short-cut across the summit of the Cayuse Range to reach their cabin on Little Eagle.

On the highest point in the range there is a sort of bald spot. Here, a microwave telephone tower had recently been flown in by helicopter and was visible on clear days from Little Eagle as well as from where the Gillmans were stuck. Using the tower as a landmark they started up the long eastern slopes of the range, Mark carrying the shovel, Christine carrying Otis in a shawl slung under one arm. Bright sun soon replaced the chill of the night. The "going" was good, through some small open grassy glades that lend a parklike character to the lower slopes of the mountains. It was quite easy, at first, to keep the tower in sight. But as the Gillmans climbed, the weather began to change. Storm clouds moved over the range and soon the tower was no longer visible.

They were smart enough to know that if they continued to climb ever upward, persistence would bring them to the tower. Above the park-like meadows now, they entered the maze of an old burn, where "jack pine" killed by fire in a distant past lay criss-crossed in a wild tangle of dead, bleached poles and limbs. Here their climb became a struggle. Mark used the shovel to some advantage as a climbing aid, but Christine began to suffer agony in both her feet. Her footwear was a pair of badly worn tennis shoes from which the toe cloth gave way as she climbed through the fire-killed pines and underbrush. Within two hours of the start, crawling through the jackstraw jumble of dead pines with the burden of little Otis slung under one arm, Christine's bleeding toes finally forced a halt. They rested while she ripped up a small strip from her shawl and stuffed pieces of cloth into the holes of her tennis shoes.

They were still in the tangle of the "blowdown" hours later as darkening skies warned of an early nightfall. They cleared a spot and Mark built a fire. They ate two apples and had only two left. No other food. Christine nursed Otis and he cried a lot. In a state of misery and near exhaustion, they sat through the night huddled to a fire that demanded a continual feeding of dead pine poles as the temperature fell. A dull, cloudy dawn found them reluctant to leave their fire.

Moving again upward, hopeful of being able to locate the micro tower, the awareness of a growing hunger began to haunt their minds. The sky blackened, Christine's face felt the first vagrant flakes of snow that within minutes became a white curtain through which the blowdown "jack pines" were only a confusing blur.

Christine remembered their struggle here, she told me later, as a time in her young life when she realized she was facing the possibility of death. Late on their second day on the mountain, by pressing ever upward regardless of the obstacles of snow and dead timber, they came suddenly into view of the tower at an elevation of about 6,000 feet. The skies momentarily cleared and a panorama of snow mantled hills lay below them, the irregular dark body of Little Eagle lying crookedly in the distance. Seeing it from the summit of the range, it in no way resembled the image of the lake they were familiar with and they both mistook it for Puntzi Lake, which in fact lay far to the northeast from where they studied the lay of the wilderness. They were exhausted, cold, wet and hungry. Seeking a sunny spot in meager timber below the summit, they built a fire and rested, Christine more weary than Mark from carrying little Otis, her bleeding feet a constant agony. Despair grew as the cold hours passed from daylight to dusk to full dark for a third hungry night on the mountain.

It was here on the snowy north slope of the Cayuse Range, unknown miles from their cabin on Little Eagle, that Christine suddenly remembered the teachings of the aged squaw at Big Creek: the inner red skin of the bark of lodgepole pine contains a natural sugar. The Indians have long known this fact, which the squaw had imparted to the young woman from New York in one of their many friendly conversations when Christine was teaching school at Big Creek.

She grabbed Mark's shovel and began whacking at the bark of a young lodgepole pine. Stripping the sappy red inner layer from the tree bark, she pushed a wad into her mouth, began chewing and passed the shovel back to Mark. Mark was soon following his wife's example. Months later, when I talked to her about their hours of desperation, she told me the nourishment she received from the pine sap was miraculously fast. A squall from baby Otis, whose almost constant crying bespoke the fact the infant was starving, was silenced when Christine chewed up another wad of lodgepole bark and transferred the lifesaving juice from her own mouth to the mouth of the baby.

When Christine told me this story, I recalled the fact that when Mildred and I came to the Chilcotin in 1954, we had discovered, and were puzzled by, pine trees around Little Eagle where the Indians had cut away the outer bark, causing the pines to bleed. We learned in time this was where the Indians had obtained their "Spring Tonic." It was an ancient custom, best known to the Chilcotins of the high plateau.

Mark kept a good warming fire going their last night on the mountain. The miracle of pine sap renewed their strength and the truth of the old Indian remedy was manifest by the fact that little Otis stopped crying and slept for hours with only an occasional whimper.

Dawn of the fourth day came clear with bright sunshine. Breakfast was a mouthful of pine sap washed down with snow water. Still unsure of their position, they concluded to head for the east end of the lake that lay below them. The "going" was most difficult for Christine, whose cloth shoes were by now little more than tattered bloody rags on her feet. They walked, crawled, fell through old blowdowns; rested and chewed on the sappy inner bark of the pines. Christine fed Otis at what she guessed were approximately one hour intervals, mouth-to-mouth, like a mother bird feeding a nestling. They came into a region of dense timber as their elevation lowered and by dusk staggered suddenly into full view of a small cabin at the east end of the lake they had first viewed from the summit. This was the small shelter the enlisted men from the new radar base on Puntzi Mountain had built a few years before the Gillmans came to the country. It was usually referred to as a search and rescue base, or emergency cabin, by the airmen who built it. The Gillmans only then realized they were, in fact, at the northeast end of Eagle Lake and by good fortune had found shelter, an iron barrel stove, dry wood and bunks to rest in. They had heard of the shelter from the Indians and by that information knew their own cabin lay to the west, probably not more than five or six miles distant on the northerly shore of the lake.

The realization that they were actually at the easterly end of Little Eagle Lake and that "home and food" was not more than a half day travel through the trackless wilderness, gave them a renewed vigor. On the morning of the fourth day, they ate vigorously of pine sap, feeding Otis mouth-to-mouth as they had on the cruel slopes of the Cayuse Range and started on the final lap of the hunger march. There was no snow at the lake level. Christine had found an old woollen shirt in the cabin with which she fashioned some wrap-around protection for her feet and quickly discovered the wool made walking easier.

She told me, when we discussed their experience long after it had become a memory, they reached their cabin in about four hours, a weary, travel-worn family that might never have left the cold north slopes of the Cayuse Range had it not been for the teachings of an aged Chilcotin squaw and the miracle of life flowing in the sap of the lodgepole pines.

# Russell Fence and Case Tractor

During the late 1950s, I was visiting one day with an old friend, a pioneer of Tatla-ko Valley, Harry Haynes. I found him sitting in the shade of his cabin, down in Tatla-ko Valley and on his lap lay a double-bitted ax which he was whetting and honing with a ten inch mill file.

As I walked up Harry said to me, "Gotta repair my Russell fence. A bull moose went through it. You know, that fence was built by my father more than forty years ago and it is just about as good as ever." His remarks stirred my imagination a little bit and as the days went by I determined to research the so-called Russell fence because I had heard somewhere, I think it was from Harry, that at one time a man named Russell had patented this fence.

In my efforts to find the facts, I contacted two old friends, Doug and Karen Smith, who live on what is known as The Big Rock Ranch on Buffalo Creek, near 100 Mile House. Doug pulled out some old magazines and in one we came across an article that he knew about which inferred at least, without any positive review of facts, that a man named Russell, whose name was originally spelled Ruscle and in later years, Russell, had actually patented the so-called Russell fence. When I first went into the Chilcotin country in the 1930s, there were already miles upon miles of this fence, some of them so evolved that they would fade into a dark line over distant hills of the grasslands.

Some of them were very old, like the one at the Bill Bliss Ranch at Willow Springs, near Alexis Creek. That one was already more than eighty years old and sagging with age. Whether this man Russell actually patented the fence is still moot in the Chilcotin country, but if he did I have been unable to find any positive record that he ever collected a royalty from anyone. Harry told me that all you needed was a sharp ax and some nice pine poles and pliers to build a good Russell fence. They are quite simple.

In the articles that I read it was told rather technically that the original patent required these Russell fences, where the little poles that resembled tepees, be dug into the ground. I never found one actually dug into the ground. That is, most of them are simply set up like an old Indian woman would set up the poles of the tepee. There'd be generally three or four poles to a set and the popular distance between these little tepees was about ten to sixteen feet, with some stretched out to as much as twenty feet, depending on the size and strength of the cross-poles between them. With old haywire, which seemed to be plentiful in the country in the early days, poles were suspended cross-wise between these tepees on wire loops that hung down from the apex of the poles. It was quite simple. If you wanted to go through, as there were no gates, you simply had to lift the cross-poles out of the loops in the wire, lay them aside and pass through. If you were a gentleman, you always put them back.

Harry told me that no fence had ever been built in the Chilcotin that would stop a moose if he wanted to go through. He simply walked up, would bang into these cross-poles and go through. The same, I found, was also true of snake rail fences, built with heavier pine poles, and barbed wire fences which came into the country later. I remember one time near Alexis Creek seeing a big bull moose go through a barbed wire fence—he simply walked through it—depending on his own power and weight, and the wire snapped like fiddle strings.

There have been many changes and innovations in fences in the Chilcotin. In recent years the highway department demanded fences be included on ranchland where it bordered Highway 20, that long 300-mile stretch between Williams Lake and Anahim Lake in the west Chilcotin. Barbed wire and woven wire had replaced some of the old Russell fences and in more recent years, power-operated post hole diggers would punch holes in that hardpan soil and vertical poles would be set, hung with wire. There has always been an argument between the scattered ranchers of the country as to who should withstand the expense of some of those range fences, but in some cases the ranchers built them themselves without financial assistance.

I think the so-called Russell fence is destined to remain popular in the Chilcotin as the least expensive of all as long as there's a patch of slender lodgepole pine that is handy and the rancher still has a sharp ax.

At Redstone Reserve I took a picture of the fence a year ago, built by an Indian who is evidently proud of his ability and proud of his product. He had taken a modern chain saw and sawed off the useless tops of the poles that made the little tepee holding the cross-rails and the fence had a very neat appearance. There was about half a mile of it and, in my own mind, I envisioned that he probably saved those short pieces that he sawed from the tops, which would give his wife a good supply of stove wood during the coming winter.

Most of the old Russell fences were made with no other tool than an ax. Old haywire, which used to be found around the doors of old barns, has become scarce now that hay is rolled into big bundles with huge machines and has been replaced by what is called "fence wire," which is of a heavier gauge.

There were two kinds of fence wire on the market—a heavier gauge to hold the poles horizontally in their loops and a lighter wire to bind the tepees together at their tops. The center wires under the apex of these little tepees would be almost vertical with a series of loops, one below the other. Generally most Russell fences you will find carry four poles or cross-poles, occasionally there will be five.

If a man had sheep in his pasture, like old Tom Chignell out near Kleenakleene River on the big ranch known to old-timers as the Halfway House, smaller poles were hung close together nearer to the ground, which kept his sheep restrained.

Pine poles were available and sometimes spruce, which is also plentiful in some areas. They were used where there was a horse ranch or other livestock that needs to be held closely together.

Near Quesnel in 1944, I saw a fence built of spruce poles that were probably a foot or better in diameter and about thirty feet long. This type of fence I saw in a few other places in the country during recent years and they stretched horizontally, sometimes only three poles high between short pieces of cross-logs. The bottom one would be set on a rock to give the bottom pole a little elevation above the ground and make it unnecessary to use more than three poles. It'd be more than high enough to hold livestock. The old so-called zig-zag fences are still very popular. Some called them snake fences. Out near One-Eye Lake in recent times, a rancher devised a new style that I had not seen before. This fence is build of heavy pine. It is five rails high and, instead of being like a snake fence, built in zig-zags, the corners are squared at right angles to each other. Looking down a long line of that fence, it looked like a series of boxes with one side knocked out. The rancher told me he thought he got more mileage out of his fence poles that way, but I have never been able to figure out his reasoning.

Near Anahim Lake, one of the oldest pole fences in British Columbia has stood for over nearly a century. It is not exactly a Russell fence, except for the fact it has what you might call uprights or risers and the poles long and slim, some of them more than twenty feet in length, have their butt ends on the ground and their slender tops angling upward to the next step at about forty-five degrees. They are tightly spaced together and they are so densely placed it is difficult to see through them to observe clearly what is on the other side. I am told there is a fence like that farther north, somewhere near Quesnel, but I have never seen it.

Back in the year of 1912 or shortly thereafter, when Bob Graham of the pioneer Graham Ranch at Tatla Lake had pre-empted the old Martin Ranch, he bought what was probably the first steam tractor that was ever seen in the country. It was a Case, an iron monster weighing several tons, which Betty Graham Linder, his daughter, told me was shipped from England in the hold of a freighter. It came overland by railroad to the West Coast, up from California to Seattle, and from Seattle to Vancouver, British Columbia, on a freight train, ultimately to be unloaded at Ashcroft on the Thompson River. It was more than 200 miles from the Graham Ranch. Bob Graham went down to Ashcroft to get his new machine, which had arrived on a flat car. He unloaded it and started on the long trip home towing a trailer with a tank full of water and a pile of wood for fuel to keep the steam alive.

He crashed into the Gang Ranch country near Canoe Creek, on the only bridge that existed at that time, a small wooden affair. But en route back in the direction of Hanceville, something got broken on the machine—Betty could not recall exactly what it was—but it stalled Bob Graham's efforts to get it home, so he parked it and began to walk. He walked from Gang Ranch to Hanceville and caught a ride from some rancher back to Tatla, wrote to England for a part needed to repair the machine and spent a long winter waiting for its arrival.

The next spring, Graham went back to pick up his tractor and continued the slow march home, which took about another two weeks. The tractor was used to operate a saw mill, finishing the lumber from the trees on Tatla Mountain, with which what's known as the Graham Big House was built. Also, the lumber for a large repair shop where the ranch equipment was maintained.

In later years, when Mildred and I lived at Little Eagle Lake, this old tractor sat in the basement of the shop near the Big House and was used to heat water for the ranch house and at times to operate a generator for lights. That was long before B.C. Hydro put its power line into the Chilcotin Valley.

The old tractor sat for a long time after it became idle and after the Grahams had left the country by death. Joy Graham, who had been the wife of Bill, sold it to a collector in Williams Lake and the last I heard the old Case had become a museum piece.

# Panic in the Bush

The story was told in the plunging tracks his feet had left in the snow. It was told in the feeble evidence of small fires he had attempted to build, as a shield against the subzero cold. It was told in the blisters on his hands, where he had fought the stiff dead limbs of a tree he had clung to, circling its trunk in a final wild attempt to survive the freezing hours of night.

A small fistful of crumpled currency, part charred where he had made his last attempt at starting a fire, lay strangely mute as evidence of his final moments of panic. Had there been a light in the old Newton Ranch house he could have seen it from where he died. But the folks had not returned from the dance at Alexis Creek that dark and freezing night and, not being able to see the cabin, he fell exhausted in the snow and died. He was less than 300 yards from the ranch house door.

This was Jack Wemus Charters, a thirty-eight-year-old retired Captain of the Imperial Army Reserve, who Jack Bliss found dead the morning of November 26, 1948. It was ten degrees below zero. Medical science would say Charters died as the result of exposure. That was the coroner's verdict. Old-timers in the Chilcotin, like Jack Bliss and his brother Bill, would tell you Charters died because he panicked.

Charters' car was found on the old Chilko road about fourteen miles back in the bush. It had stalled in deepening snow. Failing to get it started, Charters had started to walk, alternately running, to find shelter.

His foot tracks from where he had abandoned his disabled car, indicated he had walked rapidly to keep warm and that he had finally panicked and began to run. In places on the old road the snow revealed he had stumbled and fallen, to rise again and stumble on. Jack Charters, being a military officer, must have had experience in the disciplinary command of men he out-ranked. I am inclined to ponder the notion that he had lacked the ability to command himself in his personal hour of peril.

Dead matches scattered in the snow around his pitiful attempt to start a fire with his crumpled Canadian currency were almost directly under the dry and pitchy dead limbs of the pine tree below which he died. Any experienced woodsman could have survived here using this dry source of a quick fire.

# Alvin—The Precocious Pine Squirrel

We have always been "suckers" for animal pets: horses, many dogs, a few cats (in the domestic field), as well as some wilderness birds and mammals. Not the least among these latter was a red pine squirrel we named Alvin, for no particular reason, but probably because we had been intrigued by a recent phonograph record featuring the comical conduct of a singing chipmunk.

Our acquaintance with Alvin began in September of 1959, when we were in our new cabin. In those days we had no road to our land and getting there was by canoe from a wild meadow at the west end of the lake. We would load our seventeen-foot Grumann with tent, grub, tools, gas, oil, sleeping bags and most everything essential to a camp-out, and paddle the mile east to our homesite. Here, in the shelter of some big, thick northern spruces which afforded a good wind break and dry ground, we had originally pitched our seven-by-nine umbrella tent and set up camp-keeping while clearing and burning brush where we would ultimately lay the big spruce logs of our wilderness home.

One frosty morning in September, I opened my eyes to the shadow of a pine squirrel, plainly visible against bright sunlight warming the tent fabric above our sleeping bags. Alvin, as we would dub him before an hour had passed, was thumping around near my head. I reached up, snapped a forefinger directly under the spot his shadow told me was his belly. The reaction was sudden—a lightninglike pounce on the spot where my finger snap had struck. I chose another spot a few inches away and snapped again. Alvin leaped to a new attack, scratching vigorously where my finger had popped the canvas. It was a lot of fun that morning and later, setting out some cold flapjacks and a big dab of peanut butter was all it took to convince Alvin he had a couple of weak-willed campers to contend with. From that day until his death in 1966, Alvin lived with us.

He never deigned to take over our log house when we built it, preferring our woodpiles and deep holes under the big spruces for food storage and his own warm home. He was quick to appreciate some of civilizations inventions, one of which was the thick yellow blanket rolls of fiber glass we used to strip the "chinks" in our log cabin. He had his bailiwick heavily lined with fiber glass filched from our supply cache long before we had put it to its intended use. I believe Alvin probably had the first "modern insulated" squirrel home in the Chilcotin. In later times, we have come across squirrel nests in the dense branches of the spruces skirting the shores of the lake, where the smart females had lined them with soft yellow fiber glass "wool" pulled out of the chinks between our cabin logs. Here the young are born to perpetuate the pine squirrel population in our part of the country. That is, if they survive the attacks of the crows that flock in here in early spring. Those big nests have a special attraction for crows when the tender young squirrels have arrived. My wife and I have often rushed out to drive off the crows before murder was committed. We didn't always succeed.

Alvin's particular weakness was peanut butter, sunflower seeds and hard candy, in that order. He did not particularly care for peanuts in the shell. It was not long before he would come to Mildred's call. At times, completely out of sight in some dark recess deep in the thick foliage of the particularly big spruce near our back door, he would suddenly pop into view if Mildred would simply call "Boy!" and step outside. Then a handful of sunflower seeds would bring him quickly to a sitting position on the woodpile—from whence he would dash to where Mildred knelt at the foot of the spruce, to reach up and take one seed at a time, sample it with a few nibbles to be sure it was a good one, then dash off to his underground storage to deposit it and quickly return for another. This went on until all the seeds had been taken from her fingers—one at a time—each carefully nibbled for certain sampling and separately carried underground. You didn't fool Alvin with any "duds" and he never made a dry run. It had to be good or he rejected it.

In time, Alvin developed somewhat taking ways. Got so he liked to drag off socks which had blown from the clothesline in the occasional high winds that whipped across Eagle Lake in summer. Once we saw him tugging manfully at a scatter rug which had blown from the line. A gunny sack, fouled by a chunk of wood in the woodpile, he reduced to shreds in efforts to haul it underground. Once we had carelessly left the cab door of our pickup open. On the seat had been a pound plastic bag of mints, each of the small round red and white striped candies wrapped in the maker's branded wrapper of light transparent plastic.

I went out to shut the cab door when it looked like a shower was imminent. Alvin had been there. On the seat was the litter of possibly 100 mint wrappers. Alvin had cut off the twisted ends of each wrapper to sample the candy within. And all had been carried off, one at a time. Months later, while digging around the big spruce to set a line of posts for a roof gallery extending from our ice house, I came upon quantities of the candy wrappers among the litter of several inches deep of spruce cone scales covering one of Alvin's underground caches. He must have had a sweet time. A whole pound of mints had gone underground in his raid on the truck.

Then, there was a later time when Mildred's mother, Mary, came to spend some balmy fall days with us and slept in a tent out under the spruces. I heard Mary screaming one afternoon and ran out to see what all the commotion was about. Mary had put out a small washing of her personal things, including some scanty panties, and had discovered Alvin trying to drag them underground. Later she discovered a pair of her best nylons were missing. They turned up eventually as I dug into our winter woodpile. They were ruined by then, of course. Alvin had stowed them in the woodpile for some reason best known to his squirrel mind.

He had become possessive after a fashion. There were times when we had neglected to be prompt with handouts and then he would come into the cabin and race around the walls. Not infrequently Alvin came to our open door in warm weather, to stand, front feet spread, ready to pounce, staring up at us as if to remind us he could just possibly be a little hungry, which I doubt he ever was, judging from the bulbous wobble of a fat little paunch.

Alvin had his natural enemies—the crows—the dark minks that raced through our aspens or along the edge of the lake occasionally; the big marsh hawks and the great horned owls. But it remained for a bald eagle to give him his chief worry in daylight hours, though it was a hawk that finally did him in.

The eagle, which had its nest in a craggy dead fir about a mile up-lake from our cabin, would come looking for the squirrel (or any other suitable food) and we got to watching for the big bird.

Alvin was also fully aware of his danger and at one time when the eagle had been persistent in his overhead patrol, Alvin took refuge in the very thickest part of the big spruce by the ice house. Here, near the bushy top of the tree some sixty feet above the ground, Alvin would make his stand, setting up a loud, prolonged and abusive chatter, the tone of which seemed to indicate he was giving the eagle some unadulterated cussing. Once I saw the eagle sail quickly into the spruce top, its big wings actually crashing among the stiff branches and knocking brittle twigs into the air, only to emerge with feathers ruffed and damaged, to fly off in apparent disgust, while from the dense depths of the big spruce Alvin could be heard screaming epithets that seemed to say something like, "Never touched me, you big brute!"

Then one day Mildred called "Boy!" in vain. We finally concluded Alvin was gone and wondered about it. Months later I found his skull—all that was left of him—in the litter under the big spruce and from the nature of the evidence concluded that this had been the work of a hawk, a bird that seems to have a greater ability to maneuver in heavy cover.

# "Three Little Satisfies"

Mail day was one of the main events of any two-week span of dead winter time on Old Tatla. Sometimes, if the snow was deep, the two weeks stretched into three. Hodson's big truck and the mail would arrive eventually and Betty Linder would sort it into the open boxes of the shelves in the little cubby hole that was our post office while white folks and Indians sat around the old general store palavering, as usual, about the weather.

Betty, a daughter of the pioneer Graham's whose white-face herds were known by the horse shoe "walking horse" brand, was herself a generous and thoughtful person. She had provided a bench for weary walkers and you generally found it occupied by aged Indian women and old men on mail day. They were among her most loyal friends.

Nostalgic memory of the old store recalls the sweet fragrance of the smoke-tanned leather that greeted your nostrils when you entered the heavily cluttered interior—moosehide moccasins, colorfully beaded gauntlets and fancy beaded jackets with their fringe-laced sleeves, hung among an assortment of buckskin chaps, hand-braided headstalls and hackamores, the product of Native Chilcotin craftsmanship.

The appetizing fragrance of slab bacon mingled inoffensively with the odor of kerosene, Fort Gary Coffee, denim jackets, boots and rubbers. You could actually sniff a little and identify a lot of good things that by their odors did much of their own advertising.

I chanced to walk in one day during the deep cold of the hard winter of 1964—it was forty-five degrees below zero—while the store was at one of its busiest days of the current freezeup.

There had been no mail for two weeks. Betty was at the moment busy trying to finish sorting the mail and filling the weekly outgoing grocery orders for folks down in the Tatla-ko Valley and Joy Graham, who always helped during these rush days, was counting out a bundle of pine squirrel pelts for a young Chilcotin boy. Squirrel skins were bringing in twenty-five cents apiece that winter.

In the midst of her efforts to fill an order for an Indian family living in the back country beyond Choelquoit, Betty came onto an item in the wrinkled grocery list that had her puzzled. It was a request for "Three Little Satisfies."

"Now what in the world does Old Joe mean by that?" she asked no one in particular, obviously puzzled by the scribble on a piece of brown paper. "Three Little Satisfies." Well, most of Old Joe's friends were aware of the fact he had spent a lifetime in the remote wilderness of Chilcotin, as a band member deprived, by a lot of understandable circumstances, of the advantages of book learning. Mobile, prefabricated school houses and bus transportation for kids were unknown when Joe was a boy.

Betty handed the slip of paper to me.

"Three Little Satisfies."

"Betty," I said. "Did you ever chew snoose?"

She shook her head. "No. Of course not!"

"Well then," I said, "I guess you are not familiar with Copenhagen's slogan." I reached for one of the little round pocket tins of snuff stacked in neat columns on the tobacco shelf and pointed to its shiny lid where the words "A Little Satisfies" was clearly stamped.

"This is what Old Joe wants," I said.

Like a lot of old-timers in the wilds of our high plateau, some of their meager literacy had come through memorizing or copying the letters off of labels, on canned goods, flour sacks and such.

My friend Cassimil Lulua would be passing through Choelquoit country with his pack horse and that's how Old Joe would get his groceries—including his "snoose"—in a day or two and then be "satisfied."

# Rendezvous at Tatla Lake

## *A Hiyu Time Was Had by All*

It was early February of 1966 when the Cattlemen's Association
was gathered in the Community Hall at Tatla Lake for their
annual business meeting. In these days the event was usually
held combined with the traditional fur rendezvous. It was nine
degrees above zero. A light frozen snow lay over the plateau.
Our son Chuck and his wife Wilma were holed up with
Mildred and me in our cabin at Little Eagle Lake. We heard the
stomp of horse feet in the crusted snow and looked out to see
three Indians on saddle horses leading a fourth, heavily laden
with travel gear covered by a manta held secure by a single
diamond. The riders, a man and two women, I recognized as
Cassimil Lulua, accompanied by his wife, Margaret, and a sister
whose name I do not recall. They were en route to Tatla for an
event of entertainment, which few Indians would miss if there
was any way of getting there in this lonely country even when the
region was held in the grips of Manitou. The fur buyers would be
there to gather up the annual catch, doling out cheap wine and
other adulterated hootchum, calculated to get the Indian trappers
in a free-wheeling generous mood, willing to part the meager
supply of red pine squirrel skins which were bringing only 25
cents per pelt that winter, in addition to a few others in this
country which in my time had been badly over-trapped.

I invited them into the warmth of our cabin. Wilma had
baked-up some sourdough bread. I dug a can of strawberry jam
from our food cache and boiled up about a gallon of black tea
which I knew they would relish.

Cassimil, who I had known since first coming into the Chilcotin, was affable and talkative. The women, for the most part,
sat silent. They had been two days on the trail from Nemiah
which they habitually call "Me'mia," traveling up the lake ice on

their horses, only avoiding the open pot holes of hot springs near our cabin, when they took to the woods on the way to Tatla. They devoured Wilma's bread which was still warm from the Yukon oven and heavily plastered with the sweetness of strawberry jam. They rested an hour and they were on their way. We did not attend the rendezvous.

The rest of this story I got secondhand from some of the observers who had attended the big annual blow out. As usual, it began with a business meeting of the Cattlemen's Association who petitioned the provincial government to halt all further alienation of Crown land to new settlers to preserve their badly overgrazed wild meadows. The meeting wound up the afternoon and evening with a dance in the Tatla Community Hall during which the fur buyers plied their rot gut to get the Native trappers in a generous mood. An amateur group furnished music for the dance that began in early evening and Ken Haynes and his young wife Mary won the prize for the best waltzing couple on the floor. The hall was crowded with Indians and whites and the wall flower benches were lined with ranch wives, many of them with sleeping children on their laps and hope in their eyes that someone would ask them to dance. The affair grew a trifle wild near midnight as hootchum warmed the blood and fighting spirit of some of the males. At about this time, it was said, my friend Cassimil and his brother-in-law, Edward Sill, got into an argument because, it was alleged, Edward had slapped his wife who was Cassimil's sister. In a moment, Sill was on the floor with blood flowing from a knife wound. When someone said let's get him off the floor, they hauled Edward through the side door and applied fresh snow to his wound which soon blooded the snow. During the early hours of morning someone managed to get Edward over 140 miles over the Bella Coola wagon road to the hospital in Williams Lake where they sewed him up and sent him home when he was finally sober.

It was about this juncture in the celebration that an aged Chilcotin squaw got to her feet which were cased in brightly beaded moose hide moccasins over which she had drawn a pair of store-bought commercially made white man's rubbers. She was wearing an almost full-length mother Hubbard. She raised her arms above her head and, on the balls of her feet, she tippy-toed in rapid rhythm of an old tribal custom, the while chanting in Chilcotin words that few white people would understand. During her dance in which the musicians sat silent, the old woman paraded up and down the wall flower benches as she drew a knife from a fold in her mother hubbard; as she danced, shuffling up and down the rows of spectators, she passed the knife within inches of the throats of the wives of the white ranchers. There's not much more to this story.

The "Mounties" at Alexis Creek eventually investigated but did nothing official other than report the incident and thus ended another chapter in the long record of police indifference to the age-old habit of tribesmen quarreling among themselves. It was obvious to me the police were more or less indifferent to disputes among the Chilcotin Natives, rather taking the attitude it is better to let them settle their own affairs as they had been doing for centuries before the white man arrived.

A few days after the big bust at Tatla, we found the tracks of a horse passing through the woods, well north of our cabin, presumably heading for "Me'mia." We saw no riders and assumed of course, the rider was Cassimil going home. To this day, although suspicion remains strong, none of the people who witnessed the fracas in the community hall could ever say definitely whose knife had cut Edward Sill, whether it was Cassimil's or Edward Sill's.

# The Bennett Wagons

I'm told that when R. B. Bennett was prime minister of Canada back in the hard, dark years of the Great Depression—when money had become scarce and automobiles stood idle with dying batteries and dry tanks—Bennett had suggested Canadians should revert to the simple, old-time luxury of horses and wagons.

The loyal opposition made much of the Prime Minister's remarks about "going back" to a "horse and buggy" level of life and the term "Bennett wagons" soon became the jocular title of any horse-drawn farm or ranch vehicle seen on the dirt roads of the Big Country.

The first Bennett wagon Mildred and I saw was in the 1940s when we first came into the Chilcotin Interior. This was near Chilanko Forks, west of Alexis Creek.

We were tooling our old '36 Chevy slowly over the rough road, easing it along in second gear, when we came onto some zig-zagging tire tracks that wobbled in the dust.

"Looks like someone has had a flat tire," Mildred remarked. I said it sure did. The tire tracks swerved all over the road, seemed most inclined to veer off to one side. Then we saw it "parked" near the Chilanko Trading Post.

"That's a wagon on car wheels," Mildred said. This was a Bennett wagon. The chassis of an old Model-T Ford surmounted by a wagonbox of heavy planks securely bolted, supporting three homemade "jack pine" bows to carry a canvas top. The canvas was missing. Up front stood two rather old bay horses whose rib bones told of a hard winter of "rustling." Their harness was old hame straps and britchen wearing repairs of old rope. From the neck straps swung a yoke and tongue of hand-hewed pine, bolted to the "wishbone" of the chassis. The steering wheel had been discarded along with the motor and metal body, now replaced by a box full of straw which, I thought at the time, was probably a lot more comfortable for the old man and several children who occupied it with all their camp gear, than the factory Ford body would have been.

As we came alongside, there seemed to be dogs yapping and barking all around us. I was about to stop and offer some help on the "flat" when a young Indian came out of the woods with a double-bit ax in one hand, a pine pole about fifteen or so feet long on his shoulder. He shoved one end of the pole under the rear axle, while Grandma, a really big and very fat old lady, stood a block of wood upright for a fulcrum about four feet back of the axle. Then Grandma toddled to the outer far end of the pole and sat down on it. The "Bennett's" rear end raised right off the road and the young man went about the business of "changing" the deflated tire.

Grandma seemed to be enjoying her part in this roadside emergency, laughed and waved to us as we drove on. The old man smiled too and the kids in the wagon were laughing and yelling at their dogs. A young girl, a teenager perhaps, would not look at us—just turned her face away.

Well, it's a rare thing to see a Bennett wagon anymore. Most of the Chilcotins are driving pickups now and quite a few families are seen in comfortable looking cars. With "blacktop" fast replacing the rough gravel of the old Chilcotin road between Williams Lake and the Anahim country out west, the sight of a Bennett wagon is a rare event. They are fast disappearing into the limbo of things that used to be; transition is in full swing.

# Hootchum

Soap Olallie. Old Chinook. Soup Olallie. Hooshum or in Chilcotin dialect, Hootchum.

Generally a luscious orange-red by late September, the low bush fruit known variously as soup olallie or soap olallie by white folks quoting old-time Chinook, or as "hooshum" by the Chilcotin's dialect, the wild fruit that thrives in our woodlands is legendary from the Rockies to the Pacific.

And strangely enough, as hooshum or hootchum, there are connotations involving not only the ferocity of the grizzly bear, who has an avid appetite for the fruit, as well as the miners of historic Klondike who coined the word "hootch" a full thirty years before it became identified with prohibition in the United States of America.

As soap olallies they are readily mashed to a smooth and soapy lather, whipped to a thick consistency with the addition of sugar (and some clean snow if available). It is sometimes eaten as Chilcotin ice cream by those whose taste is agreeable to the tart flavor of the berries. My old friend Scotty Shields insists "they are simply delicious!" but many will disagree.

Hooshum, or hootshum, is undoubtedly of tribal vernacular, which has a way of shifting in its pronunciation from one locality to another in the tribal world.

The Chinook word for bear is siam.

But the Indian inserts a T in front of S—as tsiam. Hyas means "big." Hyas tsiam = big bear. The grizzly. "Crazy bear," old *Ursus horribilis* himself. A vernacular alteration of hyas tsiam becomes hyas shum or hootshum. Now come on up to the Yukon country for some retrospection on the gold rush of 1898.

My old granddaddy, who was a veteran Klondiker, told me thirsty miners in snowbound winter cabins at Poverty Bar made moonshine from sourdough and at times of wild drunkenness from the potency of the "white lightning" that dripped from the "worm" of the still, went so completely berserk the Indians likened them to hootshum, the crazy bear.

In the Klondike hootshum eventually became "hootch." In the blind pigs (places where bootleg liquor was available) of the big American cities, such notables as Scarface Al Capone and others of his feather engaged in such pastimes as the Valentine's Day massacre and similar shootouts that marked the history of bootleg competition in the United States of America during the colorful years of prohibition.

Hootch! Possibly few still know the true origin of the word, or that the hootshum berries and old Griz had so much to do with it.

Fall Foliage
Soap
Olallie
=
"Hooshum"
=

# Epilogue
## *Twilight of a Frontier*


One day back in the 1960s I attended a community meeting in Tatla Lake when some heated demands were being made for improvement to the old Chilcotin Road. A rancher was describing the pioneer route with a string of adjectives just as well omitted here, but clearly picturing the road as the worst in all British Columbia.

Then, Phil Gaglardi, our highways minister at the time, got up to defend his department and well remembered is the prophesy of his reply:

"You're going to get a paved road out here, just as soon as we can get the money to build it. But I want to tell you something maybe you haven't thought about. When that day comes you people are going to lose a treasure you've always had: the quiet peace of your ranches and the freedom of your open range will be forever gone."

In the intervening years since that day, Gaglardi's prophesy has seen the hard, fast surface of blacktop paving extended, at this writing, 120 miles west from Williams Lake to Pyper Lake at the foot of Bear's Head Hill; ultimate destination Bella Coola. In the limbo of nostalgic memory are the groaning, swinging cables of the old suspension bridge at the Fraser Crossing, long since replaced by solid high steel. The dizzy switchbacks of the old wagon road that climbed the perilous canyon walls of Sheep Creek are but a memory. The hill is now surmounted by one long, easy 8 percent grade where high gear is readily maintained in all but the most heavily loaded trucks.

Sod-roofed cabins of pioneer days fall to decay in the shadow of new homes of sawmill lumber. The "country" stores where harness leather and hardware hung from rafters, where you could buy such things as coffee ground in a red iron mill, an Indian beaded buckskin jacket, moccasins or gloves, chewing tobacco or kerosene for your lantern, have disappeared. B.C. Hydro's miles of copper power lines now glisten in summer's sun, their energy flowing to home refrigerators, lights and irrigation systems and the self-serving bins of frozen produce in our "new" stores. You can find a pay phone booth on almost any back-country road and aluminum TV antennas shine from roof-tops throughout the region.

The old-time Chilcotin cowboy in moosehide chaps? He travels in a jeep or a "half-ton" equipped with "C.B."; wears Hawaiian flowered shirts and his old spurs rust in the tool box.

Thankfully there are facets of the old frontier that have not perished in the alchemy of years. We still thrill to the first blush of autumn as the aspens turn to copper and gold; to the wail of loons and the wavering cries of southing geese as new snow caps the Niuts; the slap of beaver tails on Little Eagle at eventide. And there is music in the festive chorus of coyotes as the little wolves greet moonrise over Splinter Mountain.

Shoreline willows gleam in diamond frost and winter's first snowfall renews the white silence of our cabin woods.

We are older, a little softer. These days we go south more often to spend some leisure time with loved ones and old friends. And sometimes we linger, aging bones rejoicing in the warmth of winter sun.

But "come breakup" in the old Chilcotin! In the valley of Little Eagle! Listen friend, and you'll hear the windsong of a warming Chinook breathin' among the pines. It sings of old ice a-crackin' up, of grouse a-drummin'. Sunrise still turns our snow peaks to ruddy gold and the turquoise deeps of Little Eagle still mirror the friendly cotton of clouds lazin' in the blue Canadian sky. In the heady balm of wakening earth the old spell—the lure of wilderness—comes all persuasive, as in the image of Old Hasseyampa we're once more headin' north!

W. D. J.
LITTLE EAGLE LAKE, 1987

# MORE GREAT HANCOCK HOUSE TITLES

**My Spirit Soars**
Chief Dan George
ISBN 0-88839-233-8

**NW Native Harvest**
Carol Batdorf
ISBN 0-88839-245-1

**Power Quest**
Carol Batdorf
ISBN 0-88839-240-0

**Spirit Quest**
Carol Batdorf
ISBN 0-88839-210-9

**Tlingit: Art, Culture & Legends**
Dan & Nan Kaiper
ISBN 0-88839-101-6

**Totem Poles of the NW**
D. Allen
ISBN 0-919654-83-5

**When Buffalo Ran**
George Bird Grinnell
ISBN 0-88839-258-3

*Northern Biographies*

**Bootlegger's Lady**
Sager & Frye
ISBN 0-88839-976-6

**Crazy Cooks & Gold Miners**
Joyce Yardley
ISBN 0-88839-294-X

**Descent into Madness**
Vernon Frolick
ISBN 0-88839-300-8

**Fogswamp: Life with Swans**
Turner & McVeigh
ISBN 0-88839-104-8

**Lady Rancher**
Gertrude Roger
ISBN 0-88839-099-8

**Nahanni**
Dick Turner
ISBN 0-88839-028-9

**Novice in the North**
Bill Robinson
ISBN 0-88839-977-4

**Ralph Edwards of Lonesome Lake**
Ed Gould
ISBN 0-88839-100-5

**Ruffles on my Longjohns**
Isabel Edwards
ISBN 0-88839-102-1

**Wings of the North**
Dick Turner
ISBN 0-88839-060-2

**Yukon Lady**
Hugh McLean
ISBN 0-88839-186-2

**Yukoners**
Harry Gordon-Cooper
ISBN 0-88839-232-X